THE BREAKAWAY GUIDE TO
TROUBLE FREE TRAVEL

Roger Macdonald

By arrangement with the B.B.C.

When it comes to holidays, the British have never quite lost the Dunkirk spirit. Little short of a disaster is needed to turn them into true professional travellers, determined not to make the same mistakes again next year.

Unfortunately, much of that determination is soon dissipated in a sado-masochistic exercise in which the shortcomings of a trip become an action replay for relatives back home, or an endless catalogue of complaints posted to their long-suffering travel agent.

For the British have made holiday misfortunes a new art form. Stoic to the last, they savour a holiday's shortcomings in horrendous detail, once safely back on this side of the Channel.

This book may spoil that scenario for ever. It goes back to basics, making no assumptions. In its pages you will find out all you ever wanted to know (and some things you will wish you didn't know) about how to prepare for the journey, how to select your mode of transport, how to read between the lines of a glossy brochure and how to tell a good travel agent from one that simply wants your custom.

You will learn some of the tricks of the travel trade—why the British are always the first to be moved to another hotel when too many tourists are chasing too few bedrooms; why the flight you have booked sometimes simply ceases to exist; why the cheapest holidays in the brochure are seldom available.

The pitfalls of travel are spelled out in painstaking detail. Whether you take your own car across to the Continent, or go by rail, or face up to the rigours of international airports, there is a section for you. Whether you are living it up on a cruise or down in a tent, driving a house on wheels or renting a villa, *Trouble Free Travel* should enable you to take it all in your stride.

CONTENTS

There is a sound reason for such confidence. It is not simply that I have had many years of producing radio and television programmes on travel with a seemingly endless supply of other people's misfortunes as material, but that I, too, have built up an almost unbelievable catalogue of errors of my own.

I have left my passport at home, forgotten visas and vaccinations, had to telephone my insurance broker from Dover to arrange a Green Card minutes before crossing the Channel; written off a car in Yugoslavia without being in it at the time; flooded a hotel in Italy, been bodily thrown out of one in France by the original Basil Fawlty, been overbooked in Amsterdam; missed the call to get on a plane in Athens, and with it the flight; had exhaust pipes fall off, windscreens shatter, engines boil, and more punctures than spares; lost airline tickets, had motorail tickets stolen, been robbed, lost credit cards, and sometimes my temper.

Which is why, above all, this book has advice on how to get your own back on people who have given you a personal nightmare through their mistakes and incompetence. But then if you learn by my blunders and take the tips packed into the pages of this book, there may be nothing left to complain about. In which case you have only yourself to blame for having had such a boring uneventful holiday!

Roger Macdonald

Roger Macdonald is Editor of the travel programmes 'Breakaway' and 'Going Places' on BBC Radio Four and Producer of 'The Travel Show' on BBC Television.

'Breakaway' (Radio 4 UK, 200kHz/1500m, 92-95VHF Saturdays, 09.05) was launched on 29 September 1979, and has run continuously since, with two regular presenters, first Barry Norman and later Bernard Falk.

All imperial and their equivalent metric measurements in this book are converted exactly, even when the calculations are based on approximate figures.

Produced by the Publications Division of the Automobile Association

Editors: Roland Weisz and Maggie Comport

Art Editor: M A Preedy MSIAD

Illustrations by K A G Design. Cover model by Chris Maughan. Cover Photography by Andrew Huston. Soft cover illustration by Quadgraphic

Research by Caroline Daly, Judith Macintosh and the Publications Research Unit of the AA.

Phototypeset, printed and bound by Purnell & Sons Limited, Paulton, Bristol, BS18 5LQ

Maps produced by the Cartographic Unit of the Automobile Association.

The contents of this book are believed correct at the time of printing. Nevertheless, the publisher cannot accept any responsibility for errors or omissions, or for changes in the details given.

Published by the Automobile Association, Fanum House, Basingstoke, Hampshire RG21 2EA

Country	Symbol
Albania	AL
Andorra	AND
Austria	A
Belgium	B
Bulgaria	BG
Czechoslovakia	CS
Democratic Republic of Germany (East)	DDR
Denmark	DK
Federal Republic of Germany (West)	D
France	F
Gibraltar	GBZ
Greece	GR
Hungary	H
Irish Republic	IRL
Italy	I
Liechtenstein	FL
Luxembourg	L
Netherlands	NL
Poland	PL
Portugal	P
Romania	RO
Spain	E
Sweden	S
Switzerland	CH
United Kingdom	GB
Yugoslavia	YU

The AA is grateful to the following for the use of photographs in this book:

Austrian National Tourist Office
BBC Hulton Picture Library
Danish National Tourist Board
British Caledonian Photographic Library
British Tourist Office
Belgian National Tourist Office
Cyprus Tourist Office
Dan Air Services

French Government Tourist Office
German National Tourist Office
HM Customs & Excise
Interfoto MTI Budapest
Irish Tourist Board
Italian State Tourist Office (ENIT) London
Malta Government Tourist Office
Media Bureau

Monaco Government Tourist Office
National Bus Company
National Tourist Organisation of Greece
Norwegian Tourist Board
SNCF/French Railways—Couchart
Spanish National Tourist Office
Swedish National Tourist Office
Swiss National Tourist Office

GETTING READY

Going abroad?
Get set for a
wonderful adventure –
or will it turn
into a nightmare?

First check your passport, assuming you can find it. That may not be as odd as it seems: the vast majority of holidaymakers use their passport only once a year, and forget where they put it.

If your passport is out of date, or you do not have one, obtain an application form from your local post office. You will need a copy of your birth certificate, your marriage certificate if you are married; two identical photographs of yourself, not more than 63 × 50mm (2½ × 2in) and not less than 50 × 38mm (2 × 1½in), with a statement on the back by some reputable person such as your doctor or bank manager saying that you are who you claim to be.

4761957

All this can take time, and if you do not live conveniently close to one of the five mainland passport offices in Glasgow, Liverpool, London, Newport or Peterborough, your application will have to go by post. In peak summer periods it can be as long as two months before your passport is returned.

If you are due to go away in a few days and your passport has not come back, ring up the office you sent it to—try to call at 9 am when they are open. They are not obliged to help, but if you are persistent and make your case seem urgent they will expedite your

DON'T FORGET THE TICKETS!

application and get it off to you. The Passport Office in London has officials on duty on Saturday morning for urgent cases, but you would need to turn up in person with a convincing story.

Alternatively, if you are visiting Andorra, Austria, Belgium, Bermuda, Canada, Denmark, Finland, Gibraltar, Italy, Liechtenstein, Luxembourg, Malta, Monaco, the Netherlands, Portugal, San Marino, Spain, Sweden, Switzerland, Turkey or West Germany, you can obtain from any main post office a British Visitor's passport, valid for one year.

A passport can include your spouse and children under sixteen, a considerable financial saving. The disadvantage is that they might all need passports in a hurry, if, for example in an emergency, they could no longer travel with you. Separate passports for children under sixteen are valid for only five years but can be renewed for a further five.

Visas can cause last-minute problems, too. They are needed for some countries that one might expect would admit British subjects freely—for example, Australia. And the process of obtaining a visa cannot usually begin until your passport is submitted to their embassy, which can mean a

further four to five weeks' delay. However, some travel agents will undertake to obtain visas at short notice—at a price. If you are travelling in a group that contains someone not conforming to the pattern of the remainder—for example, a foreign national—make sure that they have all the necessary entry papers, even where you may not require a visa. Problems can occur from quarters you would least expect, such as those that plague British citizens born outside the UK, or citizens of the Republic of Ireland. When you do need a visa, always ask for it to be validated for longer than your intended visit, to avoid problems caused through unexpected travel delays.

If you have lost your passport, report it to the police. In the UK, you will normally be allowed to complete a fresh application form and given a passport that is valid for one year only. If your original passport has still not shown up after twelve months, the replacement will be renewed for a further nine years without additional fee. If you are abroad, the British Embassy or Consulate will check your identity before issuing you with temporary documents for your return journey, after which you will have to re-apply for a new passport.

Use an elastic band to keep any vaccination certificates you may need (see page 23) ready inside your passport, as health checks in most countries are carried out in conjunction with immigration. Also keep a copy of your travel insurance certificate in the same place, if only on the gloomy premise that if you are too ill to look after yourself, or are involved in an accident, an indication in your passport of your entitlement to private medical care could save your life.

The advantages and disadvantages of foreign currency, travellers cheques and the Eurocheque system of cashing cheques are discussed on page 20. However, a shrewd traveller may like to have the option of using all three, as well as a credit card (such as Barclaycard) or a charge card (such as American Express) that will provide cash in an emergency. Now that Access and Visa are widely accepted throughout the world, carrying a credit card is in itself a form of insurance against unexpected expense. In the United States, not to possess at least one credit card is to be regarded as a social outcast by hotels, petrol stations, car hire companies and airlines.

Travel tickets are placed in the same category as money by some insurance policies and need to be looked after with the same care. Tickets you have bought yourself direct from a ferry or airline company may in some circumstances be refundable, so that a thief could turn them into cash. Should you lose an airline ticket, the carrier may ask you to sign a form indemnifying them against loss—for example, by someone illegally using your ticket without detection—before they will provide a replacement.

The loss of a voucher

confirming your entitlement to pre-paid hotel accommodation can cause even more problems, especially if it was provided by a travel agent, whose offices may be closed at the time you plan to depart.

If you are taking or hiring a car abroad, you need several other documents. First, a driving licence, without which you will almost certainly not be allowed to hire a car, motor cycle, or, in some countries, a scooter. Even with a valid licence, many hire companies will not lend to anyone under 25, having learnt their lesson the hard way.

You can drive a car at seventeen in Denmark, Germany and Luxembourg, but must be eighteen in other Continental countries. In Italy you must be over 21 if your car is capable of speeds of above 112mph (180kph). In the USA the minimum age varies from state to state. On the Continent, riding a powerful motorcycle (the interpretation of powerful varies from country to country, so check in advance) is almost always forbidden under 21. Driving under age is tantamount to driving uninsured and may result in arrest.

If your driving licence is due to expire while you are abroad, you can apply for a new one anything up to two

months in advance from a Vehicle Licensing Office. Do not leave taking action until just before your departure because, even at the best of times, your application will take a week or two.

An International Driving Permit is also advisable, although not absolutely essential, if you are travelling in western Europe. However, should you be stopped by the police, an IDP is likely to be more favourably received than a UK licence alone because it is printed in several languages and contains your photograph, whereas the British licence, almost alone among those of European countries, does not. Even in countries where the UK licence is officially accepted—for example, in Austria—the police sometimes refuse to accept that it is valid, and proving your point hours later can scarcely improve your holiday.

An IDP also relieves you in Italy and Spain of the need to carry an official translation of your UK licence. For Spain, this translation has to be stamped by a Spanish consulate, an eccentric time-consuming exercise that actually costs more than the fee for an IDP. The IDP can be obtained from your motoring organisation (provide two passport size photographs) for a small fee and is valid for one year, after which it must be replaced.

Next in importance to deal with is the

vehicle registration document. If your vehicle licence is due to expire while you are abroad, you can apply to relicense it up to six weeks in advance. If, at the time you go on holiday, you are in the process of renewing your licence or changing your address, you can obtain a document from a Local Vehicle Licensing Office to cover the use of the vehicle abroad. Ask for form V379, except when you are still waiting for the original registration document (for example, when taking delivery of a new car) when you want form V204. If time is really short, your motoring organisation can issue an International Certificate for Motor Vehicles, for a small fee.

While you are checking car documents, don't forget to obtain a GB plate of the approved pattern and size (see page 27) from your motoring organisation, the car ferry company, or a motor accessory shop.

Car hire companies normally do not like their UK registered cars being used abroad, even though the business of moving your family and your luggage by ferry and collecting a car on the other side can be traumatic, outweighing even the advantage of a lefthand drive vehicle for use on the Continent. However, if you do persuade a company to lend a car in this way, they will not give you the original registration document—you might sell the car! A photocopy of the registration document will not do: what is required is a Hire Car Registration Certificate (VE 103), available, for yet another small fee, from

your motoring organisation.

If you have persuaded Aunt Agatha to lend you her Rolls-Royce, then you need a letter from her confirming her foolhardy fit of generosity. If you are going to Yugoslavia, this letter needs to be counter-signed by your motoring

Find out which documents you need and make sure to pack them

organisation. If you are going to Portugal, a special certificate is required, which the motoring organisations can supply free of charge.

In western Europe, Customs documents are no longer needed for cars temporarily imported by tourists. However, a Customs document, called a *Carnet de Passages en Douane* (again obtainable through your

motoring organisation), is recommended for Spain, where the Customs authorities have an unpleasant habit of demanding deposits against a whole range of goods, including radios, tape recorders and television sets. Even if you return through the same post, the bureaucracy involved in recovering these deposits is horrendous. A carnet must be properly discharged at each frontier and, after the holiday is over, returned to the issuing organisation correctly discharged to avoid Customs problems and expense later.

A carnet is also advisable for Greece, where the interpretation of Customs regulations seems erratic. Technically, though, under Greek law, provided that your stay does not exceed four months, all that is required is a note in your passport of your date of entry.

The Green Card, the popular term for an international vehicle insurance certificate, is compulsory only in Greece, Portugal, Spain and Yugoslavia of western European countries, although any visitor by car who chooses

Nightmares

If only to show that the most expert traveller has the occasional lapse, it must be recorded that Eric Tobitt, doyen of the BBC's Motoring and Travel Unit, unwittingly set out for the Paris Air Show without his passport or his travellers cheques. He got into France by furnishing himself with an identification card, complete with booth

photograph and duly stamped by Townsend Thoresen on departure. This meant that he either had to leave France within 60 hours, or he had to make sure that another member of the BBC team travelling later brought out his passport, which they did. However, it will be a long time before he remembers that episode without some embarrassment.

Wise Words

Check list of documents:

passports

visas

travel tickets

hotel vouchers

credit cards

Eurocheque card

UK chequebook
or Eurocheques

foreign currency

travellers cheques

driving licence

International Driving
Permit

car registration document

Green Card (+ bail bond
for Spain)

vehicle recovery
insurance

travel/medical insurance
(see page 10)

customs carnet (some
countries)

International Camping
Carnet

caravan documents
(see page 62)

Certificate of British
Registry (for boats)

Helmsman's Certificate
of Competence

The Eurocheque system has helped to foil bank frauds

to travel without one is foolhardy (see page 11). Similarly, any motorist who does not take out vehicle recovery insurance (see page 11) and insurance against the cost of getting his party home, such as is provided by the AA's 5-Star Service, is taking an unreasonable risk. In Spain, a bail bond is also essential (see page 11).

If you are camping, the International Camping Carnet, available from the motoring organisations or from the Caravan Club, is often accepted at camp sites in place of a passport. This could be useful as it would release your passport for use elsewhere, such as at a bank while changing money. In Italy and Yugoslavia, however, a passport is still required, and the carnet itself is a legal requirement in the state forests of France and on camping sites in Denmark. A discount for carnet holders is sometimes offered outside the peak holiday months of July and August.

Finally, find a pen. You need this to sign your new passport, Green Card (everyone insured should sign) and any other documents with a space for a signature. Do all the signing now. It may be too late when an official requires to see a document. You also need the pen to make a list of numbers and other main details of every document you are taking—passport, credit cards, tickets, insurance, together with the numbers of your car keys.

Leave a copy of this list with a relative or friend in the UK so that, even if you lose the list, you can phone home and still save the day.

Nightmares

There are a few countries where you will need a visa even if you have no intention of staying there —for example, China. An American on a flight from Tokyo to Islamabad in Pakistan discovered this to his cost when the airliner touched down at Peking to refuel. Even though all the passengers remained on board, the Chinese authorities arrived to check everyone's passports and, on discovering that he did not have a visa, they took him off the plane. He was fined 1,000 US dollars and had to pay on the spot in travellers cheques before the authorities would allow him to reboard.

10 Any insurance is better than none, but many travellers make serious mistakes in their choice of policies or on the date when they take them out. In every case, once you are committed to specific dates, travel insurance is *essential* to cover the cost of cancelling your arrangements because of some problem back home. Time and time again, holidaymakers delay buying their insurance until just before they are due to depart, depriving themselves of one of the most important benefits of a policy.

Possibly because of problems arising from clients who have failed to take these precautions (resulting, in some cases, in their not having the money to pay for the holiday that they can no longer take) many tour operators now offer travel insurance themselves. It is a profitable

GOOD COVER IS WORTH EVERY PENNY

sideline, enabling them to earn a substantial commission. But watch out, because on some booking forms the client may have to tick a box to indicate that insurance is *not* required: if he does not he may find the premium automatically added to the price of a holiday.

The attitude of tour companies differs widely. A few, especially for skiing holidays, insist that you insure with them—although you could try refusing. Others may insist that you buy some other insurance if you decline to take out the one they offer.

Although travel policies do not vary substantially, the few clauses in which they do may prove crucial. For example, the Extrasure policy was the first to offer unlimited medical cover. This is of particular advantage for tourists bound for the USA where major surgery costs a fortune.

However, the same policy will not pay your salary or average earnings should you be unable to work because of an accident on holiday— vital to some self-employed people. But other policies will do this.

Some policies have clauses that exclude certain categories, such as the elderly or pregnant

women. An illness contracted a long time ago, but which has recurred on holiday for the first time, can be interpreted as a 'pre-existing condition', disqualifying the client from benefiting. Dental treatment may be excluded unless it can be shown that the situation was truly an 'emergency'. Some policies do not provide cover for potentially dangerous sports such as skindiving or climbing, or for being a driver or a passenger on a hired motorcycle or scooter.

Holidaymakers planning a flight-only trip, which is not covered by inclusive tour guarantees, may need to look for additional insurance covering the possibility of the airline going out of business (as befell Braniff and Laker), although some policies do now include this cover without extra charge.

Compensation for delays also varies from policy to policy, and so does the qualifying period of the delay. Only a few policies actually insure you against the consequences of missing your train or your flight.

Policies also vary in the number of days they cover at particular rates: a day or two longer on holiday may in some cases put you in a higher charge band, while on some policies it does not.

Some policies offer lower rates for children—a particularly attractive facility if you happen to have a large family.

Apart from cancellation and health risks, most policies also cover personal possessions, though not all offer full replacement value. Some conditions on compensation for loss or theft relate to reporting the theft (see page 21).

No policy will cover you against extreme carelessness. If

Wise Words

To cover possible cancellation costs, take out insurance the moment your holiday is settled.

Beware of insurance premiums automatically added to the price of some package tours.

Take out an insurance policy tailored to your particular needs.

Read the small print on illness: some policies may not cover you.

On an activity holiday, make certain that you have cover for potentially dangerous sports.

When travelling by car, never rely solely on your UK insurance.

If you are going to Spain take out a bail bond.

you are shown to have been grossly negligent in safeguarding your property, the insurance company may be able to avoid liability.

If you are travelling by car, additional insurance is essential. Although in the EEC (except Greece) domestic motor insurance policies are valid, they offer only minimum cover—which for UK motorists does not include damage to their own vehicles, even though they have comprehensive insurance at home. A Green Card is no longer mandatory, but is just as advisable to take with you now as it was before Britain joined the EEC, and you will need it for several other countries as well.

Some Green Cards, such as those issued to policy holders with General Accident and Eagle Star, have the advantage that if you do make a claim, it will not be taken into account when assessing the extent of your next no-claims discount. This can be an attractive advantage because Continental claims can take a very long time to sort out, and recovering uninsured losses (such as the policy excess—often the yardstick by which companies decide whether or not a motorist technically is partly to blame) can be extremely difficult.

Indeed, the pitfalls of Continental motoring are such that if you have only third-party insurance at home, it is often worth trying to alter the policy for the duration of the trip to provide fully comprehensive cover. In any case your insurer will issue you with a Green Card.

Alternatively, Norwich Union issue a Green Card under an arrangement through Extrasure that gives comprehensive cover irrespective of the cover in force on the owner's insurance. This can be particularly useful if you take abroad—and prang—Aunt Agatha's ageing Rolls-Royce!

A Green Card with comprehensive insurance may protect you from the worst consequences of damage to your car, but it may not prevent your holiday from being ruined. Fortunately, the costs of transporting your car back to the UK, or travelling out again to collect it, are covered.

But the costs of continuing your holiday by hire car, should your own not be immediately repairable, can be enormously expensive. The AA, the RAC and Europ Assistance all provide cover against mishaps abroad, and the AA 5-Star Service also offers a replacement hire car should your vehicle break down or be involved in an accident in the week before you are due to depart—a classic nightmare situation.

Motorists intending to visit Spain also require a bail bond, a financial guarantee that their insurance company will pay up should they be held responsible for an accident. As the Spanish police are liable to arrest foreign motorists and hold them until they are sure that certain liabilities have been met, failure to take a bail bond can have dire consequences.

One curious anomaly crops up when driving in the Republic of Ireland. It depends entirely on your insurance company as to whether they need to extend your domestic cover: some do, some do not.

The cost of full cover for vehicle and occupants against virtually all risks (including even travelling by public transport)—is no insignificant sum, but anyone who has had to make a claim after a disagreeable experience will never again begrudge the outlay.

Nightmares

A disabled lady from Middlesex booked an extensive coach tour in the USA for herself and a friend. When the booking was confirmed, she arranged Advance Booking Charter flights with Wardair to coincide with the beginning and end of the tour. To her horror, the company wrote again soon afterwards saying, sorry, there were no spaces left on that particular tour after all. Re-arranging her flights cost the lady and her friend an additional £1,500, including cancellation fees with Wardair. She had taken out an Extrasure insurance policy, but then found a specific exclusion in the cancellation insurance if the cancellation was due to changes made by a tour operator in the holiday arrangements. It pays to check every detail of a policy: you have been warned!

12 All too few potential holidaymakers appreciate that their choice of travel agent is almost as important as the holiday itself. Although not every agent can be judged by the company's surroundings, in the majority of cases these do provide a clue to his circumstances. A reputable agent will regard substantial, well-furnished premises as essential to his reputation and the comfort of his clients. If he has skimped on the building, he may skimp on the arrangements for your holiday, also.

What do you know about his company? If it is affiliated to, or part of, a larger organisation, you have an alternative source of redress should things go wrong, and there is less chance of the agent going bankrupt— perhaps after collecting your money but before passing it on to a tour operator.

Is the agent a member of the Association of British Travel Agents? Not every agent who belongs to ABTA is

CHECK ON YOUR CHOICE

outstandingly efficient, of course, but access to this body gives the customer a degree of protection—especially against the effect of an agent's bankruptcy or as a channel of arbitration on an unresolved dispute.

Do his staff hold any professional qualifications? Throughout the travel industry there are many incompetent sales staff, whose inaccurate advice is sometimes faithfully reported by the Consumers' Association in their periodic checks on travel agencies. But a reputable agent has taken care to make certain his staff hold the ABTA Certificate of Travel Agency Competence (COTAC), which indicates a minimum level of service and experience.

How can you know how efficient and competent your assistant is? If you are simply handed some brochures, or if one particular holiday is persistently recommended, here are indications of poor training already.

The first priority with clients is to assess their age, person- ality and—more difficult— financial circumstances; to discover whether they are looking for an active/ sedentary, family/single, sun/sport, single/multiple destination holiday, and indeed whether their preliminary inquiries

suggest that they are perhaps aiming at the wrong holiday. In that case, the counter clerk should be attempting to point them in a different direction. Above all, the customer should expect to be offered four or five different choices at four or five different destinations, and with at least three different tour operators.

If he is doing his job properly the travel agent is certainly not going to be shy about persuading you to make up your mind on the spot. A cynic might suggest that his enthusiasm is motivated only by a selfish desire to clinch the sale, to prevent losing you to another travel agent. The reality is that while you are on the premises you can be shown the full range of possible holidays to suit your taste and pocket, and have all your questions answered. You can also refine your choice to the kind of holiday you really want to take. By delaying making a decision you might miss a specific holiday bargain or opportunity.

Nonetheless, you may still prefer to take some brochures (see page 16) home, having narrowed the choice with the help of the agency staff. Read the sections of the brochures on booking conditions (usually in small print at the back) to assess the attitude of the tour operators to unexpected problems: do they, whatever the law may allow, accept adequate responsibility for your flight and your hotel? Too many exclusion clauses can alert you to possible difficulties later. At the same time, make certain that you know the full price for the holiday you intend to take, including airport taxes, insurance, room and peak period supplements, if any. As brochures are complicated and confusing in their pricing, can

the travel agent confirm that he has not by any chance overlooked a child reduction offer that could make another holiday more attractive?

Do not imagine, however, that you will be offered every conceivable holiday in the category and area you prefer. No retail chain could possibly stock the whole range of goods an industry produces, and there has to be some kind of product policy. In the same way, many agents concentrate on the slice of the tour operators' market that offers the chance of high-volume sales because, by doing so, they can exercise far greater control over the quality of the product. Companies who have lapses in standards or who lack the technology to provide an instant response to booking requests, will be among those whose brochures are not on display. If, nevertheless, you want more information on a particular company's holidays, you can be sure that a reputable travel agent will do his best to obtain full details of the holiday and, if asked, make a booking for you.

Unless, that is, the tour operator concerned is not a member of ABTA. In that case the travel agent who is a member will be prevented by the rules of his association from booking a foreign package holiday run by that company.

This is a two-way agreement, for, just as ABTA agents agree to sell only the holidays of ABTA tour operators, operators in their turn undertake to sell their products only through ABTA agents. This system is called Stabiliser, and came to prominence following the spectacular collapse of a major

tour operator, Clarksons, in the 1960s, which led to renewed efforts by ABTA to try to stabilise the industry by offering the public financial protection if the tour operator they booked with went bust. Although this system has been under attack, ABTA have been able successfully to demonstrate its effectiveness in court.

If you have been unable, or unwilling, to make up your mind about your holiday on your first visit to the agency, an effective travel agent will want to contact you at work or home to offer further advice and to encourage you to make up your mind, especially in holiday periods when vacancies are being snapped up and time is short.

Even if bookings are slow, however, do not expect the travel agent to offer a discount. He will probably be party to an agreement with the tour operator concerned that he will not offer their holidays below the brochure price. And, if he is part of a major chain of retail agencies, he will not have the discretion to strike a bargain, because such agencies do not as a rule offer discounts. All that he may be prepared to entertain in some circumstances is a discount on your travel insurance and even then, before accepting, you should examine the policy being offered carefully, to make certain that it will provide full cover.

That is all very well, you may say. But what about my well-heeled neighbour, Willie Hardbargain? He has just been on a world cruise with the wife, and their travel agent

provided a free Rolls to Southampton, vouchers for free swimwear and camera films, free excursions at the ports of call, flowers and champagne in their cabin, and a crate of wine waiting at home. Wily Willie made sure of this deal by taking the cruise company's brochure into his little local agent, saying he had already made a provisional phone booking and if the agent wanted to

pick up his commission, well, he had better make it worthwhile for Willie to let him fill in the reservation form.

Willie may have got a discount on everything except hard cash, but did he get a bargain? Even if the cost of the cruise was prohibitive and did not compare in value with others, the shipping company would hardly want to talk him out of booking or mention a rival. And the travel agent, faced with having to cut his commission to secure the deal, would be in no mood to suggest to Willie a more modestly priced cruise that might have suited him just as well.

Even though tour operators do as a rule print their telephone numbers in their brochures, and accept direct bookings, many of them will still give the prospective customer a reservation number and tell him to go to his local travel agent to complete the paperwork. A direct booking is still a long way from a direct-sell operation, which is one where the tour operator *only* sells direct and does not take bookings through travel agents. This, of course, means that he can no longer offer the complete protection of the ABTA umbrella, although many such companies are still

solidly financed—none more so than Portland who, while they offer a direct-sell operation, are part of the Thomson holiday empire.

Allowing for this obvious drawback, there are circumstances in which a prospective holidaymaker can save money by booking direct. He will be faced, however, with doing much of the legwork himself; for instance, ringing round for brochures and sending off for information in response to TV or newspaper ads; above all, having to rely entirely on his judgement on what to choose. If he wants a standard high season package, he may be quite satisfied with what he gets, but if he is looking for special offers for children or is in any way uncertain about his destination, then he may regret not having an agent to rely on.

The main drawback is that the direct-sell operator, however knowledgeable his staff may be about their programme of resorts and hotels, is interested only in selling his own holidays.

In addition, if something goes wrong with a booking made through a travel agent, your relationship with the agent may prove a key factor in obtaining compensation (see page 152). Although the law is still unclear, a travel agent is

unlikely to offer any compensation himself for a ruined holiday unless, that is, you can prove you received misleading information at the time of booking. If you paid the travel agent by credit card (such as Access or Barclaycard, but not American Express or Diners' Club, which are charge cards, not offering credit) and the tour operator, or someone else the agent dealt with, goes bust, you may, in the last resort, be able to claim from the credit card company.

Even though your agent is unlikely to compensate you directly, his support is likely to bring a faster and more favourable response from the tour operator than you might achieve on your own. If that travel agent happens to be part of a powerful chain, the tour operator will ignore the agent's intervention at his peril.

Nightmares

It may not be much consolation to know that travel agents themselves occasionally have a rotten holiday. In 1975 a group of ABTA agents went off to Mexico on what was supposed to be a VIP tour to encourage ABTA to hold its 1977 conference there. Unfortunately, the hotels were not finished, the tour arrangements were a shambles, and three of the wives went down with Montezuma's Revenge. Some of the ABTA travel agents later sued the organisers for the extra cost they had incurred when they abandoned the trip and went off to Florida to recover.

Surcharges

Holiday brochures are put together at least a year before you can take any peak season package tours which, at times of fluctuating exchange rates and unpredictable rises in the cost of aviation fuel, makes operators extremely reluctant to guarantee their prices.

Only in years when business is below expectations—1983 was a conspicuous example—have most companies been prepared to promise that there would be no increases of any kind. This, of course, did beg the question that if they could manage such a step one year, why had they to impose surcharges on other occasions?

Since the summer of 1981, ABTA tour operators have been obliged by their association's code of conduct to specify the 'main cost heads' of any surcharge and to provide on request in writing a reasonable explanation for each additional charge under those headings.

What might seem 'reasonable' to the operator has, in many instances, proved to be only the vaguest indication of why a surcharge had to be made. Some surcharges have even exceeded the level the operator promised would be the maximum he would apply.

If you do receive a demand for a surcharge, contact the agent who did the booking, insist on a written explanation from the tour operator and keep asking for more details. On what date did the operator fix his original prices? Has sterling fared better against other currencies included in the costs, allowing the operator to reduce the surcharge for your holiday? Did he buy any of his foreign currency at a fixed rate in advance, allowing him to avoid the effects of a change in the exchange rate? Does he have fixed price contracts with airlines or hotels?

If the answers seem evasive, complain to ABTA and to the Office of Fair Trading, at Field House, Bream's Buildings, London EC4A 1PR.

Tour operators have been known to reduce surcharges, if only on a selective basis, when faced with awkward questions.

Wise Words

Size up the efficiency, competence and probity of your travel agent.

Watch your rights if you go to a small direct-sell operator.

Don't be beguiled by tempting offers when booking your holiday. They may not make the cost as cheap as it seems.

Do not expect miracles even from a good travel agent, but do demand impartial, sound, expert, professional advice.

Selling a package holiday differs from selling a washing machine in one vital respect: once the machine is made, the manufacturer, distributor and retailer have a vested interest in actually getting rid of the object to a customer. Therefore, they may all be prepared at various times to trim their profit margin to shift the goods. In contrast, the package holiday may exist only on paper—in the brochure. Rather than sell it below a certain figure, the tour operator may prefer to abandon a particular package holiday altogether.

This is because two or three times a year the tour operator has either to take up or give up his options on airline seats and hotel beds. If he cannot be certain of filling enough seats and beds on each holiday to make a profit, he is likely to cut back on both and concentrate on hardening his prices for his remaining holidays. Even in years when the travel industry had an undeniably uneasy time in

READ BETWEEN THE LINES

the early Eighties, the holidaymaker could not be certain that by holding out to the last minute he would obtain a real bargain. He could find he was paying as much as those people who booked early, possibly more in areas subject to surcharge, with far fewer places to choose from.

The package tour industry in recent years has become a bizarre game of brinkmanship. In 1982, the industry as a whole overestimated what it could sell, began panicking in May and June and offering

large discounts as an incentive to buy, only to find there was a huge rush of late bookings for all holidays anyway, making many of those discounts completely unnecessary. In 1983, tour operators who had the previous year hung on to spare capacity and lost money, took fewer risks and cancelled some flights and reduced hotel accommodation early in the year. As a result, a last-minute rush for Easter holidays was hopelessly oversubscribed at the new, lower capacity.

The prices in the brochures have become as negotiable as the holidays themselves. The discounts of 1982 were followed, in the winter of 1982–83, by a huge re-launch of their entire programme by one of the largest tour operators, Thomson Holidays. They stopped the print run of their summer brochure and trimmed almost all their prices, forcing other operators to follow suit.

Reading between the lines of a brochure has, therefore, become an art in itself. The would-be holidaymaker needs to be knowledgeable, alert and sceptical before he can recognise true value for money.

First of all, it is essential to accept your limitations on dates. If you must travel during the school holidays, you are already among that disadvantaged majority who will always need to book early at peak prices. However, children can be kept away from school legitimately for two weeks a year. Teachers, of course, try to discourage parents from taking this step, even though it may not affect the children's education in most cases, except when examinations loom near. Taking work with them can be a sensible compromise, even if

The brochures tell all—once you have learnt to unravel the information packed in their pages

parents do end up doing algebra in the Algarve.

If you are flexible, or can make yourself so, the quietest weeks are invariably after Easter, late April, May or early June. The attraction of this period may wane if you are determined to find a place in the sun. For the truth is that there is no reasonable certainty of fine weather anywhere in the Mediterranean until well into June.

These quiet weeks are the holiday periods that provide the low 'come-on' prices shown on brochure covers. They are also the holidays most vulnerable to cancellation or alteration, when tour operators combine flights and change hotels to avoid being stuck with unwanted rooms or aircraft seats.

But they do provide a clue to a method of obtaining an even cheaper holiday than is offered in the brochure. The majority of tour operators have a number of 'dead legs'—that is, the return flight of their first aircraft out which obviously has no holidaymakers to bring home; and the outward flight of their last aircraft of the season, which equally has no clients going off on holiday. Usually they will be happy to book passengers one-way on the 'dead leg' at a nominal price, as they have already spread the cost of the empty flights across the whole of the season.

Having fixed one cheap flight, either back early season or out late season, you need to search the brochures for another company flying to the same or a nearby destination earlier or later, and who therefore might have some spare capacity on the other

flight you need to complete the trip, though obviously not at rock bottom 'dead leg' prices. Although this leaves you with the problem of booking your own accommodation, the full cost could still be substantially below a brochure package price.

Even if you are going on an official brochure package, it is essential to unravel the printed information. Many package holiday flights take off in the middle of the night, which may require you to book a hotel near the British departure airport for the whole family to make the journey tolerable, and leave you spending miserable hours waiting for your resort hotel room to become available. Worse still, on the return you may have to vacate your room up to eighteen hours before your flight home. Some 'fourteen-day' holidays are in reality only eleven nights abroad, with two overnight flights making up the difference.

To avoid being taken in by

exaggerated claims, ask your travel agent to show you the *Agents Hotel Gazetteer*, covering resorts and hotels. This is the travel agents' bible, and it is likely to give you a more realistic assessment of the holiday you have in mind.

First recognition that a brochure did not always coincide with reality came refreshingly from Sovereign Holidays in their winter sun brochure for 1981 and then in their summer brochure for 1982. These both included a section entitled 'What it's really like'.

Admittedly, this candid section appeared towards the back of the brochure and was not always consistent with descriptions on the glossier pages. For example, the Promenade Des Anglais in Nice, described as 'famous, palm-fringed', at the back became a 'howling inferno with traffic lights'. Switzerland's 'sparkling air' and 'shining blue waters' was augmented by an admission

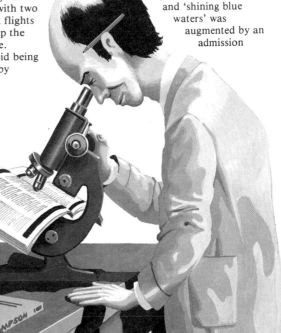

that 'it rains quite often'. The 'brilliant sunshine' of the Greek mainland was qualified by the observation that it was 'insufferably hot in summer'. Sadly, some of the contents of 'What it's really like' were toned down the following year or omitted altogether—in particular, the comment on Spain that 'The natural warmth and dignity of Spanish manners has been overlaid by a pre-occupied frown—the frown of people torn between the itch to make another million and the desire to pack the whole damn thing in.'

Sometimes, also, it pays to study the brochures carefully, preferably at leisure at home, if necessary by collecting handfuls of them from a travel agent, or by using one of the telephone numbers that follow holiday advertisements on television. Ask yourself:

Does the price quoted in the brochure include airport taxes, transfers, and, if compulsory, insurance?

Do the children's discounts apply to the weeks I want to go?

What do I get for my money in the way of meals?

What time are the flights and what type of aircraft is it?

What facilities am I actually promised at the resort hotel?

Am I liable for any surcharges? (see page 15)

In recent years, many companies have offered a no-surcharge guarantee as an inducement to book early. Alternatively, they may give an undertaking to allow you an option to cancel if surcharges go above, say, ten per cent of the price, but this may leave you with no suitable holiday at all if you take them at their word and cancel.

Also, in return for a no-surcharge guarantee, you may be tempted to pay for the entire holiday at the time of booking, when you could have invested the money for the remaining months at a higher rate of return than any likely surcharge! In these days of fluctuating currencies, the safest holidays are those either levying a surcharge without conditions, or no surcharge.

Never rely on your friends' comments on a tour company: they will rarely admit they made a disastrous choice; that the hotel was next to a railway line and the food inedible.

A careful reading of the brochure may not prevent you from making the wrong choice or being misled, but it can give you a hint of the attitude of the company you are dealing with. If its booking conditions appear in minute print and are couched in 'legalese', its price tables incomprehensible, its vital data on flights obscure, its descriptions suspiciously effusive . . . well, you have been warned.

Better the candid observation, such as the one in the Small World brochure, that 'maintenance, one suspects, cannot be translated into most Mediterranean

Wise Words

Try not to travel in school holidays. Holidays cost more, and discounts are virtually non-existent.

Make the most of off-peak holidays by booking yourself on 'dead leg' flights.

Ask to see the *Agents Hotel Gazetteer* for unbiased information on resorts and hotels.

Study the brochures at leisure to determine the full cost of the holiday and its hidden drawbacks.

Do not rely on friends to tell you the unvarnished truth about a package tour. They seldom admit they have chosen badly!

languages. No one thinks of repairing anything until it is broken, and then a long period of gestation is necessary before action is taken.'

Brochure photographs are an art form in themselves, sometimes taken by professional photographers using telephoto lenses to obtain the one angle that cuts out the sewage farm adjacent to the hotel, or foreshortens the long trek to the beach to a matter of yards.

John Hill Holidays took the bold step in 1983 of including snapshots taken by their own clients on previous holidays rather than professional pictures, in a brochure that was often brutally frank about some of the shortcomings of the holidays offered.

Take, for example, one hotel in the Algarve, where, said the brochure: 'If you wish to try for any service at all, a

crash course in German is suggested. Car hire highly recommended, in order that you may legitimately escape from the watchful eye of the camp commandant.'

But there is no accounting for taste. John Hill were amazed when the first booking they received from their new brochure was for . . . the very same hotel!

Nightmares

A leading chain of travel agents, Wakefield Fortune, decided one year not to accept tour operators' descriptions of hotels in brochures, but to compile their own *Recommended Resort and Hotel Guide*. It proved to be a startling frank publication. For example, of a Mediterranean hotel, it said: 'No words can describe this appalling hotel. Do not recommend under any circumstances.' But, when a television crew

arrived at the hotel, they discovered that by and large the British clientele were quite content with their lot. They also found the owner was an Englishman, who was quite beside himself with fury when he discovered what had been said about his hotel. Although Wakefield stuck to their assessment, they may have wondered privately about the wisdom of being quite so candid about an establishment with a British proprietor.

Up until May 1983, there was little doubt that the most attractive method of spending money abroad was by cashing personal cheques backed by your domestic cheque guarantee card. Because of the time lag between the date when you received the money and when the money was debited from your account—two to three weeks on average—it was possible to obtain some spending money on credit. For years, irresponsible customers have been cashing cheques abroad with impunity, knowing that the cheques could not bounce and that they had achieved a temporary overdraft without even the risk of a sharp letter from the bank manager.

Alas, those halcyon days seem to have gone for good because all the major clearing banks have now followed Barclays (whose Barclaycard, a credit card as well as a cheque card, never guaranteed cheques cashed abroad) by requiring customers who want to cash cheques abroad to apply for a Eurocheque encashment card.

The Eurocheque encashment card allows customers to cash up to two cheques, each for £50 or less, every day, written in sterling, at any overseas bank displaying the 'EC' symbol in its window. This arrangement has enabled the

PAY UP, WITHOUT LOSING OUT

banks to reduce the number of stolen cheques in circulation and to exclude customers whose financial acumen was likely to desert them in the face of Continental temptations, thereby potentially saving the clearing banks millions every year. At the same time, the banks have speeded up the process whereby they can debit the home account of customers. People who draw too much can suddenly find their accounts in the red, then face not being issued with a new card the following year.

Not that the Eurocheque system is necessarily the most attractive or advantageous source of funds. The plain truth is that banks take longer, charge more, and are less flexible than other agencies. On the Continent, banks always seem to be open when you do not need them. What with early opening and long lunch hours, or no lunch hours and early closing, or fête days or public holidays or bank holidays and Monday

closing (if it is a Monday) or Saturday closing (if it is a Saturday), they have us all beaten from time to time.

Unless, that is, you happen to be a customer at the Midland, Northern, Clydesdale, Allied Irish Banks or Bank of Ireland. They issue Eurocheques to go with their Eurocheque encashment card, and these can be used in shops and hotels as well as banks. Each cheque, which you write out in local currency, is good for £75, and you can use several at once. The snag is that most customers have to pay for the Eurocheque card, and pay another small charge for each cheque cashed abroad.

Holders of a National Giro account with a Girobank guarantee card can use Giro postcheques to obtain foreign currency at European post offices and at Western Union offices in the USA—an advantage as post offices are frequently open when banks are closed.

For most travellers abroad, however, a combination of cash and travellers cheques is the most sensible solution. In the USA dollar travellers cheques are a must. Elsewhere, travellers cheques in the currency of destination are of advantage during particularly poor periods for the pound, when British people abroad will find themselves having to cash sterling travellers cheques at appalling rates of exchange.

The clearing banks are more than happy for their customers to take travellers cheques, because they have the use of your money from the moment the cheques are debited from

your account to the moment they arrive back from some other bank or retail establishment. This can be up to six weeks which, multiplied in millions, provides the banks with an enormous interest-free float for much of the summer.

This fact makes it all the more indefensible for the major banks to take so long to make refunds on lost travellers cheques, even if the client has carefully counter-signed them only at the moment of encashment, and kept a separate record of the numbers. All of the banks require the time-consuming paraphernalia of telexing the issuing bank, which, of course, can happen only during banking hours back in the UK, and takes half a day at best. After that, Barclays and National Westminster do offer on-the-spot refunds through another bank, but Midland cheques can take a week to replace. Lloyds, if a little quicker, actually make you liable for the loss unless you can show that anyone has accepted them negligently (such as with a signature blatantly not your own). Other banks may be even worse: at least two Italian banks took more than a year to refund stolen travellers cheques, and one refused any refund.

Thomas Cook and American Express are considerably faster at refunding than any bank, and if you buy your travellers cheques from them your own cheque will not be cleared for a day or two, giving you a little extra credit. As a useful last-minute service, Thomas Cook sterling travellers cheques are available at post offices on the spot for cash over the counter. Where

American Express have the edge on Cooks is that they have an arrangement with Avis and with Holiday Inns (USA only), for an emergency refund to keep the holidaymaker from starving at night or on Sunday until their local office or agency re-opens. American Express offices also assist travellers to cancel lost or stolen credit cards, to obtain a temporary identification card, and to send a free cable home as part of the service—extremely useful if you are robbed of everything at once.

However, cash remains the only uniformly acceptable way of settling bills, especially as the point at which credit card transactions are turned back into sterling can cost you several pounds if the currency is weak, and still not be at a really favourable exchange rate even if sterling is strong. Consult your bank about taking foreign currency as many countries have regulations controlling its import and export. And if you take cash, it is vital to make certain that you are covered on your travel insurance.

Nearly every insurance policy now requires that any loss of money or cheques or even travel tickets is reported to the local police, and that a report from them accompanies a claim. This was clearly drafted by people with no idea of the potential hassle involved in getting anything in writing out of Continental police, even in major cities where they speak some English.

If the police are unhelpful, no one can expect you to ruin your holiday by sitting around half a day while they find an English-speaking officer and a typewriter. If they will not

Wise Words

Don't get caught without cash—check bank opening hours and holidays.

Insure your cash.

When ordering travellers cheques, ask your bank which denominations give more favourable rates.

Look up exchange rates when cashing cheques or changing money.

Always be sure of the amount you are paying out in local currency.

produce some sort of report in half an hour, thank them politely and leave. Make a surreptitious note of the name or number of the policeman you speak to, and immediately tell your tour guide or hotel manager about your dilemma. Insurance companies may quibble a little about the absence of a report, but if you have enough circumstantial evidence plus some documentary evidence, they should eventually pay up.

The key to carefree holiday money is that it should be hassle-free! It is never worth joining a long queue for the sake of a few percentage points on the exchange rate, which will add up at best a pound or two on your total expenditure. Cash travellers cheques at your convenience, keeping a good float of well-insured local currency and holding your Eurocheque and credit cards in reserve.

Take a calculator and work out what you should be getting when you do change money: you may be surprised at how often banks make mistakes.

Nearly half the people who go abroad each year fall ill while they are away, or shortly after their return. Visitors to Tunisia and Morocco are extremely likely to become ill, travellers to Spain more likely than not, while one in two tourists in Greece are at risk of catching a tummy bug. Even though the statistics are less depressing for other destinations, every possible precaution should still be taken.

The Department of Health and Social Security has a leaflet, SA30 with form CM1, which, provided your National Insurance payments are up to date, can be used one month before your trip to obtain form E111. This in turn is supposed to ensure that you can obtain reciprocal free medical treatment throughout the European Economic Community.

Alas, it does not. First, potential patients seeking help under a social security scheme are regarded as second-class citizens in some EEC countries, particularly in Greece. Even the DHSS 'strongly recommends' private medical cover for Greece, where other treatment can be extremely rudimentary. Second, you need to find a doctor registered with the sickness insurance scheme, and many are not. Third, in the majority of cases, you will have to pay on the spot for treatment and recover some of the money later. Fourth, you will have to pay the local pharmacy or the hospital for any medicines used, and the costs of these, together with doctors' fees, X-rays, etc, will have to be entered on a signed statement of treatment which you send to the DHSS back in Britain. Fifth, any refund, which may well take three months, could be only 70 per

MODERATION PROVIDES THE BEST PROTECTION

cent of the total expenditure.

Some insurance companies encourage policy holders to take out form E111 because they could recover some of the cost of claims. The realistic position is that anyone trying to use form E111 is likely to be given inferior treatment and subjected to a disagreeable level of bureaucracy far out of proportion to the benefits involved.

As many people will be insuring their luggage, and against cancellation, the actual cost of obtaining additional insurance against the need for medical treatment may be very little more. Anyone who does not do so is taking a quite unrealistic personal risk, with their own health and with the health of others of the family involved.

Many package holidays include an optional insurance —optional, that is, in that you may be able to choose an alternative policy of your own, but some kind of insurance may be obligatory. These policies are only summarised, and not printed in full: ask to see a complete version of all conditions.

Policies which offer some kind of emergency telephone service must be highly recommended. Do not hesitate to use the number, however

brief you expect the illness or disability to be. Your diagnosis may be wrong and, if only to reduce their later potential bills, any prudent insurance company will make certain you receive expert treatment from the start of any sickness.

You may need to be taken home: make sure that any repatriation clause applies equally to other members of the family. There may be a three-way conflict of interest between the needs of the patient, the wishes of the insurance company (who obviously want to keep down their costs) and those of the get-you-home service (who want more business). If you suspect that your treatment is inadequate, ask your hotel to send a cable or a telex to the insurance company demanding repatriation. It may strengthen your claim for compensation later and may well influence their attitude in your favour.

In other respects, do not expect any help beyond sympathetic noises from your tour operator's local representative, your hotel manager, or the nearest office of the British Consul. The reality is that they simply have far too many people to deal with to give specialised assistance.

If you do not take out a policy where the insurance company undertake to handle all the bills, such as with Europ Assistance, you may be required to pay quite large amounts in advance by travellers cheques, credit cards or Eurocheques. In the United States, especially, it is quite common for people to be refused medical treatment on the grounds that they do not have the means to meet their bills.

Do not, under any circumstances, allow anyone in

your party to be admitted to a hospital or to be given any treatment unless you know exactly what is involved. Your aim must be to ensure that they receive first-class treatment, whatever the cost of this or, if this is not available, to get them home. Argue about the money later on.

Prevention is worth any amount of care or cure. Tour operators and travel agents will, of course, indicate compulsory vaccinations, because holidaymakers without them could be sent home and therefore be looking for compensation. Any other vaccination recommended is ignored at your peril.

The DHSS produce a useful leaflet, SA35, listing recommended vaccinations and precautions. Many people may have the impression that the Mediterranean is free of serious diseases. In fact, visits to Morocco and Tunisia need vaccinations against cholera, typhoid and polio, and tablets to prevent malaria; for Spain, Italy, Greece, Yugoslavia and Mediterranean France vaccinations against typhoid are needed. Vaccinations should be completed three to four weeks before your holiday to avoid discomfort when travelling and to make certain that they have had time to take effect.

There is, however, no real prevention for travellers' diarrhoea. Its symptoms, apart from the obvious, are general nausea and stomach cramps, sometimes lasting two or three days. Kaolin for children, and morphine, available in liquid or tablet form for adults without prescription, can reduce the symptoms; or, for a severe case, use streptotriad

tablets. It is cheaper to buy medicines from a UK chemist.

The tourist 'trots' cause dehydration, as does air travel and hot temperatures. It is most important to replace lost fluid by drinking large amounts of pure water or alcohol-free drinks. Bottled mineral water is much cheaper than in the UK and ideal in most cases. Avoid all heavily chilled drinks.

Tap water in large cities, major tourist hotels and almost everywhere in northern Europe is usually quite safe to drink; but rather than worry about whether it is or not, prudent travellers tend to stick to mineral water. They also avoid two common traps: ice in drinks, which may not have been frozen from pure water; and cleaning their teeth with tap water.

Body salts are also lost in hot climates: again, sachets of oral-rehydration salts can be bought at chemists' shops.

All raw food is a potential source of infection, especially shellfish, salads, unpeeled fruit and icecream. Unboiled milk, too, can be dangerous unless you are quite certain that it was sterilised before being bottled.

Mosquitoes can carry malaria and, contrary to some advertising claims, there is no safe preventive against being bitten. Insect repellent (which can also repel fellow travellers) may keep most of them away; antihistamine cream may help to reduce swelling. Mosquitoes are more active after dark and are invariably attracted by light.

The most dangerous bites, however, are from animals. Rabies has made such inroads abroad that no area is completely safe. If you are

bitten by a dog, or scratched by a cat or some other animal, assume the worst: go to a local doctor and pay for a series of anti-rabies injections. Even an animal lick on an open wound can be fatal. So stay away from all strange animals abroad, watching children— who are usually attracted to animals—especially carefully.

Health precautions are also a matter of moderation. Too much alcohol, too much 'exotic' food, too much sun and too little sleep can all contribute to poor health. Equally, a paranoid obsession with avoiding every possible risk can spoil a holiday more effectively than bad weather and indifferent accommodation. The trick is to avoid the pain while still partaking of the pleasures!

Wise Words

Disregard the procedure that gives limited cover in the EEC and insure as for any other country.

Take out insurance which offers a telephone emergency service, and do not hesitate to use it!

Read the small print on the insurance policy: under what circumstances will they bring you, and your family, back home?

Be aware that the Mediterranean is far from free of nasty contagious diseases.

Take plenty of non-alcoholic drinks for diarrhoea or dehydration. Do not drink tap water, or take ice in drinks.

Be careful of uncooked food of all kinds.

Stay away from animals.

Give some thought in advance to whether you will want to drive a hired car abroad. Although it may seem convenient to take a car hired in the UK abroad or to hire in one Continental country and drive to others, you must advise the rental company of your intentions when booking in order that they may obtain any relevant documents and this can prove complicated and costly.

If you want to hire when you arrive, still make some preparations. Don't forget to take your driving licence and a current International Driving Permit (see page 7), plus good maps and metric/imperial conversion tables, and to find out about motoring regulations in the country or countries you intend visiting.

There are rather more pitfalls than you might expect in hiring a car. It is not simply the choice between an expensive, but reliable, car from one of the major international companies, or a cheap, potentially troublesome vehicle from the local firm.

First, there is the deposit. Tempting though it may be to use a credit card to pay the deposit—by signing a voucher in which the total has been left blank—in doing so you will have abandoned your major bargaining power if things go wrong. Although you might be able to dispute a bill paid in this way, especially by Barclaycard or Access, under the terms of the Consumer Credit Act, it can be a prolonged and tedious business. Better to leave a sum of money or travellers cheques to cover the deposit, and to fight hard to keep the amount around or below what you actually expect to pay.

Next, insurance. It is difficult to prevent the less

ASK FOR A TEST DRIVE

reputable car hire firm from making a profit on your insurance, because the risk of being involved in an accident in a foreign country is really too high for you to refuse to take out the Collision Damage Waiver, by which you reduce your excess (that is, the amount you have to pay, however large the claim) to nothing or next to nothing.

But do ask to see a copy of the insurance policy covering the car and passengers, and look carefully at the extent to which injuries to passengers and other third parties are covered. In the USA, especially, cover in this respect is often inadequate.

Then there is petrol. The usual system adopted by car hire firms is to fill up the car before use, then to refill it at the end, and to charge for the difference. However, in hot countries, petrol expands as it heats, so if they re-fill the car early in the morning, it could

Wise Words

Pay your deposit in cash or travellers cheques.

Read the insurance policy details carefully.

Hire only when you can get a full day's use out of the car.

Check the car over—especially if it is hired from a small company.

cost you five per cent more in fuel. Some less reputable companies also fix the fuel gauge so that it shows full when the tank could actually take 25 per cent more petrol; when they come to fill it up, they make a gallon or two on every rental.

Most rental companies work on a 24-hour basis from the time of delivery, so using a taxi on the first and last days of your holiday—when all you may want to do is the relatively short journey between the hotel and the airport—can save two days' rental.

Whatever kind of car you get, check it as though your life depended on it—it probably does! If you go to a local hirer, ask a representative of the company to let you drive the car round the block and attempt an emergency stop to test the brakes. Check the tread on the tyres and the pressure on the spare; try out the jack and see if the wheel brace will actually undo all the wheel nuts.

Other items to check include sidelights, headlights, windscreen wipers and washers, horn, and whether you can adjust the seat to a comfortable driving position. As you may wish to lock your belongings in the car, check that all the locks work, including the lock on the boot, assuming there is one.

All this may seem unnecessarily cautious, but any kind of mechanical failure can cause you inconvenience. A small firm may simply be unable or unwilling to provide an instant replacement. Remember also that a badly tuned car can waste petrol, and in countries where the price of a gallon is higher than in the UK, the additional cost can be considerable.

SETTING OFF

**By rail, boat,
car or plane,
the choice is yours –
but what price the journey?**

You will not be able to load up your car and drive away in a carefree mood if you are worried about the security of your home. The best defence against burglary is not to leave your house empty. Encourage relations to come and stay while you are away (assuming you can trust them not to do more damage than a potential burglar) or let your house through a specialist estate agent who will demand the highest references, and insist on a deposit against breakages. Your short-term tenants (and make sure they are short-term) can be asked to water the plants, feed the animals and look after the garden as part of the deal. Or, if you can't get anyone to stay, ask your neighbours' children to do these things for you, and to check that no milk sits on the doorstep, despite cancellation, or mail and hand delivered leaflets are left sticking out of the letterbox.

Do not hope for the best when it comes to securing the house. Seek advice from the crime prevention officer at your local police station; fit new locks to doors and windows if he says they are needed. Do use your locks: incredible though it may seem, many cases of theft arise because the back door, or even the front door, was left unlocked or actually open. Do not, though, lock inside doors: a burglar once inside the house has time on his hands to break them down, and you will come home to a lot of damage—and your worldly goods will still be gone! Outside, lock away all your tools, especially hammers, chisels and ladders.

As well as visiting a locksmith or specialist security firm, you may need to go to a good electrical store. Buy two or three automatic time

GOING BY ROAD

For the freedom to have a flexible timetable, and visit some places en route, the sheer convenience of travelling by car is hard to beat.

switches which, connected to the lights and a radio, may effectively deter burglars and vandals.

As well as giving thought to the home you are leaving behind, consider the car you are taking with you. The trail of British vehicles strewn across the Continent every summer after failing to last the course emphasises the need to have your car properly prepared for the journey. Not only should it go in for a service in adequate time before you depart, but your garage should be made aware of the mileage you intend to complete—in some cases, five or six times the average for a fortnight. Put your intentions in writing, so that the garage is aware you may have a legitimate claim for redress should they make a foolish mistake.

If you have had your car looked at in the crucial few days before you set off on holiday the chances of a mechanical breakdown on the road will have been substantially reduced. But just because you think the car is in tip-top condition at the outset does not mean it will soldier on throughout your holiday without needing to be pampered from time to

time. The car handbook gives a list of essential checks but, as a general guide, here's what you should not neglect.

Daily checks
Check tyres for damage, brake fluid and coolant levels, oil and petrol. Clean windows, lights and mirrors. All these routine examinations can be best remembered with the code word POWER—Petrol, Oil, Water, Electrics and Rubber.

Weekly checks
Check brake and clutch fluids, battery distilled water level, windscreen washer bottle, tyres for flints or stones in the tread, and see the treads have at least 2mm of tread depth. Check tyre pressures, fan belt tension and the free movement of both brake and clutch pedals (see owner's handbook).

Even if you are a complete duffer when it comes to mechanical matters, you can at least carry spare parts which will allow someone better qualified to restore you to the road if you do break down.

An emergency kit is easy to store in the boot and will

Nightmares

It is possible to be too eager about leaving your home safe. By all means switch off electrical wall sockets and remove plugs and aerials, but don't follow the example of one thorough couple who turned off their electricity at the mains. Not only did this defeat the purpose of having carefully installed automatic timing devices for the lights and radio, but the contents of their large freezer degenerated into a soggy write-off.

always come in useful. Here is a checklist:
fanbelt
complete set of bulbs
set of fuses
top and bottom hoses
two spare wheel nuts
set of ring spanners
strong jack
wheel brace
length of electric cable
a roll of insulating tape
pair of windscreen wiper blades
torch
fire extinguisher
tow rope
first aid kit
warning triangle

A first aid kit is compulsory in Austria, Belgium, Bulgaria, Czechoslovakia, Germany, Greece, Portugal, the USSR and Yugoslavia and only sense to carry, anyway. You are expected to carry a set of replacement bulbs in Italy and must do so in France, Norway, Spain and Yugoslavia. A fire extinguisher is compulsory in Belgium and Greece. A warning triangle is compulsory more or less everywhere.

If, despite all your precautions, your car lets you down on the open road you must be prepared for it to happen in some remote spot with no garage, phone box or habitation in sight. Thrown on to your own resources, the only solution is to roll your sleeves up and get on with it. The most inept motorist is able to change a fuse (look for their position in the car handbook) or repair an obviously broken cable; with practice, you can even put on a new fan belt.

The wheel brace, jack and wheel nuts are part of the scenario at a puncture where invariably the jack buckles under the weight, the brace will not budge the wheel nuts, or if it does, a nut rolls down a bank and out of sight. Testing the jack and undoing all the nuts (then doing them up again tight, of course) before you set off can avoid problems and possible disaster in, say, a busy Parisian street.

A GB plate must be displayed on the rear of your car: these can be obtained from motor accessory shops, the ferry company or your motoring organisation. The plate is required to be a white oval, at least 175mm (6.9in) wide and 115mm (4.5in) high, the characters black Latin capitals with a minimum height of 80mm (3.1in) and a stroke width of 10mm (0.4in). Police with time on their hands have been known to

MYO 131B

measure GB plates and to fine offenders.

You will also need to take headlamp beam deflector and colour conversion kits, both available from motor accessory shops. France may penalise motorists not displaying yellow headlights, while left-dipping headlights are not permitted abroad. You will probably have time to fit these kits and put on the GB plate while waiting for the ferry.

One other important item to consider is a nearside wing mirror, which must be attached before you set off if your car does not possess one. On the Continent this is a major safety factor. In Italy it has been required by law for some years on all vehicles, whether imported temporarily or not, and in 1983 the Italian police began to fine motorists without one.

Before you set off inspect your tyres particularly carefully. Apart from the safety factor, it is a serious offence to drive in certain Continental countries with significantly worn tyres. If they are marginal now, they could be dangerous before you complete the trip. Find out the correct increased tyre pressures which will compensate for the weight of passengers and their luggage and fast motorway driving and pump up the tyres when cold. Pay special attention to the spare, as finding that it is almost flat when you have a puncture could leave you stranded.

With regard to luggage, check your cases and everything you intend to pack at least two weeks before you travel. Does anything need repairing or cleaning? Does it still fit or, if it is new, did it ever fit? Make a list of what you need to take and add to it as you go along.

Always take a separate case for each person travelling, because packing is simpler and the weight is more manageable. Luggage in a car may be difficult to unpack on the way, so taking an overnight bag will save you discomfort. To keep you self-sufficient for 24 hours or so, it should contain a change of everything, a toilet bag, your camera and films, sunglasses, aspirins, paperbacks, and a small alarm clock.

When planning what you will take, bear in mind that there are limits—both practical and legal—to how much you can load into and onto a car. Exceeding your car's regulation weight limit can create safety risks and make you liable to on-the-spot fines. You would also be obliged to reduce the load before you could go on your way. An overload of passengers could get you into trouble, too; it is an offence to carry more passengers than the vehicle is intended to seat.

Packing the car is a major battle between necessity and logic. A variation of Parkinson's Law says that absolute necessity rises to pass available space, particularly because the family always regards a car as an unbridled licence to take everything bar the kitchen sink. Do not take a roof-rack unless packing without one proves quite impossible, because they are time-consuming to load and unload, vulnerable to weather and thieves, and devour petrol. If you must take one, ensure that it is loaded in a way that will not upset the vehicle's stability, strap down everything under a waterproof cover and make it as streamlined as possible. Any projections that are not obvious must have attention drawn to them in some way.

A roof-rack, however, is preferable to blocking the rear window with cases or restricting the driver's leg room. What may be acceptable for a shopping trip could prove dangerous on a long Continental drive. When you have decided on the maximum safe amount of luggage, a day before you depart work out how it will all fit into the boot. Try to ensure that emergency items, such as the warning triangle, can

Wise Words

What have you forgotten? Here is a useful check list: house keys; spare car keys; camera; films; some sterling; spare spectacles; needle, safety pins; cotton; aspirin; indigestion remedy; plasters; insect repellent; anti-histamine cream; sun oil; anti-diarrhoea medicine; sleeping pills; make-up; shampoo; toothpaste; toothbrush; nail scissors; soap; shoe polish; sunglasses; razors; shaving foam; hairbrush; comb; handkerchiefs; dressing gown; swimming costume; hair dryer; phrase book; address book; pens; raincoat. For a list of documents you need to take, see page 9. For items for children, page 138.

be removed quickly. (Unfortunately, almost every car has an inaccessible spare wheel, adding to the aggravation of a puncture.) Wedge soft bags with crushproof items such as beach wear or towels between the cases to stop them shifting and to keep metal items from rattling. To avoid moving the bulk of the luggage more than once, the last bag to go in should be the one full of essentials for an overnight stop.

Then come items stored inside the car to make the journey as trouble-free as possible. Road maps, with your intended route marked in bold red ink—they may be a useful source of reference next year, too. Maps do not weigh much or take up a lot of room, so carry large and small-scale folding maps or atlases covering the route and your destination. Try to buy those with a publication date inside that suggests they are up to date. It would be a pity to miss, say, 20 miles (32km) of brand new motorway.

Another list of items can make the trip as hygienic as possible: toilet paper (often missing from public loos), half-a-dozen large boxes of paper napkins, a packet of plastic rubbish bags with ties to seal their tops, plastic containers for decanting tea, coffee, milk or orange juice, paper plates, paper cups, refresher tissues, a wet flannel and a wet leather for cleaning the windows.

Add to this two corkscrews (you are bound to lose one), a bottle opener, some old knives and forks, a new sharp knife, a tin opener, some old drinking glasses (wine tastes awful in paper cups), a

vacuum flask, salt, pepper, powdered milk, instant coffee packets, tea-bags, cans of soft drink, crisps, biscuits, and cling film for wrapping sticky foods.

If you are travelling across mountain passes, keep some thick sweaters in the car for the colder sections. For younger children, you will need many more items for the trip (see page 138).

Lastly, to cut down on the risk of being burgled, tell as few people as possible that you are going away, and never talk about it casually in pubs, shops or anywhere you might be overheard. Pack the vehicle discreetly. Some families make such a performance of their preparations and packing that their departure could not be more conspicuous if they took out an advertisement in the local newspaper.

On the great day itself, check petrol, water and oil, and whether the boot or tailgate lock opens easily. If it does not, take the time to oil it—if it jams on holiday it could spoil your arrival at your destination on that day. Put all your

Wise Words

Do not take too much with you.

Stow essential car spares in the boot.

Wedge soft bags between hard cases to stop luggage rattling.

Put an overnight bag in last.

Buy good up-to-date maps.

Make a list of 'comfort' items for the journey.

documents in a folder under the driver's seat and, for peace of mind, check them all one more time, before you set off.

Estimate a safe margin for reaching your departure port in bad weather and heavy traffic and advance that time by an hour for everyone else. You will probably still only just make it!

Any port in a storm, but which port for your holiday? Depending on your ultimate destination, you can substantially cut the amount of Continental driving (though not necessarily the journey time, as the longer sea crossings are slow). For example, using motorways where available:

Paris is 178 miles (297km) from Calais, 120 miles (200km) from Dieppe

Rennes, in Brittany, is 41 miles (69km) from St Malo, 172 miles (286km) from Le Havre and 249 miles (415km) from Calais

Amsterdam is 49 miles (81km) from the Hook of Holland, 158 miles (263km) from Zeebrugge, 170 miles (283km) from Ostend and 229 miles (381km) from Calais

Barcelona is 427 miles (711km) from Santander, 764 miles (1,273km) from Cherbourg and 860 miles (1,432km) from Calais (via Lyon).

The longer the crossing, usually the higher the price—but balance that against the

CHOOSE AND USE THE RIGHT TOWN

fact that there are tolls on many motorways, including most in France.

Calculating the exact cost of your ferry, even once you have decided on your route, can be complex. Ring the companies for quotes and check with more than one travel agent to arrive at accurate figures. Many fares are seasonal, and if you can shift your date of travel marginally (avoiding school holiday periods in summer) you may save money.

The day of the week and the time of day can also have an important effect on the cost, though no one should underestimate the

the dearer ferry one way may be the cheaper ferry coming back. Weigh up the cost advantages of a shorter crossing and the frequency of services. If you miss a boat on a short sea crossing, unless you are really unlucky at the height of season, you will be able to travel on the next one. Miss a longer crossing, and you may have to wait several hours or several days.

Even with meticulous planning and packing the odds are that, by the time you get on the road for your final journey to the port, you are already behind schedule. Do not panic, though you should always aim to meet the check-in times of 45 minutes or more before departure. These are based on the assumption that the handling procedures work most efficiently if the arrivals can be spread, and that by the law of averages, a few stragglers are inevitable. So, if you arrive with only fifteen minutes to spare, you will have to be very unlucky not to be allowed to board. But do not get into the habit of cutting it fine . . .

The layout varies slightly from port to port, but your procedure should always be the same. Unless you are frantically behind schedule

price you pay in fatigue for a late night, overnight or dawn sailing without a cabin.

Do not automatically book with the same company in both directions; because of tariff and seasonal variations

your first requirement is a petrol station because you do not want to waste time filling up abroad in unfamiliar surroundings. The days when ferries were so unstable that petrol tanks had to be only two-thirds full have gone long ago, but filling right to the brim can result in slight spillage, causing ugly stains on the bodywork. Many ferry companies prohibit the carrying of a full spare petrol can, however secure, as it constitutes a fire risk; so take an empty can and fill it on the Continent.

Re-check oil (see page 48) and water and tyres (see page 28)—again because a potential problem identified in the UK may be a lot less hassle to rectify here than it is on the Continent.

Stock up with cans of soft drinks, sweets and crisps for the journey. Pay for these items and the petrol by credit card; you may be glad later that you kept your cash.

If you have plenty of time and have not yet changed your money, at many ports there will be an opportunity to do so.

When the time comes to check-in, look for a sign indicating the company you are travelling with, as at most ports individual ferry operators handle their own clients. The principal exception is Dover where, at the main departure point, the Eastern Docks (services to Dunkerque and some Sealink

have not booked, you could be allowed through on standby on the premise that someone is bound to fail to turn up). There is normally no Customs examination on the outward journey (that is an experience to cherish on your return) so you proceed to emigration. Here you will be asked to produce the passports of everyone travelling, and the passport officer will usually check the expiry date.

At Continental ports the passport inspection for incoming and outgoing passengers may be cursory or even non-existent, on the assumption that as every person leaving or arriving in the UK is thoroughly checked, there is little to be gained from repeating the exercise.

After emigration, you are now in limbo—physically still in the country you are leaving but technically on your way abroad. At some ports, there may be an opportunity to visit a duty-free shop, where products of the country you have just left, so to speak, may be cheaper than on the ferry. At others, you may be

removed from your ticket holder; the inconvenience of obtaining replacements, especially at a foreign port, can be horrendous.

Make use of the time in the queue. Re-organise the inside of your vehicle so that items you need on the other side, such as the relevant maps, are now easily to hand. Ensure that any valuables and any items you feel you may need on board the ferry are properly organised, as every second can count once you do embark. Clean the windscreen and all lights. Fit the

services to Ostend leave from the Western Docks), all arrivals are handled by a single computer. Once your tickets have been checked, and your reservation confirmed, a sticker is placed on your windscreen indicating the company you are travelling with and your status (if you

directed into an appropriate queue, where your tickets, already checked, will now be collected.

It would be silly to assume that officials are infallible. At the risk of looking foolish make certain you are in the correct queue: missing the boat is a bad way to start a holiday. Check that only the relevant voucher has been

headlamp beam deflector plus colour conversion kits and GB plate (see page 28), if you have not already done so.

Boarding times are unpredictable at Continental ports, so do not allow the family to wander off. Never park close behind the car in front because if you do, you can be sure his car will not start and you will be left cursing your luck.

32 British ferry ports

The choice of departure port depends on your initial starting point—obvious, perhaps, but many motorists leaving from Manchester and Bristol still travel through Dover when their most direct route would be from Portsmouth or Southampton to Le Havre. If their destination is almost anywhere in the Mediterranean, Le Havre is already at least 50 miles (80km) closer to Paris than Calais. By the same token, the Suffolk port of Felixstowe, with its connection to Zeebrugge, may prove the most direct route for motorists travelling to Scandinavia or Germany. The shortest route between London and Paris is not via Dover but by way of Newhaven and Dieppe. However, Dover does have one real advantage—the frequency of sailings. The Dover Harbour Board promise that motorists who turn up without a reservation, or miss their sailing, will be away on another ship—perhaps not to the planned foreign port, but you cannot have everything—within three hours of their original departure time.

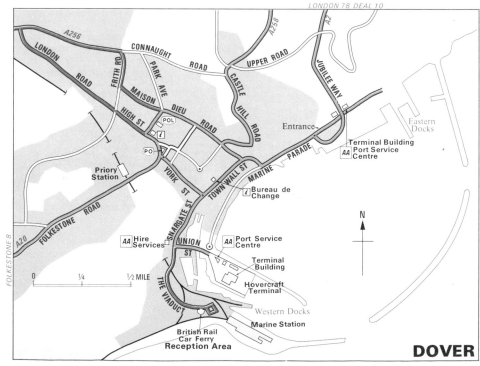

LEGEND					
Motorway		Other road		Police Station	POL
Throughroute	A253	Pedestrians		Post Office	PO
A road	A260	Tourist Information Centre	i	Level Crossing	L.C.
B road	B1315	Hospital	H	Road Service Centre	AA 43

DOVER

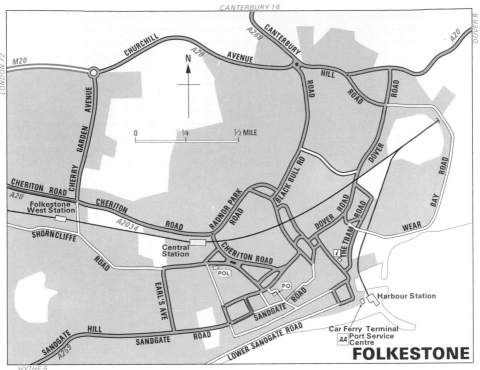

FOLKESTONE

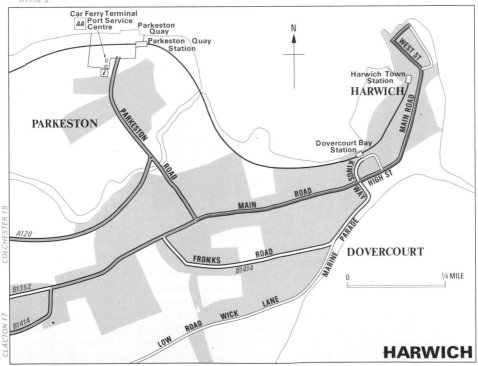

HARWICH

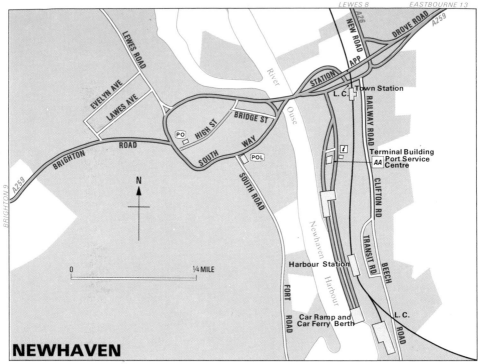

NEWHAVEN

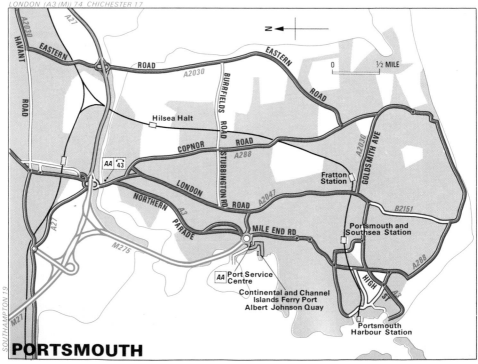

PORTSMOUTH

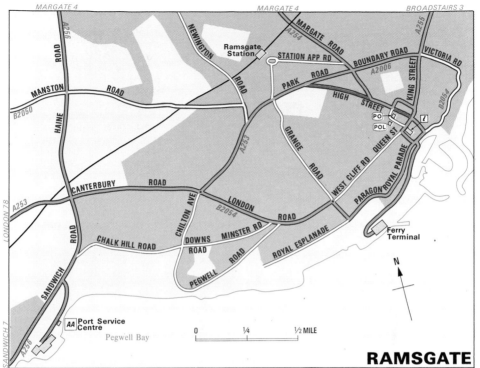

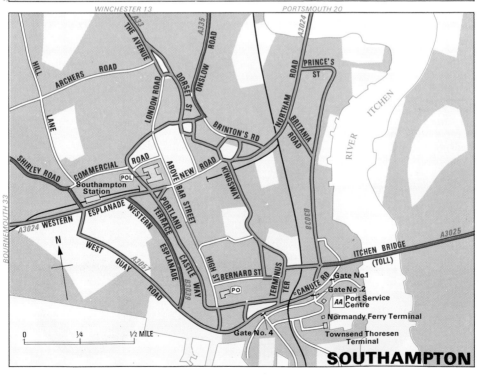

While you have been waiting by your car on the quayside, the ferry that you are sailing in has been a scene of frenetic activity. Supplies of food and drink are replenished and all the passenger areas thoroughly cleaned after the last trip. As one purser remarked while surveying the debris left by the departing passengers: 'To think I used to believe that flotsam and jetsam were found only in the Channel . . .'

The busiest crossings are also the shortest (see page 115). Townsend Thoresen hold the record on the Blue Riband route from Dover to Calais with a time of little more than 50 minutes from harbour mouth to harbour mouth, and delight in passing the Sealink ships. Even the full journey time of up to one and a quarter hours is so short as to make it essential for car passengers to plan ahead to get the best out of their trip.

Driving on to all the ships is simplicity itself—less bumpy than the average level crossing. A ship's officer will usually point your car in the general direction he wishes you to go: a deck hand will shoe-horn you into a precise spot. He wants you straight and no more than a few inches behind the car in front. Park with handbrake on, in gear, lock all

HAVE A GOOD CROSSING

the doors and the boot.

This is where precious minutes are wasted, even by experienced travellers. Everyone has a vague idea of what they want on board: food and drink, duty-free goods, to change currency, or to find the loo—but apart from that pressing need, the order can be critical.

Eat first: that is the advice of a very experienced ship's purser. His reasoning is that a high proportion of passengers on every crossing, faced as they are with a long journey

ahead, are anxious to have a meal. This activity is therefore the least flexible, takes the longest to complete, and on a busy day may well have the biggest queues.

On really crowded crossings, the restaurants with waiter service offer the most comfortable environment. Put simply, they are the one area where passengers cannot collect in crowds. Restaurant seats, of course, fill up quickly as the ship sails. So, before you all get out of the car, dispatch one of your party to stake a claim to a table.

The same principle applies to self-service cafeterias. Queuing a long time is never pleasant, and the food will undoubtedly be at its best in the opening minutes of the voyage. Again, the ideal solution is for one member of your party to climb the stairs quickly to find a place in the queue: if you are lucky, your meal will be on the table by the time you have the children, their paraphernalia and grandma up the first flight.

The restaurant or the cafeteria makes a good base for sending someone on reconnaissance to see how long the queues are for the money

Having a meal on the ferry helps the crossing pass quickly and can save you time on arrival

change and the duty-free shops, usually divided between alcohol plus cigarettes and other goods such as perfume and cameras. Except on the busiest days, queues never last for the whole voyage; and, on most ships, the duty-free shops do not close until the ramp comes down in harbour.

Her Majesty's Customs and Excise have a major role in determining how soon a ferry company will allow passengers on board. In British ports, they impose rigid rules on when bars may open and duty-free goods be sold. Strictly speaking, nothing should be on sale until after 'Harbour Stations' have been called on the way out of port. For this reason, most companies do not allow outgoing passengers on board more than ten or fifteen minutes before sailing, because they will only be irritated if they find shops and bars shut.

In contrast, Continental Customs officers seem quite happy to have duty-free drink sold in harbour, so you may be allowed on board 30 or 40 minutes before sailing. Coaches usually have priority, but their passengers are invariably obliged to carry their duty-free goods around with them for the duration of the voyage. A particularly

efficient car party could finish their duty-free shopping and stow the goods in their vehicle before the car decks are shut for the crossing.

It is worth giving serious consideration to the idea of buying duty-free goods intended for home on the outward trip, if you have room in the car to keep them. Alternatively, you could decide to succumb to the temptation and sample the Scotch or open the king size, or they can be useful for unexpected gifts—perhaps to a helpful mechanic who comes to your rescue when your car gives trouble just as you are down to your last few francs.

On longer sailings, even the most disorganised passengers usually find time to buy their duty-free goods and have a meal, keeping their lounge seats by the thoroughly anti-social (but very British) way of leaving some of their clothes on them. Some companies actually send enthusiastic young officers round the ship on busy days to collect offending cardigans and free the seats: so you have been warned.

At peak periods, the advantages of a day cabin may be considerable. They are frequently available at little cost, and they provide a place

to relax and keep your belongings. The advantages of a cabin on night sailings are obvious.

Perhaps the sternest challenge of all, however long or short the crossing, may be finding your car. It really is essential to make a note of the deck where you parked and the exit you used, even to count the number of staircases you climbed. Otherwise you will join the ranks of refugees clanking up and down corridors in search of a car they can call home, and in the process holding up whole lines of vehicles waiting to disembark.

38 Continental ferry ports

A quick study of your map on the cross-Channel ferry can save a lot of time by making certain that you take the best route out of town to the nearest motorway—assuming, that is, you are in a hurry and want a direct route. From Ostend, the A10 motorway to Brussels begins on the outskirts of town. From Dunkerque West take the N1 towards Dunkerque town, then join the N225 expressway for the A25 11 miles (17km) away to Lille and the first leg to Paris. From Calais take the N43 to the A26 for Paris; this begins 14 miles (23km) away just south of Ardres. From Boulogne, the fastest (though not the shortest) route to Paris is to join the same A26 near St Omer, 27 miles (44km) distant.

From Dieppe, the A13 for Paris lies some 44 miles (71km) away, south of Rouen. From Le Havre, the fastest route to Paris is via the Tancarville bridge to join the A13 near Pont Audemer, 27 miles (44km) south. From Cherbourg, the nearest motorway is at Caen, 75 miles (121km) drive on N13, for Paris by way of the A13.

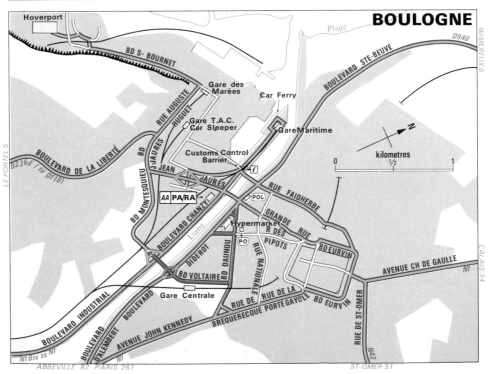

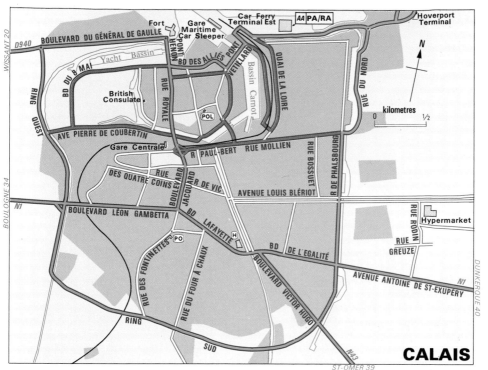

CALAIS

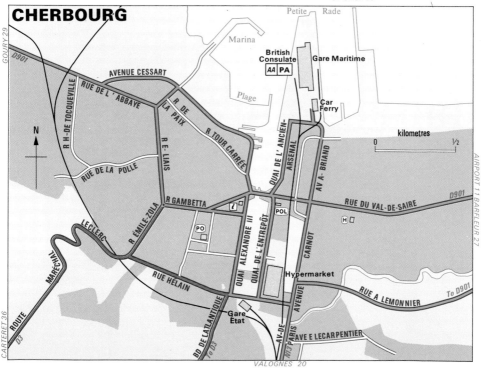

CHERBOURG

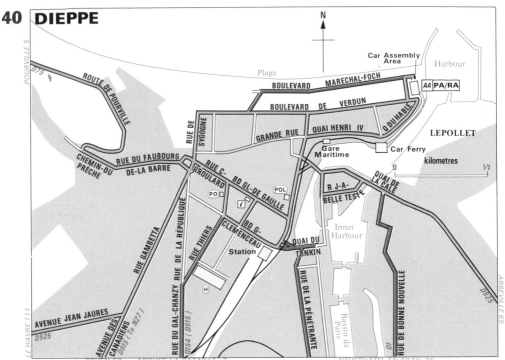

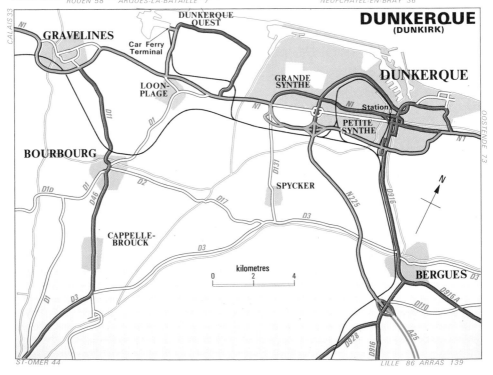

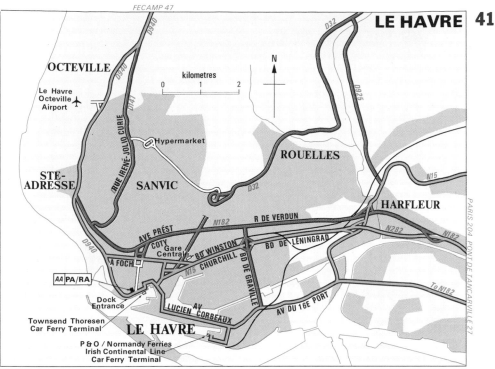

OCTEVILLE

Le Havre
Octeville
Airport ✈

kilometres
0 1 2

N

RUE IRENÉ-JOLIO CURIE

Hypermarket

ROUELLES

STE-
ADRESSE

SANVIC

HARFLEUR

D32

R DE VERDUN

AVE PRÉST

N182

BD DE LÉNINGRAD

COTY

Gare
Centrale

BD WINSTON

A FOCH

AA **PA/RA**

N15 CHURCHILL

BD DE GRAVILLE

Dock
Entrance

AV
LUCIEN CORBEAUX

AV DU 16E PORT

Townsend Thoresen
Car Ferry Terminal

LE HAVRE

P & O / Normandy Ferries
Irish Continental Line
Car Ferry Terminal

PARIS 204 PONT DE TANCARVILLE 27

To N182

D32

N15

N282

N182

D925

D940

D141

D940

D940

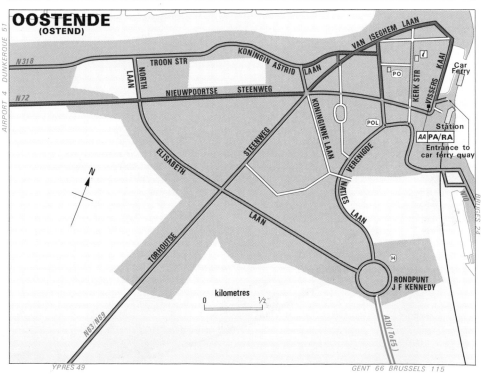

OOSTENDE
(OSTEND)

N318

N72

TROON STR

KONINGIN ASTRID

NORTH

LAAN

LAAN

NIEUWPOORTSE   STEENWEG

VAN ISEGHEM LAAN

VISSERS KAAI

Car
Ferry

KERK STR

PO

POL

Station

AA **PA/RA**

Entrance to
car ferry quay

KONINGINNE LAAN

VERENIGDE

NATIES LAAN

ELISABETH

STEENWEG

LAAN

TORHOUTSE

N

kilometres
0   ½

RONDPUNT
J F KENNEDY

H

AIRPORT 4 DUNKERQUE 51

BRUGES 24

A10 (To E5)

Ostend

Main shops	Adolf Buystraat, Kapellestraat.
Market	Thursday morning, around the Wapenplein; smaller version Saturday and Monday.
Supermarket	Delhaize, Leopold II Laan, quite close to ferry terminal.

Calais

Main shops	Divided between the two centres, Rue Royale in Calais Nord (near the ferry terminal) and Boulevard Jacquard and Boulevard Lafayette in Calais Sud. Free bus to both from the terminal.
Market	Calais Sud, Place Crèvecoeur, Thursday and Saturday Calais Nord, Place d'Armes, Wednesday and Saturday morning.
Hypermarket	Continent, Avenue Guynemer, 1½ml (2.4km) east of Calais. Good crêperie bar (wheel in your trolley if you are lucky). Best sections—wine, cheese, kitchenware. Free bus service from the ferry terminal. Open 9am—10pm Monday—Saturday.

Boulogne

Main shops	Rue Faidherbe, Grande Rue, Rue Thiers.
Market	For food, Place Dalton, Wednesday and Saturday morning For clothes, Boulevard Clocheville, Wednesday and Saturday.
Hypermarket	Auchan, at La Capelle, 4ml (6.4km) from Boulogne, just off N42 in St Omer direction. Best sections—charcuterie, cheese, fish, electrical goods. Will take sterling but exchange rate poor. Bus connection from town centre. Open 9am–10pm Tuesday–Saturday; 2pm–10pm Monday. Also Champion, in town centre.

Dunkerque

Main shops	Place Jean-Bart.
Market	Place du Théâtre, Wednesday and Saturday.
Hypermarket	Auchan, 3ml (4.8km) from Dunkerque, on N1, between Port West and town. Good cafeteria. Open 9am–9.30pm Tuesday–Saturday, 2pm–9.30pm Monday.

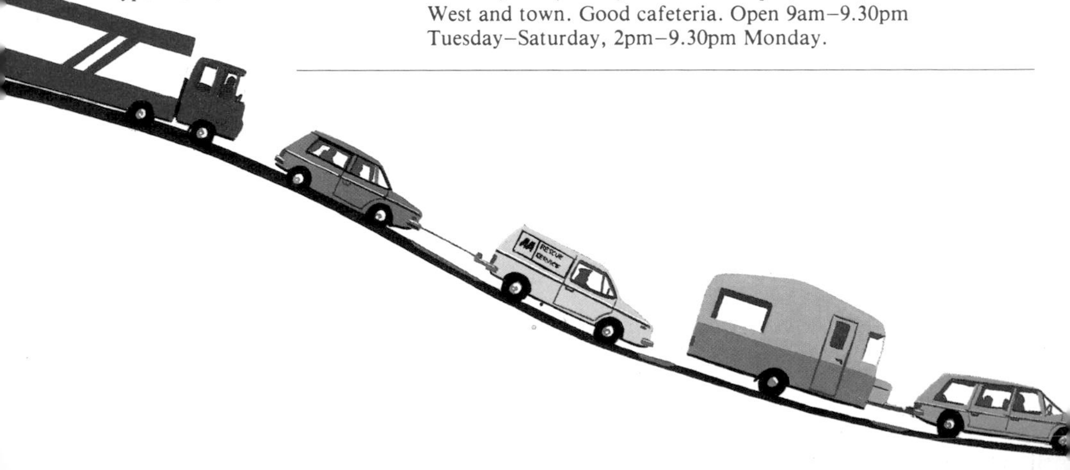

Dieppe

Main shops	Grande Rue, Rue St-Jacques, Rue de la Barre.
Market	Grande Rue, Rue St-Jacques, Place Nationale on Saturday; smaller version Tuesday, Wednesday and Thursday mornings. Exceptionally good.
Hypermarket	Mammouth, 2ml (3.2km) from Dieppe, on the N27 towards Rouen. Best sections: wine, cheese, electrical goods. Will take sterling, and has bureau de change. Open until 7pm weekdays, 6pm Saturdays.

Le Havre

Main shops	Rue de Paris, Place Gambetta.
Market	Cours de la République, daily; Avenue René Coty, Tuesday, Thursday and Saturday mornings; Place des Halles Centrales, under cover, all day.
Hypermarket	Auchan, 2ml (3.2km) north of Le Havre. Take Cours de la République through a tunnel and follow signs to 'Centre Commercial'. Well-stocked food section. Open Monday–Saturday, 10am–10pm. Mammouth, Vallée de la Lézarde, at Montvilliers, a suburb of Le Havre. Not as extensive a selection as at Auchan.

Cherbourg

Main shops	Grande Rue, Rue Gambetta, Rue du Maréchal Foch.
Market	Monday, food.
Hypermarket	Continent, Quai de l'Entrepôt, near the harbour. Superb charcuterie. Other good sections: wine, cheese, kitchenware, garden equipment. Open until 10pm, Monday–Saturday.

St Malo

Main shops	Rue Clemenceau, Rue Ville Pépin.
Market	St Malo Ville, Tuesday and Friday; Place Rocadey, Monday, Thursday and Saturday mornings.
Supermarket	Champion, Centre Commercial, Avenue du Général de Gaulle.

CONTINENTA

The secret of shopping on the Continent, especially in France, is never to be in a hurry. The French like to be regarded as human beings and to have their products appreciated. Passing the time of day, exploring a choice of items, is all part of an accepted way of life. It simply does not matter if there is a long queue of people waiting behind: their turn, eventually, will come. If you fall in with the atmosphere, if you regard shopping as a charm not a chore, an art not an agony, you will never fall out with the shopkeeper.

La charcuterie
As well as cured and cold, cooked meats, provides cooked entrée dishes, including salads and other vegetables.

La poissonerie
The fishmonger who always seems to have an inexhaustible supply of fresh fish, however far his shop is from the sea.

Le traiteur
Goes in for cooked dishes in a big way, sometimes providing a delivery service of full meals.

La boucherie-chevaline
Is what it seems, a seller of horse meat. This is rather stronger in flavour than other meats, but in no way disreputable. Not, however, to be confused with an ordinary boucherie.

La cordonnerie
A shoe-mender's. Expect repairs to take a few days.

Le garage
For car repairs.

L'épicerie
The nearest equivalent to the British grocer's, with a variet products, usually including m Most people use UHT (ultra-heat-treated) which keeps indefinitely until opened. Fre milk comes either with a red which is full cream, or with a blue top, which is skimmed. Various other milk products also usually on sale, including cheese (there are at least as m varieties as days in the year), yogurt and butter. Also tinne food of every kind, and sometimes fresh vegetables.

La librairie
A real bookshop.

La fleuriste
The florist, for flowers and plants. Remember that the import of some of them into the UK may be prohibited.

La pharmacie
A dispensing chemist with only a limited range of the products on sale in British chemists' shops, although he does usually sell baby foods.

La parfumerie
As well as perfume, beauty aids of various kinds.

Le station service
Sells petrol and is unlikely to manage more help than an oil change.

La boucherie
Sells a selection of meat and usually poultry.

La pâtisserie
A French cake shop puts its British equivalent to shame by specialising in superb hand-made tarts and eclairs. Usually they provide a full sweet course rather than a snack.

La crémerie
In larger towns, a specialist dairy shop with every variet milk product.

La boulangerie
Bread is so important here it merits its own shop and is usually made on or near the premises. Baking usually take place every day or twice a day the French take fresh bread f granted. Try croissants, cresc shaped pastry rolls, for breakfast.

IGH STREET

Start early or go late. The British system of opening at 9 am, staying open all day, closing early and never opening on Sundays would be regarded as an anathema by the average Frenchman. Outside Paris, most shops open around 8 am,

close at midday or 1 pm for anything up to four hours, then re-open for another four. Food shops may open even earlier, close longer for lunch, and be open even later. Many are

open on Sunday mornings and, to compensate, may close on Monday mornings or even the whole day. The concept of lunchtime shopping simply does not exist in France, or, for that matter, in other Latin countries such as Italy, Spain and Portugal. Lunchtime is for lunch.

Le supermarché

Self-service, and offering a wide choice. For truly comprehensive shopping find a hypermarché — a huge all-purpose store with a car park, usually on the outskirts of a town.

Le pressing

Have your clothes cleaned and pressed here. Sometimes a 'service wash' is available.

La maison de la presse

Magazines and a few books plus newspapers, although in some areas the French have their daily paper sent overnight by post as there are no deliveries. UK newspapers generally cost three times their face value.

La blanchisserie

A laundry, and certainly not cheap. Launderettes (blanchisseries automatiques) are, however, few and far between because so many French homes have low-priced washing machines.

La mercerie

Haberdashery shop with needles and pins, buttons, zips, sometimes wool. A department in a big store.

Le cours des halles

In large towns only, a shop specialising in fresh fruit and vegetables.

SUPERMARCHÉ · PRIX UNIS · PRESS · PAUL SANSOMA · LIVRES · Blanchisserie · MERCERIE St PAUL · COURS DES HALLES

QUINCAILLERIE · LINGERIE · DROGUERIE R. BOULIN · BOUCHERIE - CHARCUTERIE · JEAN DU BOIS · MARCHAND DE VIN · P T T

La lingerie

What it sounds like, a specialist in women's underwear.

La quincaillerie

A kind of ironmongers, selling tools, screws, more or less anything DIY and metallic.

L' alimentation

Baffles visitors, because no two ever sell the same. Nearly all have tinned food, crisps and biscuits; some may offer eggs and even vegetables - except when you want them.

La boucherie-charcuterie

In addition to meat and poultry, also offers pork, ham, bacon, sausages and pâtés.

La droguerie

Does not sell drugs, but some products associated with chemists' shops, such as soaps, scissors, hair-pins. In fact, household goods of all kinds including paint, polish, brushes, detergents.

Le P T T

A general post office.

Le marchand de vin

Sells wine, beer, spirits and bottled water. A supermarket is cheaper but has less choice.

Le tabac

A tobacconist. To avoid confusion, just ask for a *packet* of cigarettes: they all contain 20. Tobacconists also sell stamps, but may not always know the correct postage rate.

One unexpected source of danger to the British motorist on the Continent can be . . . other British drivers. Some of them drive on and off ferries at breakneck speeds; they have not bothered to study the various relevant motoring regulations and consequently infringe them; they are either exhausted or under the influence of alcohol or both. Above all, they offer the frightening possibility that in an emergency they will respond automatically and swerve to the left rather than to the right.

The closer a British driver comes to a Channel port, the more likely he is to encounter another British driver behaving badly, simply because there are more of them around. But the truth is that all nationalities of drivers on the Continent present a variety of extra risks. The Germans are unused to having an upper speed limit, so go too fast; the Italians, once passed, turn into grand prix drivers until they get their revenge; the Swiss are neurotically slow, and consequently incompetent; the Spanish run cars with defective steering, tyres and brakes; the French are to be avoided after a good· lunch; and Belgians of a certain age may be avoided with difficulty because when they should have been taking a driving test, well, Belgium did not have one.

The busier the European roads, the more likely you are to be involved in an accident— particularly one of those multiple shunts started by a motorist 22 cars back and where your vehicle has dents front and rear. The school holiday period from the middle of July to the end of August should be avoided like the plague. Not only do you face the prospect of collision

THE SURVIVOR'S GUIDE TO MOTORING ABROAD

but every main road at one time or another has a huge traffic jam. A Continental traffic jam is no circus side show, over and forgotten in a few minutes; it is the grand spectacle, certain to last for hours, with the spectators built up to a frenzy. Traffic jams happen at ludicrous times: one of more than 40 miles in length, for example, occurred north of Bordeaux at breakfast time on a Saturday morning. Ironically, it consisted almost entirely of Parisians who had left the capital on Friday night to avoid the main rush.

With the French rediscovering the attractions of domestic travel after their government placed restrictions on the amount of money they can take abroad, evasive action is essential on the peak weekends of July and August. There are alternative routes to motorways and main roads, all thoughtfully signposted with little green arrows by the French department of transport. They even offer a free map of France showing all the routes, which is usually available at the ports or at tourist offices in France. It is called the Bison Futé, or Wily Buffalo, a character who is

supposed to be an American Indian who knows when the palefaces (the tourists) will be on the warpath and has ways of avoiding them. However, beware the possibility of everyone taking evasive action at the same time, reviving the nightmare cartoon image of scores of drivers nose to tail on tiny country roads.

You can, of course, ignore these routes and stay on either the major, direct roads through France or the motorway network. France has a great many fast, straight roads, but with very bumpy surfaces. The surfaces are indicated by a sign 'chaussée deformée', the equivalent of our 'temporary road surface' except that for the French it is not temporary. Many roads also slope sharply in both directions, making the centre of the road the only comfortable place to drive— which is why you constantly need to swerve to avoid oncoming vehicles doing exactly the same.

With the completion of the motorway almost to Ardres, south of Calais, it is now possible to drive continuously by motorway to the toe of Italy. At a price: Austria, France, Greece, Italy, Spain, Portugal and Yugoslavia all charge tolls on most stretches of motorway. In France, toll fees are the same for all passenger cars, but cars towing caravans can expect to pay some 50 per cent more. In Italy, cars under 1300cc are charged less than the rest, except if towing a caravan, when they are automatically charged the large car rate. However, in order to stimulate tourism, the Italian government have been running a scheme of tourist coupons which include a certain number of motorway vouchers, access to a free breakdown service, and petrol coupons giving a substantial discount.

The package for southern Italy, with additional vouchers, has been much more generous than that for northern Italy alone. The tourist coupons have been made available through the motoring organisations in the UK, Barclays Bank and Italian automobile club offices at the frontiers. When buying the coupons, drivers have been required to produce both their passport and their vehicle registration document (if that is a snag, see page 8). To prevent abuse, the coupons are not on sale in Italy, except on the black market, aided and abetted, it must be said, by tourists with coupons left at the end of their holiday. In the past, the Italian government's response to abuse was to abandon the scheme, and this could happen again.

Negotiating motorway toll booths is an art form in itself. There is no set game plan to get you through quickly, let alone to ensure that you have paid the correct sum of money, as receipts are rarely issued. On some motorways, you push a button at the first checkpoint to obtain a tariff card that tells the gateman at your intended exit where you entered the network. On others, you pay in advance for a predetermined stretch of road ahead. On still others, there is an optional toll booth that is fully automatic, into which you throw the correct number of coins to raise the barrier. Spotting a gate with a fast-moving queue can save quite a lot of time on busy roads.

One word of warning: traffic police hang around toll gates and check entry and exit times at random. If the evidence is there in black and white that you have exceeded the speed limit—for example, if you have driven from Calais almost to Paris in under two hours—he may fine you on the

spot. Even without such misadventures, carrying some appropriate foreign currency is essential to meet the toll charges as, apart from a few toll booths situated on frontiers, most of them accept only the domestic currency or Eurocheques.

Petrol costs substantially more on motorways than at garages on ordinary roads, almost without exception. Self-service stations are, however, uniformly cheaper than those with pump attendants. The price of petrol in the UK has risen so much that there is no longer a great saving to be made by filling up at, say, Dover, and running the tank almost dry on the return journey to the port. Nevertheless, without putting yourself to great inconvenience, when you have a choice of country to fill up in, the following observations are likely to remain valid, however much the actual price of fuel changes.

Germany is cheaper than Austria, Belgium, France and the Netherlands but more or less the same price as Switzerland; Switzerland is cheaper than France and much cheaper than Italy, although Italian petrol coupons ensure a 20 per cent discount; France is cheaper than Spain and Spain is cheaper than Portugal; the UK is cheaper than France.

The real bargains, however, are Luxembourg and Yugoslavia, both substantially cheaper than anywhere else in western Europe. Luxembourg also has a major differential between four and two-star petrol, making a minor diversion for motorists whose cars run on two-star really worthwhile. In Yugoslavia, the pump price is more or less the same as Luxembourg, but petrol coupons give a further 27 per cent discount, making their petrol extremely cheap. These coupons are obtainable at the frontier, from branches of the Stopanka Bank, or from the Atlas, Kompas and Putnik travel agencies, on production of your passport and vehicle registration document. The discount is so large that motorists can hardly ignore the coupons and anyway, strictly speaking, they are not allowed to buy petrol in Yugoslavia without them.

Carrying petrol in cans in your car is prohibited on Continental motorail trains and on ferries. It is also against the law to carry petrol in cans in Greece, Italy and Portugal.

What can and should be carried, however, is engine oil. Not only is this much more expensive on the Continent, but it is sold in bigger cans, so merely topping up can be an extremely expensive exercise. Drivers of automatics should carry a supply of transmission fluid as this is not always readily available.

The huge distances motorists frequently travel on a European holiday, combined with the generally higher price of petrol and oil, do make fuel-saving measures highly desirable. A roof-rack adds substantially to fuel consumption, far more than a small trailer attached to the rear of the car, although that would increase charges on many ferry routes. Carrying a lot of luggage also uses extra fuel, especially when accelerating or climbing hills. Bear in mind that it takes a certain amount of energy to get a car into motion and that applying the brakes creates further waste when more energy is used to regain speed. The key to economical driving is to accelerate gently and to change up to the highest gear the circumstances will tolerate as quickly and smoothly as possible. A sensible cruising speed also affects your fuel consumption. At 70mph (113kph) many cars use about a third more petrol than they would do at 50mph (80kph).

This chapter has so far not mentioned the most obvious distinction between driving in Britain and abroad, which is, of course, that Continental motorists drive on the right or, rather, drive in the middle of the road until forced by oncoming traffic to drive on the righthand side. It is mentioned only at this stage to keep it in proportion. Many British motorists travelling on the Continent for the first time are reminded so frequently of the awe-inspiring task ahead of them that they are nervous wrecks before they complete the first kilometre and have quite unnecessary accidents.

There is nothing to it. After the first few minutes, you get used to the idea of sitting on the side nearest the kerb. In fact, you may even grow to like it, because you can pass cyclists, parked cars and pedestrians much more safely and on narrow, hilly roads you may even have a better view than other drivers.

There are two snags. The first, and biggest, is in overtaking. Although a driver would be foolish to rely entirely on the judgement of his front-seat passenger and leave no margin at all, unless he intends to proceed at a snail's pace he must allow his passenger to give him frequent guidance. It follows that putting anyone without good eyesight and road sense in the front is likely to end in disaster. After overtaking, always return to the inside lane; in France, failure to comply will incur an on-the-spot fine.

The second snag is in turning left. Turning left in the UK is one of the easiest and safest manoeuvres. Abroad, you must curb any instinct simply to turn left without any indication to the vehicles behind you and straight across the path of oncoming cars—a speciality among first-time drivers abroad. Instead, go through the procedure you would normally use for turning right. That is, straighten up in the

outside lane (on the left, of course), indicate in good time, study the oncoming traffic and make the turn in a single, decisive movement.

Driving on the right also, in most Continental countries, means giving priority to the right. This should relate only to roads of approximately equal status but, particularly among ageing Belgian, French and Spanish motorists, it can result in vehicles shooting out of side roads without a second glance and forcing cars on the main road to come to a sudden stop. A yellow diamond with a white border indicates that officially your road has priority, but do not count on it. A yellow diamond with a black bar across it indicates that your road no longer has priority, and that is the moment to take extreme care.

Although roundabouts are not used much on the Continent, where they are in operation priority to the right will mean that traffic already on the roundabout gives way to new traffic, except in France from May 1984.

Forgetting which side of the Channel you are is a remote yet dangerous possibility. It can happen when you are turning back on to the road after a lunch or petrol stop, on entering a wide, empty road from a narrow one, or on a deserted country road. It can also happen when you are tired, or have had too many glasses of wine. It can happen as a reflex action when you are faced with a sudden emergency. Putting up with constant reminders from the rest of the tour party is better than one possibly fatal moment of forgetfulness.

However careful you are, an accident is always possible. Looking after casualties must always be the first priority. If the engine has caught fire, you may be able to tackle it with a fire extinguisher. If there is fire anywhere near the petrol tank, the risk of explosion is considerable, and you must move everyone as far away from the vehicle as possible and go with them.

Otherwise, move injured people or anyone suffering from shock as little as possible. Post someone away from the scene of the accident to warn oncoming traffic, and set up your compulsory warning triangle about 50yd away. Many accidents are compounded by other vehicles piling into the back of crashed cars, or inflicting further injuries on casualties lying in the road.

Move the vehicles involved only if they are a serious danger to fast-moving traffic. Before doing so, mark their position or take photographs from several angles. Round up any witnesses and, by sign language if necessary, indicate that you wish to make a note of their names and addresses. As spectators show a marked reluctance to get involved, especially with foreigners, this may take some persuasion on your part.

An accident must be reported to the police if the law of that country requires it. Anyway, if it is serious enough, the police will be called, and they will almost certainly insist on taking any uninjured members of your party back to the police station to make statements. Your attitude to a statement will depend on the circumstances. If you are convinced that you are in no

Wise Words

Avoid travelling in busy periods—school holidays, national holidays, Friday nights.

Study Continental motoring regulations.

Always remind yourself which side of the road you are driving on.

Carry sufficient change of the right currency to pay motorway tolls.

Watch out for petrol-saving opportunities.

Don't forget to stow a regulation accident warning triangle.

Carry a can of top-up oil.

way to blame, saying so in writing presents no problem. If your Green Card (see pages 11 and 62) covers any damage to your vehicle without affecting your no claims discount, as many do even if you are partly at fault, you can suffer no financial penalty on your insurance. However, your insurance company will not thank you if you admit liability and you are certainly not obliged to incriminate yourself. In any case, your immediate impression of what happened may be wrong.

In these circumstances, invoke your emergency insurance. Obtaining the services of a lawyer may well be the wiser course, however tempting it may be to sign a statement—or even to exchange statements with the other driver on the standard European accident form—in order to be allowed to go on your way.

50 Break the Continental motoring regulations at your peril. Although the day has not arrived when endorsements and disqualification are applied on an international basis (with a speeding offence in, say, Italy, being taken into account under the penalty points system in the UK), the penalties for infringing the law can be quite severe.

While British motorists cannot be disqualified for drinking and driving offences committed on the Continent, a conviction of this nature will certainly affect their insurance rating in the UK, and can result in a prison sentence on the Continent—even when no injury is involved. The only sensible advice is to avoid alcohol altogether when driving. Remember that some Continental drinks, for example beer, can be much stronger than their British counterpart and the level of alcohol at which prosecution is automatic is sometimes lower than in this country.

The niceties of stopping motorists only when there is good reason to believe that they have been drinking and driving totally escape the Continental police. Random testing is widespread, and sometimes police will set up road blocks to check every motorist for a whole variety of potential offences. It is wise always to carry your passport and usually mandatory to carry a driving licence (plus IDP, if applicable), car registration documents (or International Certificate for Motor Vehicles) and evidence of insurance, and anyone found without these may be immediately arrested. There are signs that visiting motorists—hitherto exempt —may be treated just as harshly so don't go by car for an evening out and leave your

ON THE RIGHT SIDE OF THE LAW

documents behind at the hotel.

The driving licence requirements are explained in detail elsewhere (see page 7). Even motorists guilty of only technical offences—for example, an out-of-date UK licence or IDP—have been forced to abandon their vehicles.

With the single exception of Sweden, the police have

sweeping powers to fine motorists on the spot. Even in those countries where domestic drivers are usually given 'tickets', and expected to pay fines by the purchase of special stamps at post offices, the police may levy 'deposits' from visiting motorists to make certain that they actually pay the fine before leaving the country. Nor are these fines modest amounts. Expect to pay the equivalent of a three-figure sterling sum for minor speeding offences. Never travel without sufficient local currency to cover this contingency—sterling, travellers cheques, or credit cards are not acceptable. In France you should be prepared for roadside courts, too. The French have introduced these in an effort to reduce road casualties, with magistrates sitting at trestle tables dispensing justice on the spot.

In Spain, if you do not have sufficient funds to meet a fine, your car may be seized. However, the Spanish police do operate a discount system whereby, if you pay on the spot (not that you have any real choice), the fine is reduced by 20 per cent. There is absolutely no truth in the suggestion that if you do not insist on a receipt, much larger discounts are offered. It is not only the police who can levy fines in Yugoslavia. Any employee of the Department of Internal Affairs can demand money on the spot if he sees you committing an offence such as illegal parking.

Although parking tickets are often cheerfully torn up by the visiting motorist in the safe knowledge that they will not find their way back to the home address, or even if they

European Driving Regulations

Country	Minimum driving age	Speed limits mph (kph)			On spot fines	Seat belts	Warning triangle	First-aid kit	Minimum age child in front seat
		Urban	Country	Motorway					
Austria	18	31 (50)	62 (100)	81 (130)	yes	yes	yes	yes	12
Belgium	18	37 (60)	56 (90)	74 (120)	yes	yes	yes	yes	12
Denmark	17	37 (60)	49 (80)	62 (100)	yes	yes	yes	no	—
Finland	18	31 (50)	37 (60)	74 (120)	yes	yes	yes	no	—
France	18	**37 (60)	**56 (90)	**81 (130)	yes	yes	yes	no	10
Germany (West)	17	31 (50)	62 (100)	*81 (130)	yes	yes	yes	yes	—
Greece	18	31 (50)	49 (80)	62 (100)	yes	no	yes	yes	—
Italy	18	***31 (50)	62 (100)	***87 (140)	yes	*no	yes	*no	—
Luxembourg	17	37 (60)	56 (90)	74 (120)	yes	yes	yes	no	*10
Netherlands	18	31 (50)	49 (80)	62 (100)	yes	yes	yes	no	12
Norway	18	31 (50)	49 (80)	56 (90)	yes	yes	yes	no	—
Portugal	18	37 (60)	56 (90)	74 (120)	yes	yes	yes	no	—
Spain	18	37 (60)	56 (90)	74 (120)	yes	yes	yes	no	*14
Sweden	18	31 (50)	56 (90)	68 (110)	no	yes	yes	no	—
Switzerland	18	37 (60)	62 (100)	81 (130)	yes	yes	yes	no	15
Yugoslavia	18	37 (60)	49 (80)	74 (120)	yes	no	yes	yes	12

* recommended	** lower if wet	*** cars 1300cc and over

do, the motorist has no obligation to pay, much tougher measures are sometimes taken in larger cities. Wheel clamps are quite common; and vehicles are frequently towed away. The paraphernalia involved in recovering a car is, of course, vexatious, time-consuming, and costly—in some countries twice as costly as a similar experience in the UK.

A word of caution on speed limits. The maximum mph shown in the table can vary, particularly on roads that fall in between categories.

Apart from Italy, Greece and Yugoslavia, where the wearing of front seat belts is strongly recommended, every country in western Europe has made them compulsory, although occasionally not in built-up areas. It is compulsory to carry a warning triangle for use after a breakdown or accident. The distance it is supposed to be placed behind your vehicle to warn oncoming traffic varies from country to country, although if you take 50 yd as an average you are unlikely to fall foul of the law.

In several countries it is compulsory to carry a first-aid kit (see table above), and it is recommended elsewhere. Although this is hardly ever checked at the frontier, should you be at the scene of an accident, however innocently, and not be able to produce a first-aid kit, you may be fined. In Belgium and Greece, you are also obliged to carry a portable fire extinguisher.

Naturally, all these measures are in the interests of road safety, and eminently sensible precautions even when not strictly required by law. A motorist who scans the regulations to see where he can 'safely' take off his seat belt, for example, is irresponsible. Similarly, the variety of legal age limits applied to children travelling in the front seat of vehicles, whether wearing belts or not, should not obscure the fact that all children ought to be riding in the back.

Wise Words

Avoid alcohol completely when driving.

Be prepared for on-the-spot police checks.

Always carry enough foreign currency to cover a three-figure fine.

Check what items Continental laws oblige you to carry—eg first-aid kit, fire extinguisher.

Make sure all driving documents—especially your driving licence—are in order.

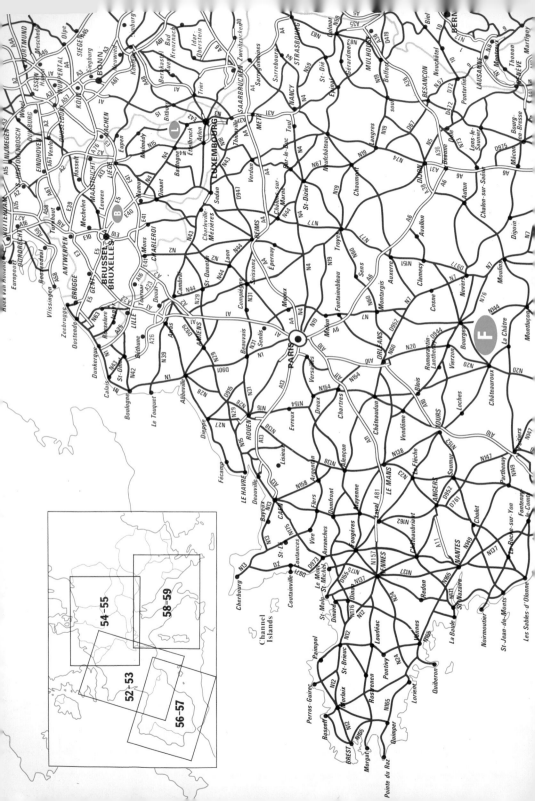

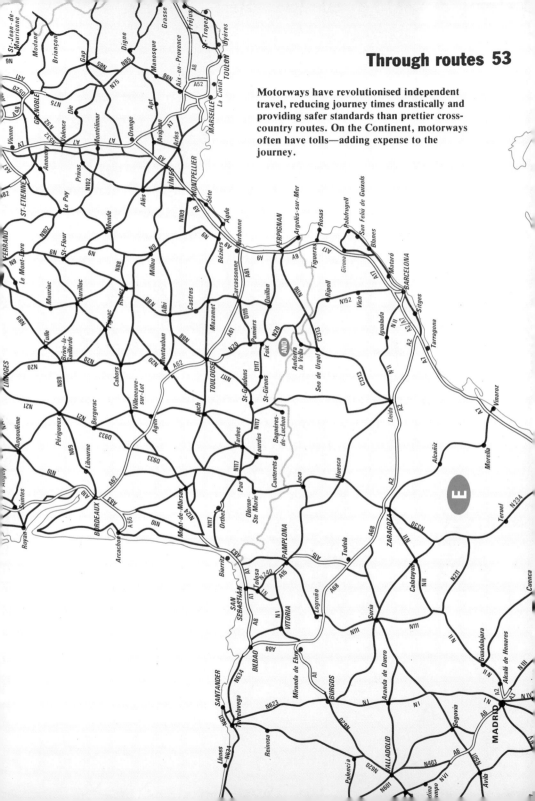

Motorways have revolutionised independent travel, reducing journey times drastically and providing safer standards than prettier cross-country routes. On the Continent, motorways often have tolls—adding expense to the journey.

54 Through routes

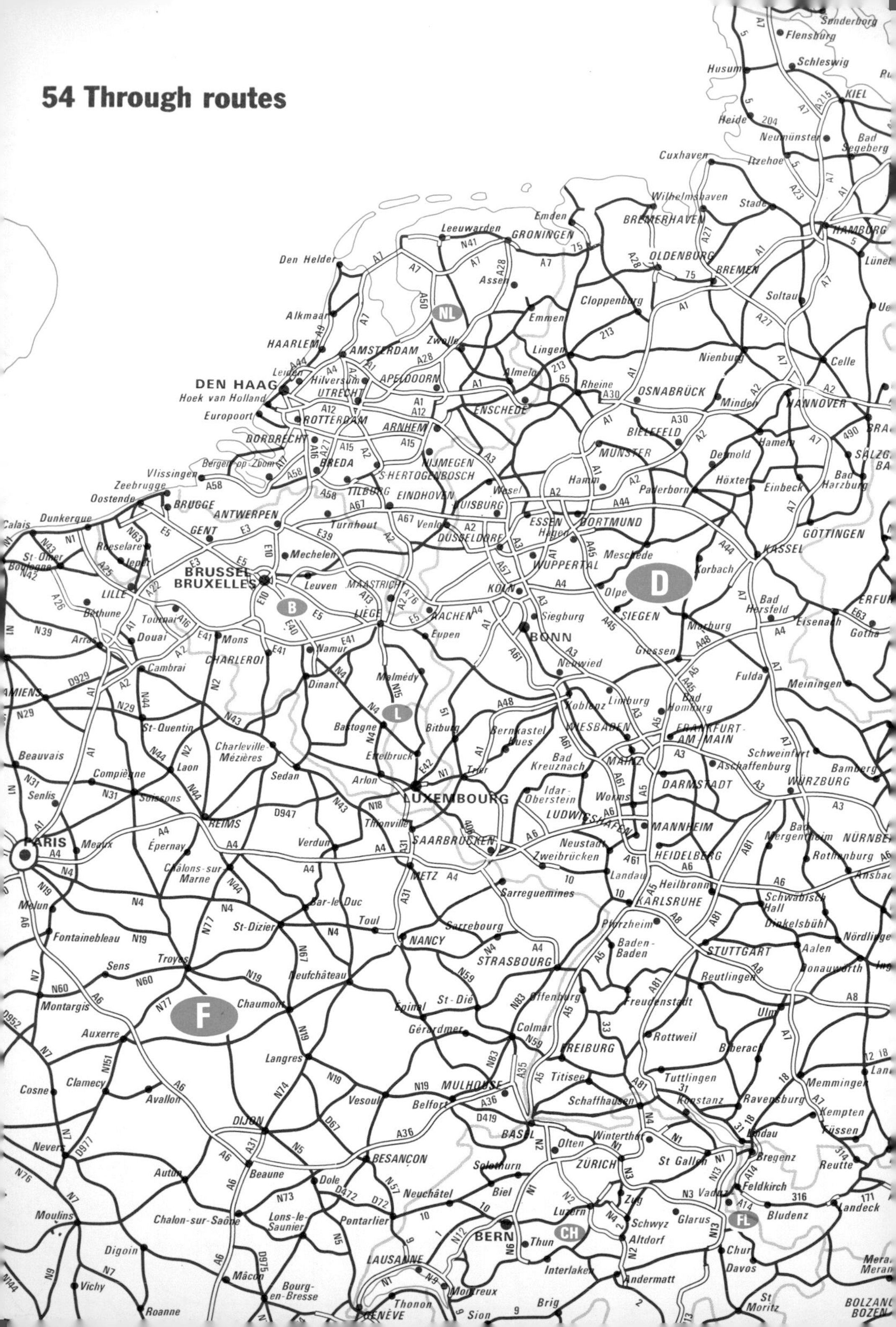

56 Through routes

58 Through routes

Marco Polo, intrepid traveller though he might have been, would never have coped with the modern concept of the caravan. To start with, he would not have understood the jargon—pitching that does not involve a tent, snakes that are not found in the grass, noses that do not appear on people's faces. He would have been even more baffled to discover that the very concept of the caravan—that of banding together for safety—is now regarded as extremely anti-social behaviour by everyone on the road.

Preparing your caravan for the Continent is a major task, and needs to be undertaken in good time. Last-minute work under pressure is likely to result in some crucial element being overlooked, possibly with disastrous consequences.

For the beginner, the task is daunting. Usually he is prudent enough to have both his car and his caravan regularly serviced and, if his caravan

TOWING WITHOUT A HITCH

is not doomed to become some rotting eyesore, he has taken it on the road enough times to know whether it is too big for his car, or—to look at it another way— whether he needs a more powerful car for his caravan. But if he has any doubts at all, or the car has seen long service, the only advice about a Continental trip is: forget it, or hire a bigger car. The journey is too long and the hills are too steep.

Owners of automatics should remember that towing makes transmission fluid hotter and thinner, so the gearbox may overheat. Check with the car's manufacturer whether you should fit a gearbox oil cooler.

The problem of a towing

vehicle resolved, take the bathroom scales to the caravan. Load up your caravan with everything you expect to take (see page 137), then place the scales on blocks of wood, so that they are just below the level at which the caravan rests when linked to your car. You are now going to check the nose weight, that is, that part of the weight of your caravan that will be carried by the towing vehicle. Not only should the nose weight comply with the car maker's recommendations in the handbook but, as a general rule, it should be about 100lb (45kg) heavier than the rear of the caravan, to avoid pitching (see later). For a good towing performance, the total laden caravan weight should really be kept at around 75 per cent of the car manufacturer's recommended maximum gross weight, although not much less than this, as too little weight can lead to general instability.

It is your responsibility to ensure that your vehicle and caravan comply with the complex Continental regulations concerning weights and dimensions. At least be

very careful about maximum weight. When loading the caravan, at all costs avoid exceeding the legal or manufacturer's limits—you may invalidate your insurance plus any warranty on your car and your caravan, and risk prosecution. An important point to watch is that information on weights supplied by a caravan manufacturer rarely takes account of any extras you have fitted.

Even when you are satisfied with the total weight and its general distribution, try to improve stability by storing heavier equipment on or near the caravan floor and by keeping as much weight as possible above the trailer axle. A road test, fully laden, the day before you leave for the Continent is a wise precaution.

Next, ensure that the caravan braking mechanism is adjusted to suit the car brakes.

Then consider the tyres. Ideally, you will have the same tyres on your car and your caravan. In reality, they may well be different. If the tyres are a mixture of cross-ply and radial, they will be safe if fitted in the following combination:

car-front	car-rear	caravan
cross-ply	cross-ply	cross-ply
cross-ply	radial	radial
radial	radial	cross-ply
radial	radial	radial

New caravans are now fitted with radials, but if you have an older model with cross-ply tyres, you should appreciate that these are virtually unobtainable on the Continent. Taking one or more spare caravan wheels and tyres is absolutely essential if you are using cross-ply on the trailer, and sensible in any

Wise Words

Prepare your caravan well before departure.

Decide whether your car is young and powerful enough to tow—even on long drives and in hilly country.

Check that the caravan's nose weight is correct.

Road-test the car and fully laden caravan before you leave.

Ensure car/caravan tyre combination is safe. Check tyre pressures and examine for damage.

Remember to check rear lights, wing mirrors, caravan number plate and GB plates.

Tell your insurers that you are towing.

Don't forget the last-minute safety check.

Know how to cope with steep climbs: plan ahead.

circumstances.

If your caravan has not been used for a long time, examine the tyres carefully for any signs of deterioration, such as cuts or cracks. Should you have any doubts at all about their condition or the depth of the remaining tread, the only sound advice is to replace them. Additional expenditure now is greatly preferable to struggling with a jack on some mountain ledge on the Continent.

Now, while the tyres are still cold, check the tyre pressures on your car and your caravan. Regard the recommended everyday pressures as a minimum and add an extra 5lb to the rear tyres of your car to

absorb the extra load when the caravan is linked up.

Hitching-up is largely a matter of practice. When the caravan is fully loaded, leave in position any blocks of wood needed to stop it rolling, but raise the corner steadies—the wind-down legs or struts at each corner. (If you have loaded the caravan without using the corner steadies, the nose is probably digging a hole in your drive by now, but never mind, you will not make that mistake again . . .) The caravan should now be resting on its wheels and its jockey wheel at the front. Reverse the car so that the ball on the towing bracket is as close as possible to the coupling; release the caravan handbrake and guide the coupling over the ball; release the coupling plunger and make sure that the coupling clicks into place. Raise the jockey wheel and plug in the electrical connection.

Next, check the lights—rear lights, brake lights, number-plate lights, indicator lights. See that the indicator flasher rate is correct—between 60 and 120 times a minute. Most standard car-flasher units will be overloaded by the extra lamps of a caravan and a special heavy-duty unit or a relay device should be fitted. If your caravan is equipped for connection to Continental mains, take a 50ft (15m) length of correctly rated cable with you to make certain you can reach the mains.

Check the rear view in your car: a variety of helpful accessories are available for use when towing. It is really most desirable to have a wing mirror fitted to the nearside of your car: obligatory for travelling in Italy, and also required in Denmark if you are towing a caravan.

Of course you may not own the caravan you are intending to take. Many people hire a caravan before buying one to make certain they are going to like the idea. This can be done through some of the ferry companies, providing a discount on the price of the crossing, and you can also hire a car with a towing bracket if your own car is not suitable. If you are taking your own car, it may need an adjustment to the suspension.

Remember that your caravan needs an identical number plate to your car, plus its own GB plate on the rear (see page 27). It must also have a chassis identification plate.

In western Europe Customs documents are no longer needed for tourists' cars and caravans, but visitors to

best to draw up one for packing, anyway.

Make sure you have all the necessary personal and vehicle documents (see page 6). For camp sites it is advisable, and in some cases essential, to have an International Camping Carnet (see page 9).

It is vital to be adequately covered by insurance so don't forget to advise your motor insurance company that you will be towing abroad and to

doubtful spots with filler compound (available from any DIY shop). Test all the cupboard and window catches

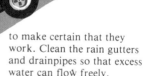

to make certain that they work. Clean the rain gutters and drainpipes so that excess water can flow freely.

If your caravan has a water pump, check the flow and flush out the system thoroughly with fresh water. Remember in re-filling the tank abroad that any doubtful water will contaminate all your remaining supply (though water from mains supplies in western Europe is generally pure enough).

Decide if you want to carry gas supplies with you, or buy most of it abroad. Up to twelve small containers, sealed and packed in an outer container, or three large cylinders are allowed and these must be adequately secured. Vehicles carrying unsealed cylinders must arrive at

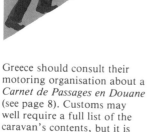

have your Green Card (see page 8 and page 11) specially endorsed for that. Austria requires full insurance for any temporarily imported caravans: check that the conditions of your policy and, therefore, Green Card cover, will meet this requirement.

Just before your trip, examine the caravan for potential leaks around the window rubbers and rooflights, sealing any

Greece should consult their motoring organisation about a *Carnet de Passages en Douane* (see page 8). Customs may well require a full list of the caravan's contents, but it is a port 30 minutes early for a leakage test.

When you actually set off try to avoid an initial fiasco, especially if the neighbours are watching. Check that the jockey wheel is pulled right up into its recess; that the hitch is fully locked on; that the caravan handbrake is off and the reversing catch is free; that all liquids are in firmly secured containers; that the tap on the gas cylinder is off; that all the caravan windows and roof vents are locked; that the van door is locked . . . and that you have the keys!

Driving with a caravan is a matter of commonsense and experience. All your movements, signals and manoeuvres need to be much more careful and deliberate than when driving a car on its own. Use the mirrors constantly.

Keep to the speed limits, wherever you are. While abroad, watch for standard limits being varied by road signs or at certain seasons. Whether towing or not it can be an offence to drive so slowly as to hold up other traffic.

Plan your route to avoid Paris (caravans are barred from the centre) and mountain roads with severe gradients. On most passes, the roads are now so well engineered that it is not the gradients, but the length of the climb that causes problems. Remember that the greater the altitude, the more a vehicle loses power—around 25 per cent at 7,500ft (2,285m). The hotter the weather, the greater the chance of overheating, so try to time your arrival at a high pass for early in the morning.

If your car does overheat on a long mountain climb, you may be able to keep the engine from actually boiling by turning the heater and fan on to maximum, keeping all the windows open. If you are brought to a temporary halt in traffic, keep the engine and fan running. If the radiator does boil, to avoid being scalded, delay before taking off the cap. Wait until the engine has cooled before adding water, or you risk cracking the cylinder block. When it has cooled, have the engine running while you pour in the water, so that it circulates quickly.

If you do break down, the Caravan Club has a scheme for helping the stranded, but AA roadside help is also available to members.

Pitching, an up-and-down movement of the whole outfit, can be started by a bump in the road. It is usually caused by too heavy a nose weight or incorrect loading of the caravan. The remedy is obvious, but if, after your trial run, shifting the weight does not cure the problem, the towing car's rear suspension may need to be stiffened.

Heavy pitching or bad weight distribution can lead to snaking, probably the most dangerous towing problem. A side-to-side movement builds up so that the caravan starts to swing like a pendulum. Trying to correct the action with the steering wheel only makes the problem worse, as by the time the movement has been felt and an attempt made to correct it, the caravan is already swinging in the opposite direction, and the correction accelerates the snake. (This is the moment when you may wish that you had flown to Benidorm on a package tour after all.) The only solution is to steer straight ahead and gradually slow down without heavy braking.

Unless it means driving a long way in the wrong direction, the prudent and discriminating motorist will plan his overnight stops so that, wherever possible, they fall within the borders of France. In terms of value for money, no other country can match France for cheap rooms and good food—though it is important to keep away from places on the main road.

France's reputation for looking after the fleeting visitor stretches back more than 50 years. In the early thirties the *Relais Routiers* were already established, with their blue and red signs outside hotels, inns and restaurants indicating that the traveller would be well looked after. Smart Parisian society went off to *'les Routiers'* at the weekend, armed, after 1934, with the *Guide des Relais Routiers*.

The *Relais Routier* is still going strong, and their guide is one of many useful reference works for the motorist planning an overnight stop. The Red Michelin guide has a huge list of recommended hotels and restaurants, and uses a red capital 'R' to indicate establishments that offer particularly good food at moderate prices. Then comes the list of *logis* and *auberges de France*, featuring some

GOOD FOOD AND SIMPLE PLACES TO STAY

4,600 family-run hotels (*logis*), and inns (*auberges*) with simpler accommodation and fewer rooms.

If you need further help in sorting out where to stay, a number of books offer precise recommendations, including:

The 'Holiday Which?' Guide to France

French Leave and *Hidden France* by Richard Binns (Chiltern House Publications)

Traveller's France and *Encore Traveller's France* by Arthur Eperon (Pan)

Travellers' Guide to Europe (AA)

Needless to say, an outstanding hotel one year could be a disaster the next. One of those selected by Arthur Eperon became so

successful that the owner sold out, the chef moved and the new owner, by general agreement, was reckoned to be one of the worst cooks in France.

Book in advance by telephone, if necessary in pidgin French. Confirm in writing, in English if your French is not good enough; French hoteliers usually regard the effort of writing a safe indication that you are going to turn up, and do not require a deposit. However, do not push your luck by arriving late. Many French hotels do not hold rooms after 6pm even if you have booked, especially during peak periods when they may have another hopeful customer hovering around the cash desk.

Always ask to see your room before accepting it. The hotelier will not be insulted; he knows that not all his rooms are of equal standard, even if they vary little in price. The later you arrive, the more likely you are to be left with the attic.

Hotel rooms are cheap by British standards, and usually cost much the same irrespective of the number of people using them. Thus a family room with two or three beds may be perfectly acceptable for a single night's stay and extremely good value.

Do not expect a luxury

Nightmares

French provincial hoteliers can be very possessive. One of them cornered a couple of his guests, demanding that they eat in his overpriced restaurant. When they refused, he tossed their cases downstairs and threw their valuables out of the window.

bathroom. The French seem less concerned than the British about private facilities, and think nothing of traipsing down the corridor in the morning to use one of the public bathrooms for a few francs. Even rooms with their own facilities are likely to have only a *cabinet de toilette*—a large cupboard with a wash basin, a bidet and sometimes a shower. Full private bathrooms are comparatively rare and relatively expensive. Whatever the arrangements, the plumbing is likely to behave eccentrically.

Small French hotels are more likely than most to have double beds but, if you want to make certain, ask for a room with *un lit de mariage*. Most beds double or single, have a bolster (*un traversin*) tucked under the sheet. If you are lucky, or the hotel has a lot of British visitors, you may find a pillow in the wardrobe, together with some extra blankets. If not, ask for a pillow (*un oreiller*). You may also discover a complete absence of soap, which French visitors are expected to bring themselves. If you have forgotten to buy soap, and the shops are shut, the proprietor

may be induced to provide a small bar (*une savonette*). Another common deficiency in small French hotels is electric light bulbs, frequently of too low a wattage to read by. Only a brave traveller will ask the hotelier to change a bulb, but there is nothing to prevent your carrying a varied set of bulbs.

Most French hoteliers will be offended if you do not eat in their restaurant (this is where they make most of their profit). However, it is extremely rare for a French hotel not to provide a modest fixed-price menu if you are trying to economise. A menu in the middle of the price-range may be the best value for money.

Once again, do not expect to be welcomed with open arms if you arrive late. Outside Paris, very few people eat dinner after 8.30pm, and many much earlier than that. Expect service to be casual, friendly, and slow—usually by members of the hotelier's family. Do not be put off if they leave you with the menu for ten minutes or more; choosing food in France is a serious business, not to be rushed. If you are on a budget, always stick to the set menus, which usually have service and taxes included in the price—an *à la carte* bill can mount up alarmingly. Local wines, and especially the house bottle (*cuvée du patron*), are always good value, but classic wines can actually cost more in France than in the UK. Coffee is always extra.

Breakfast is not normally included in the price of the room, and is frankly of poor value in comparison to dinner. It can cost a quarter as much

as your evening meal, providing for the price one croissant, some French bread, a pat of butter and a tiny container of jam (almost never English marmalade—if you cannot do without it, take your own), with coffee, chocolate or weak tea. Unless you are staying right out in the wilds, breakfast at a local café will probably be far better and considerably cheaper.

Finally, a warning about the bill. Many small hotels take only cash: no credit cards, no cheques, not even travellers cheques. If you have no francs and it is a question of sterling or nothing, they will probably ring the local bank manager at home to work out the latest exchange rate, grumbling all the time. However, if you come back again, all will be forgiven. There is no greater compliment you can pay a French hotelier than to stay with him a second time.

Wise Words

Wherever possible, try to take your overnight stops inside France, but away from main routes.

Use a reliable hotel guide to plan your stops.

Book in advance by telephone, however bad your French.

Confirm by letter.

Try not to arrive after 6pm.

Do not expect luxurious bathrooms.

Be prepared to eat early in the hotel restaurant.

Stick to the set menus and drink local wine for the best value.

No worry, no fuss, it's better by bus—unless, of course, that particular bus happens to be owned by a cowboy coach operator, has suspect brakes and steering, and, for a journey of several hundred miles, one driver who becomes so exhausted he falls asleep at the wheel.

Horror stories about such coaches have been rife, with tales of young Britons stranded in faraway places when operators simply decided that they did not have sufficient passengers to justify making the return journey.

The problem became so serious that the UK Department of Transport took action in 1982 against disreputable operators, although it was still unable to control the working practices of coaches which left from a foreign port. Moreover, for its own sake, the business has taken some steps to protect its reputation. The Bus and Coach Council's free Bonded Coach Holidays scheme offers financial security, should an operator's business fail. Check when booking to see if the operator is a member.

And the UK National Bus Company set up a network—called the European Supabus—in association with other British operators on the Continent. In every case the coaches themselves and the regulations on drivers' hours had to be approved by the governments of all the countries taking part. These were Belgium, Finland, France, the Irish Republic, the Netherlands, Norway, Portugal, Spain, Sweden and Switzerland.

Although the fares charged are considerably

AIMING AT LOW FARES, HIGH STANDARDS

higher than the lowest offered by cowboy operators, who keep down fares at the cost of safety, they are still far below the equivalent fares on rail or scheduled air services to many destinations where cheap air fares are not available, even through bucket shops (see page 77).

Regular routes include:
London-Dover-Boulogne-Paris
London-Dover-Calais-Nice
London-Dover-Calais-Rome
London-Dover-Calais-Athens
London-Dover-Zeebrugge-Munich
London-Dover-Zeebrugge-Amsterdam
London-Dover-Zeebrugge-Stockholm
London-Dover-Zeebrugge-Helsinki
London-Dover-Boulogne-Geneva (with bunks)
London-Dover-Boulogne-Barcelona

Average journey times from London are:
Geneva 19 hours
Nice 24 hours
Barcelona 25 hours
Rome 37 hours
Athens 62 hours

The largest network of regular services, however, is operated, ironically, by the railways of Europe. Called Europabus, it has regular line services connecting many of the major cities of Europe. The London connection is called Line 163, and operates at least twice a week, more frequently in summer. This goes: London-Dover/Folkestone-Ostend-Brussels-Cologne-Frankfurt-Munich, which takes just under 24 hours.

Once on the Continent, there are connections:
from Brussels to Spain and the South of France (Brussels-Waterloo-Venoy-Nimes-Figueras-Barcelona; Brussels-Dijon-Orange-Nice)
from Frankfurt to Austria (Frankfurt-Augsburg-Innsbruck)
from Ostend to north Germany (Ostend-Düsseldorf-Dortmund-Osnabrück/Minden)

There is also a British Rail/Sealink service to British Army bases in Germany, primarily intended for servicemen and their families, but open to the general public. This route goes:
London-Dover-Ostend-Brüggen, Rheindahlen-Münchengladbach-Düsseldorf-Soest-Bielefeld-Herford-Lippstadt-Paderborn-Minden (with summer connections to Münster and Osnabrück).

Many inclusive tours are operated by Europabus and by British and other Continental companies, but these

Wise Words

Don't book the cheapest trip without checking—it may not prove such a bargain.

Pick your seat carefully.

Keep anything that will make you comfortable on the journey, plus documents, with you in a small bag.

invariably bring you back to your starting point after a specific number of days, and do not allow you to break your journey in between.

Even in so-called luxury coaches—any journey by standard sized coach with more than 20 people on board cannot really be called 'luxurious'—be prepared for an uncomfortable trip. Except where specific seats are bookable, getting on early can markedly improve your choice of seats. Many coaches still have raised floors over wheel arches which give you less room to stretch your legs. Seats near the driver or the lavatory are likely to be noisy. Those in the last row may not tip back as far as the others. A window seat near the back is likely to offer the best possible chance of sleep.

Coaches, even those with air-conditioning, seem prone to sudden changes of temperature. A window opened apparently innocuously near the front on one side of the coach can cause a most uncomfortable draught on the other side at the back. Therefore, woollens that can be put on or taken off easily are essential wear. So are flat shoes, warm socks and

easy-fitting clothes, because you are going to be sitting in a more or less fixed position for long periods.

Many of the items ideal for long-distance air travel are also suitable for the coach. They include slipperettes, an eye mask, ear plugs, face tissues, an inflatable cushion and a small vacuum flask. As it may be raining sometimes when the coach stops, carry a folding or telescopic umbrella. However discouraging the weather, always take advantage of stops to stretch your legs and reduce the chance of cramp.

If you are carrying a lot of luggage, most of it will be placed in the luggage compartment in the side of the coach. Keep with you a lightweight bag for your documents, money,

paperbacks, sunglasses, toilet items, and possibly a change of clothing. In this way you will have a better chance of keeping fresh throughout the trip. If you are on a coach package tour, you will also be able to take a stroll out of the hotel, or get ready for dinner, without waiting for your main luggage to be sorted out and brought up to your room.

European coach tours and direct services still have a long way to go to match the Greyhound Bus system in the United States and Canada. All their buses have fully tilting seats, reading lights, lavatories and air conditioning, and can be used by the hardy traveller overnight as a regular hotel. Substantial discounts can be obtained by buying an unlimited mileage pass in the UK before you leave.

Nightmares

On one eventful coach trip run by a cowboy operator, the original coach left London for southern Spain six hours late, lost its only driver who decided to resign in Barcelona, and collided

head-on with a car in Valencia: the replacement burst a tyre in Alicante; broke down in the Sierra Nevada and had to be replaced again; this coach finally arrived in Malaga two days late.

For the experienced traveller, airports can be confusing; for the uninitiated, they are overwhelming. Nobody sensible wants to spend longer at an airport than is strictly necessary, but aim to make the time you must spend there as relaxed and profitable as possible.

Travelling by air requires four essential elements of advance information:

the name of the airport

the terminal from which your flight departs

your flight check-in time

the name of the airline handling your flight

Knowing which airport you are flying from may seem blindingly obvious, but each year passengers continue to turn up at the wrong airport, some of them ruining their holiday as a consequence. If your tour operator changes the travel arrangements (perhaps combining your aircraft load with another operator's if he cannot fill his own flight) you could suddenly find you are flying from another airport. The added complication is that there are a number of major European destinations with more than one airport in regular use, especially for charter traffic. So it is as well to familiarise yourself with the range of alternative airports which include:

London
Gatwick
Heathrow
(Terminal 1—mainly UK and British Airways; Terminal 2—European airlines; Terminal 3—inter-continental)

GOING BY AIR

Those who dream of faraway places, but hate stage-by-stage planning and don't want to waste precious hours on the journey, need to fly.

Stansted
Luton

Milan
Linate (European and domestic)
Malpensa (inter-continental and charter)

Moscow
Domodedovo (some domestic and Asian)
Sheremetievo (all foreign airlines, some Aeroflot)

Paris
Charles de Gaulle (Terminal 1—all except Air France and Air Inter which are at Terminal 2)
Orly (West Terminal—international; East—domestic)

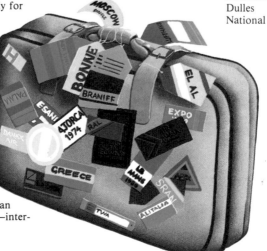

Rome
Leonardo da Vinci (also known as Fiumicino)
Ciampino (mainly charter)

Add to this the fact that East Midlands airport is entirely separate from **Birmingham**; that **Bonn** and **Cologne** share an airport roughly midway between them; that **Basle-Mulhouse** airport is not only a considerable distance from either place, but situated at St Louis in France and connected to Switzerland by a tariff-free route, and it is easy to see how travellers sometimes go to the wrong destination.

Outside Europe, cities with more than one airport in use include:

Montreal
Dorval
Mirabel

New York
John F Kennedy
La Guardia
Newark

Rio de Janeiro
Galeáo
Santos Dumont (domestic)

Tokyo
Narita
Haneda (mainly domestic)

Washington
Baltimore–Washington
Dulles
National

Some airlines have their own terminal facilities, such as TWA at New York John F Kennedy. Many airports are divided into domestic and international departures, which may be some distance apart.

Once you know exactly where your flight is leaving

from, and arriving at if you are being met at the other end, the next critical question is your check-in time at the departure airport. On the assumption that every random selection of passengers is bound to include a few who are optimistic about the time they need to reach the airport, or who get lost, or stuck in a traffic jam (check radio bulletins), airlines tend to give pessimistic assessments of the times by which passengers need to check in. An hour and a half before departure is quite common for many flights.

A key question to ask yourself is: how vital is a particular flight, and what would be the consequences of missing it? If you are travelling by charter, or on a restricted ticket, the answer may well be that the financial penalty of being late is so great that it is foolish to take the risk of being prevented from travelling at all.

That does not mean you should always assume that the check-in time remains the same on the day of departure. Push your tour operator for an airport contact number and phone before you leave home.

To speed things up, the British Airports Authority have instituted a scheme at Heathrow for several European carriers, including British Airways, known as 'gate check-in'. This means that, apart from a perfunctory check at the departure entrance, if you have only hand baggage the first point at which anyone is interested in your ticket is at the final departure gate.

So, if you arrive at the airport with time to spare, but get stuck in a queue at passport control, or take too

Check in early—though not more than two hours early!

long buying duty-free goods, as far as the airline is concerned you have turned up too late to travel. This scheme has had a significant effect on the punctuality of flights, because airlines no longer have to chase around for stray passengers who wander off secure in the knowledge that they have a boarding pass, and that, short of going missing within minutes of take-off, they will be allowed to travel.

You can also arrive too early: few airports or airlines will accept your luggage or check you in more than two hours before your departure time, and frequently later than that. Long queues form irritatingly fast, so it can be a serious miscalculation to leave the check-in area before the check-in desk opens, only to find all the passengers have suddenly materialised in front of it a few minutes later. However, if you are travelling in a party, only one person need queue and check-in for all of you. Leave them with all the tickets, passports and the suitcases (preferably on a trolley).

When you check-in, you will be issued with a boarding pass. This may consist of a folder in which your ticket

voucher is placed until it is collected at the final departure gate. Check that the boarding envelope, pass or card has your correct flight number: remedying mistakes later may involve you in unnecessary trouble.

Bags which are too big to take into the aircraft, or which you do not want to carry on the plane with you, will be weighed, taken behind the check-in counter, and from there moved along a conveyer belt out of sight. Watch your suitcases until you are certain that the correct tag for your destination has been fixed around the handle. When you receive your ticket back, check that the only voucher that has been detached is the one for the next flight. Check that all the remaining vouchers you will need are still in place. If this sounds unnecessarily pedantic, appreciate that the consequences of vouchers going astray can be formidable and are well worth avoiding at the risk of incurring a few quizzical glances from the airline staff.

If your suitcases seem overweight, remember that the airline will be interested only in the average weight of your party's cases, and will not charge you extra unless this overall total is exceeded. If you are travelling alone or with only one companion, look around for an amiable passenger with little luggage who might be persuaded to 'team up' for the check-in. Don't forget, either, that, whatever the reduction on their fares, children occupying an aircraft seat are entitled to the same baggage allowance as an adult.

The baggage allowance is 30kg (66lb) for first-class

passengers and on some airlines for business-class passengers, and 20kg (44lb) for everyone else, except on certain charters where it may be only 13.5kg (30lb). This allowance is supposed to include hand baggage, but in practice that is rarely weighed. A wide variety of items are in fact allowed as hand baggage, including:

a small personal bag or briefcase

an overcoat

an umbrella or walking stick

a small camera and pair of binoculars

a reasonable amount of reading matter

baby food, clothing and carry-cot to accompany a baby, total weight 10kg (22lb)

a collapsible wheelchair (for invalids)

Nobody has ever defined what 'reasonable' is as far as reading matter is concerned, so a fast reader might claim that a dozen books and magazines are 'reasonable' for a long flight. More unscrupulous passengers have been known to keep excessive hand baggage out of sight, behind a pillar or left in charge of a fellow passenger, on the assumption that no one will query it after check-in.

On some transatlantic flights, however, airlines have given up weighing baggage, and instead require it to conform to certain combined dimensions—height plus length plus breadth. For checked-in baggage (maximum two cases), this is usually a combined maximum of 158cm (62in); for hand baggage, a combined maximum of 115cm (45in). There is the added requirement for hand baggage to stow in the overhead luggage locker or to fit under the seat in front of you, but this is less of a problem now that many aircraft have such huge overhead luggage lockers.

The key question is: can you avoid taking anything other than

hand baggage? This is not as absurd as it might first appear. The doyen of foreign correspondents, James Cameron, wisely observed that the principle of good travel was to take twice the money you think you'll need and half the clothes. Certainly, most holidaymakers take far too much luggage with them, especially as laundry services abroad are fast and efficient and, except in big cities, not too costly.

If you are not travelling on a package tour and are able to manage with only hand baggage, the advantages can be enormous. Waiting for checked baggage can add an hour or more to travelling times, quite apart from the risk of something going astray.

A passenger with hand baggage only, and no need to wait for others with checked-in luggage, has an entirely different priority when it comes to seat selection. He wants a seat as close as possible to the exit so that he can take advantage of his freedom to leave the airport ahead of all the passengers whose luggage is in the hold. Even if boarding is by more than one entrance, especially on older aircraft, a seat near the disembarkation door, or the first-class section, if there is one (they usually are let off first), is likely to achieve the desired result.

At check-in on certain flights, you may be asked to produce your passport. This will be so that the airline are satisfied that you have the necessary visa for admission to your destination (if one is required) or they might be obliged to fly you back if you are refused entry.

Before you go through the

barrier separating the passengers from the 'wavers and weepers', make certain that you have made the bulk of your pre-flight arrangements. A departure lounge usually has fewer and more expensive shops and probably no chemist's, post office, bank or bureau de change. It will, however, almost always have a snack bar, an ordinary bar (with exorbitant prices), a bookstand, loos, telephones and a duty-free shop.

Passport control or, in Britain, a pre-passport control check, will invariably involve you in showing your ticket or boarding pass as well as your passport. You will then be subjected to a

your holiday snaps, it is sometimes possible to have them inspected by hand and passed round the machine—although not at some airports, notably, Paris Charles de Gaulle, New York John F Kennedy and Washington Dulles.

Some items which may escape the security check are nevertheless not encouraged on board. They include lighter fuels, book matches, aerosol cans and full fountain pens. When an aircraft climbs and the cabin pressure changes, fountain pens can spurt ink all over your clothes.

After the security check you

again if you have a specific, guaranteed seat.

However, while the last passenger on board may be the smartest, the first passenger to miss the flight is undoubtedly the most foolish.

On an increasing number of flights, when you check-in, you also choose your seat. The experienced traveller may tell you that they can usually obtain a seat with a particular advantage in its location or leg room. The truth is that even travel experts come unstuck because the way the seats are laid out on aircraft (the configuration) changes frequently from airline to airline and from aircraft to aircraft (see page 88). This is especially the

security check in which your hand baggage passes through a machine and is X-rayed while you pass through a body scan. Keeping calculators, metal combs and pens out of your pockets can help to avoid being felt all over by some security officer. To carry scissors or a pocket knife, however innocently, is asking for trouble.

Film and tape are now unaffected by most modern security equipment, although wrapping them in foil may prove an added safeguard. If you are still concerned about

have an opportunity to visit the duty-free shop, and add further to your hand baggage. You also need to keep an eye on the indicator board, which will show your flight number, the departure gate, and a light or sign to warn passengers that boarding is actually taking place. Even then, there may be time to sneak a last cup of coffee, or a visit to the loo or to a shop, especially if you are travelling long-haul on a full flight—because 300 or more passengers cannot be boarded simultaneously, and there are no prizes for queueing yet

case on European flights since the introduction of business class, where movable headboards and curtains can be shifted from row to row according to the demand for business-class seats. As a result, what seemed a comfortable row on the way out could be barred to you on the way back.

There are, however, some basic guidelines. At the check-in desk you will certainly be asked to choose between smoking and non-smoking seats. The trend towards non-smoking does now seem to be leaving more vacant seats in

PASSPORT CONTROL

Nightmares

A few travellers do somehow manage to get on board the wrong flight, despite the allegedly foolproof boarding pass system. Travelling unintentionally by air, however, is more or less unheard of. The person closest to managing it in recent years was a British Airways loader. A BA flight to Tel Aviv was aborted just before take-off when the crew heard knocking noises coming from the hold. When the aircraft returned to the apron the loader was found inside. Apparently, he had loaded a group of mailbags, waited for some more that never arrived, and dozed off. He was hidden by the mailbags when the hold was closed and eventually made himself heard only just in time to avoid going on a no-passport, free jaunt to Israel.

smoking than was previously apparent, so unless you are seriously affected by tobacco smoke, you may find there is more room in the smoking rows. If you are a party of two or four, consider asking for

two or four seats in adjoining rows across the aisle. It is actually easier to hold a conversation with someone separated by a few feet rather than jammed in the seat next to you, despite the drawback of

having to put up with occasional interruptions by passing trolleys or passengers. Aisle seats offer quicker access to the loo, allow you to intercept cabin staff when you want something, and give you a little extra arm and leg space. On long-haul flights, they also give a better view of the film, especially halfway between cabin bulkheads. The disadvantages are that you will have to get up to let other people visit the toilet, and you may be brushed by passengers going past.

If you are taking a long-haul flight, and are travelling alone, a window seat may

Nightmares

When you fly into a foreign city, know the local currency and what it is worth in sterling before hailing a taxi. One British visitor to Taiwan, the offshore version of China, took a taxi from Chiang Kai-Shek Airport to his hotel in Taipei and was asked to pay in local currency. As the Briton was extremely tired, and uncertain of the exchange rate, it was only some hours later that he realised that he had parted with the equivalent of . . . £600.

Pre-packed meals on crowded planes may lack finesse, but the service is convenient

offer the most restful trip, provided that you do not need to get out too often to go to the loo (see page 91). However, do not imagine that the window itself will be of much value. The view out of an aircraft is unattractive on the ground, and meaningless at 35,000ft. On those rare occasions when there is something to see, the captain may announce the fact to the passengers, so you could have people craning over the seats to share your view.

If there is an odd number in your party, or aisle seats do not appeal, you may be forced to use the middle seat in a row of three or five. This can be claustrophobic, especially at meal times, and if you can persuade all your party to sit along the aisle, even if this means sitting alone yourself, you may have a far more comfortable flight. After all, you are off on holiday, and you have another two or three weeks to talk to relatives or friends.

The next task is to settle for a particular section of your class in the aircraft. As toilets, galleys and permanent bulkheads require major engineering before they can be altered, aircraft plans are useful in indicating areas definitely to be avoided. You may need to be firm about where you want to sit to avoid being simply allocated the next vacant seat or seats numerically or alphabetically from front to rear.

The most attractive rows are those next to emergency exits, which usually have more leg room, especially on charter flights, where the distance between seats can be as little as 71cm (28in).

Seats at the front of the plane are quieter since on most aircraft they are a good distance from the engines. However, children and babies are invariably placed in the first and second rows, partly because 'skycots' can be fixed against the wall or bulkhead separating economy class from the business section. Seats at the rear are almost always near galleys, and inclined to be noisy because this is where the cabin crew prepare meals, or are by toilets, and as a result surrounded by passengers for most of the flight. Seats near the wings may also be noisy because of their proximity to the engines, offer no view at all, and on larger aircraft are close to toilets and galleys— definitely the worst of all worlds!

Wise Words

Ensure you know which airport you need.

Don't cut your check-in time too fine.

Make sure your bags are tagged correctly.

If you are not in a package tour party, try to avoid taking more than hand luggage.

Insist on picking a seat to suit your priorities.

Don't carry scissors or knives on you or in hand baggage.

ATLANTIC RUSH-HOUR

The sheer volume of traffic, especially in the peak summer months when regular scheduled services are supplemented by charter flights, is highlighted in this unusual view of all the aircraft over the Atlantic at a precise moment on a typical Wednesday night in June. At 0530 British Summer Time, when most people in Europe and on the eastern seaboard of the United States would have been tucked up in bed, no fewer than 98 aircraft were under Oceanic Air Traffic Control.

All but four were flying eastwards towards Europe, between North America and Europe – one of the busiest routes – because most flights in the other direction would be likely to reach their destination in North America in the middle of the night. It also helps to explain why in the busiest European airports such as Heathrow and Frankfurt, there is massive congestion around our breakfast time, when most of these aircraft land and disgorge anything up to 450 passengers. This is definitely a period to avoid Terminal Three at Heathrow.

The most prolific carrier on this route that night was TWA, with 16 services in the air, followed by Pan-American with 11. At the same moment British Airways had six flights airborne, closely followed by Lufthansa and KLM, each with five, and Air France with four.

All around them, well separated by altitude and distance, of course, were another 43 different airlines, ranging from Spantax of Spain to SAN of Ecuador. Plus one curiosity: a US military aircraft, a C141, with the quaint call sign of Huff 72.

This showed up on the air control scanner because it was flying at only 41,000 feet. Above it were probably many more examples of military hardware . . . and not all of them friendly!

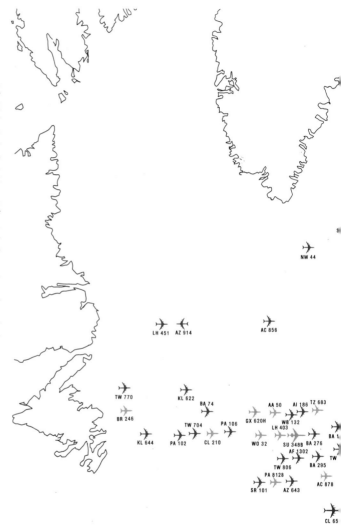

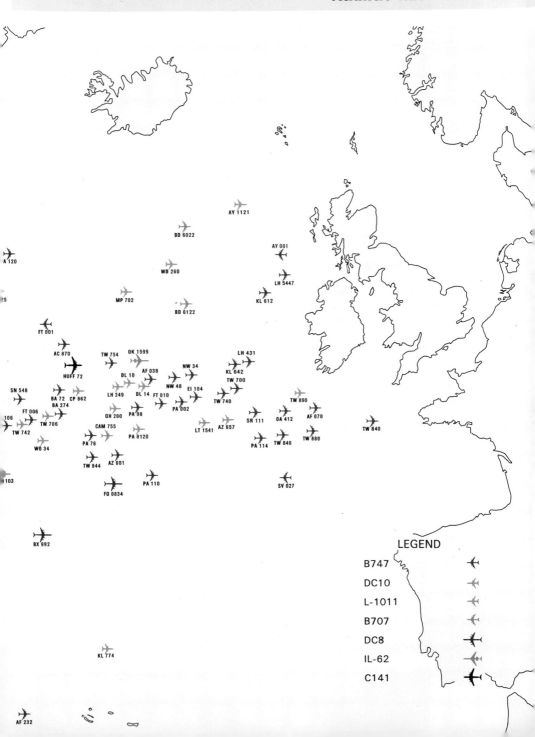

LEGEND

B747	
DC10	
L-1011	
B707	
DC8	
IL-62	
C141	

Most of us would like to travel to our intended destination in the best seats on the most modern aircraft, flying the most direct route. It follows that the only really satisfied customer will be flying first-class at someone else's expense on a scheduled aircraft that arrives right on time. For most holidaymakers, however, precise timing, comfort and the flexibility to change their travel plans at the last moment come a long way behind the price. All they ask is that the flight actually exists in both directions.

As there are several ways in which air travel is organised, it is important to know why certain fares are cheaper and to be sure in your own mind what you are prepared to settle for in making your booking.

Scheduled services do what the name suggests: operate as near as possible to a published timetable. They fly at pre-arranged times on a regular basis, and fail to operate only through extremely bad weather or when something has gone seriously wrong. In those circumstances the airline has a legal obligation to get you to your destination on the next available flight and will often look after you until that happens.

Charter flights are an arrangement whereby a travel company or group of companies pay for the use of an aircraft, either for a specific return journey between two points or for a series of journeys over a period of time. Because the number of people likely to travel can be determined with much greater accuracy, the price per seat may well be considerably lower than the equivalent journey on a scheduled service. Against that, the risk of delay, for example through the aircraft

DO YOUR HOMEWORK AND DON'T WORRY

being used for its previous journey by a different company or encountering technical problems or adverse weather, is much higher. To cut costs, companies schedule only for short, trouble-free turnarounds, and operate on too slender a profit margin to keep replacement aircraft in reserve.

Mixtures of scheduled and chartered seats also exist. As the scheduled airlines are anxious to fill as many places as possible, on some routes they block off a specified number of seats for use as a charter operation, either through their own associated tour companies, or with an independent operator. They also offer tickets that you can book very early or very late, or which are subject to a variety of restrictions on how long you have to be away, where you can break your journey, and whether, if at all, you can change the date or time of your flights. Alternatively, some charter operators offer a number of seats on their charter flights for use by the independent traveller, again with the purpose of ensuring that they fly as close to full every time the use of the plane is paid for.

Given these complexities, discovering who is offering

what to where and with what limiting conditions is a formidable and daunting task. The prospective traveller has to be prepared to make a lot of telephone calls and to do a good deal of reading and walking, if he is to be sure of a bargain.

First, he needs as complete a list as possible of the companies and airlines who offer the destination of his choice. This can be compiled from advertisements in newspapers and magazines, from information provided by the national tourist office of the country concerned (look in the London telephone directory or ring directory enquiries), and from enquiries at travel agents.

The next requirement is to list prices charged by the carriers or other companies. Some prices will be mentioned in advertisements or volunteered by travel agency staff; at this stage, all should be treated with suspicion. Often seats on charter flights are sold by brokers who are interested only in their profit margins and who could not care less if the flight is unsuitable or a prime candidate for cancellation. Many quoted figures are 'come-on' prices: either they omit some crucial factor such as airport charges, or they relate to a flight operating out of season or at very unsocial hours. Some quoted figures are simply wrong or out of date.

However, make a note of them just the same. They will be useful in forming a judgement on your target price. They will give some indication of what you may have to pay, which is, perhaps, so far above your budget that you need to revise your travel plans entirely.

If you are still on target

as to price, start with the scheduled airlines.

Competition is now so intense between the carriers that they may well have introduced some special low fares that match any being offered elsewhere. Have a precise idea when you intend to travel and when you want to come back. If you have any children, ask about discounts for them.

Now go back to the advertisements for fares to your destination shown in newspapers or magazines. Some of these will be for charters; others, discounted fares on offer at 'bucket shops'. This expression originally described the selling of suspect stocks and shares by unlicensed dealers but, in the vast majority of cases, bucket shops are reliable and so are the tickets they sell. This is because, in order to obtain their products, bucket shops always need the tacit cooperation of the respectable side of the travel industry.

The scheduled airlines farm out the tickets they cannot sell through their legitimate outlets to general sales agents, middlemen who buy in bulk at a discount, and who, as the airlines know perfectly well,

will have no qualms about passing on tickets—with their mark-up but still well below official prices—to anyone prepared to buy them. Other tickets reach bucket shops through licensed travel agents, who cannot sell them openly below the official rates but who are more than happy to split the commission on a discounted price with the bucket shop proprietor.

Some elements of the supposedly respectable side of the travel industry have tried to suggest that members of the public who buy tickets from bucket shops are encouraging a criminal act. In fact it is not illegal to buy such tickets, and the international regulations which forbid discounting of this kind may in themselves be an unjustifiable restraint of trade—certainly no one has been anxious to put these

agreements to the test by bringing a bucket shop proprietor to court.

Discounting has reached such a high level of acceptance, even among the leading national carriers, that the airlines' accounting systems suffer a great strain through the need to obscure their wholesale disregard for the rules set down by the International Air Transport Association. This, in turn, has permitted a practice known as 'cardboarding' to grow up among the shadier agencies on the fringe of the business. The agent writes out a ticket with a piece of cardboard between the counterfoil that goes to the airline and the coupons given to the customer. In this way, a much higher price could be reclaimed in revenue from the airline, in the more or less certain knowledge that the carrier would never be able to marry the counterfoil to the ticket coupon with a lower figure at which it actually changed hands; and even if

they did, they would never pursue it for fear of opening a whole can of discounting worms.

Some bucket shop tickets are sold in blatant disregard of an individual airline's own rules—for example, by back-dating the selling date to make it appear that it was sold early enough to qualify as an Advance Purchase Excursion Fare or APEX ticket. Sometimes individual tickets appear in the airline's manifest as part of a group fare for ten or more passengers, even if the

collect tickets in person. This may involve a discouragingly long journey for would-be travellers who do not live near the big cities where bucket shops are to be found, but conducting this type of business by post is fraught with danger.

Have everything confirmed in writing: the airline you are travelling on, the flight numbers, and the full itinerary, including the time the aircraft arrives and departs from each stop en route. It

Moscow or Sofia and extremely indifferent service into the bargain. The travelling time may also vary sharply: for example, between 22 and 41 hours to Australia. The lower price offered by the bucket shop may simply not be worth the acute discomfort involved in using their route.

What your ticket must have is a validation stamp—either the stamp of the airline or of the official issuing agency, which may well be a bonded

travel agent. It will come from a metal die plate of approved International Air Transport Association design. The stamp records the place and date of issue—quite possibly a much earlier date to comply with airline regulations. Under no circumstances accept a ticket carrying the stamp of the bucket shop.

ticketholders never meet any of the others in the group and perhaps do not even travel on the same flights. The chance of either of these infringements ever coming to light are, frankly, remote.

Although things rarely go wrong when discount tickets are purchased, the consequences when they do are serious as the bucket shop is unlikely to come to your rescue. Refunds are certain to be restricted, so always insure against the need to cancel your ticket through, for example, last-minute illness. Never agree to pay more than a small deposit in advance, and always

will then be possible for you to check that you are on the airline's computerised passenger list as a bona-fide traveller—have no inhibitions about ringing the airline yourself on the bucket shop's telephone to confirm the fact before parting with your money.

You can also find out in this way what you are letting yourself in for on the journey. There is a world of difference between a long-haul flight on one of the top European airlines with one refuelling stop, and a meander around eastern Europe that could involve half a day's wait in

Members of the Association of British Travel Agents have been making determined efforts to recover their share of airline ticket sales, and eventually may be successful in putting some bucket shops out of business. However, the fact is that the more successful bucket shops have sometimes been able to better the High Street agents' prices by superior homework and working out elaborate permutations that are completely within the rules.

The idea also exists that scheduled airline tickets purchased from ABTA agents are in some way more secure when, in reality, the protection offered to holidaymakers buying package tours through ABTA agents has never been extended to the purchase of flight tickets alone. This became apparent when Laker Airlines collapsed in 1982, leaving many travellers who had been sold tickets by ABTA agencies with little chance of recovering their money. Cooks and ABTA have now separately promoted insurance schemes which holidaymakers buying air tickets alone can use to protect themselves against the possibility of the carrier going bust; but the holidaymaker may have to pay extra for this, and cynics have seen these insurance policies, rather unfairly perhaps, as yet another commission-earning activity by the trade.

There is another means of obtaining low fares on scheduled flights by which the traveller does have the full protection of the ABTA bond. Many travel agents are also in effect modest tour operators in their own right, collaborating to produce a series of package tours by scheduled services. They are able to make these competitive because IATA allow the airlines to create a specially low fare for most destinations, known as the Inclusive Tour Excursion Fare, or ITX. Because of frequent abuse of this concession, in the case of flights to Spain, it is rarely available.

These fares are confidential to the travel trade, so you may get a rough reception if you simply glide into your nearest travel agency and ask to be shown the list. However, a selection of these fares is published from time to time by the magazine *Business Traveller* and included in information sheets offered by the BBC *Breakaway* programme. Clearly, if you can find out what it will cost an agent to obtain an ITX fare to, say, Paris, you can quickly see whether his overall deal including the Hotel Splendide is generous or not.

You can also discreetly try to persuade your travel agent to interpret the rules governing these ITX fares as generously as possible. He may not be able to do much about the requirement to spend at least six nights abroad, one of them a Saturday night, but the average holidaymaker would be quite happy to do that in any case.

It is in the interpretation of IATA's requirement that the ticket can be sold only in conjunction with some 'ground arrangements' that there is real flexibility. Agents have been known to issue accommodation vouchers for hotels so awful that no one would ever contemplate using them or that do not exist, so that if their clients are challenged, they can produce them in evidence; arranging car hire is another means of meeting the requirements, even if it is only for one day; a travel agent noted for his imagination regularly issues vouchers for drinks in a series of Continental bars. The risk of being challenged is once again remote, and the saving

Today's complexities of air travel are nothing compared with the rigours of early flights as this one between London and Paris

on the fare is sometimes more than 50 per cent.

On longer routes, scheduled tickets on which the carrier has not placed a lot of restrictions have another advantage over charter flights —the flexibility to make intermediate stops and to vary your route to pass through interesting places at little or no extra cost. This is possible because of Maximum Permitted Mileage or MPM, which allows a passenger a choice of routes and carriers to his destination, up to a prescribed mileage which may be as much as 20 per cent longer than the most direct route. As long as he continues to fly in the same general direction, he may well find even quite substantial diversions add nothing to his fare.

Because IATA set their own exchange rate for airline tickets, which tends to lag behind the normal rates of exchange, and because one

country may have access to promotional fares when another does not, it is sometimes possible to cut the cost of a ticket by travelling via a neighbouring country, such as the Netherlands or the Republic of Ireland. It is even possible to purchase by post from Irish or Dutch travel agents tickets that start and end in these countries— preferably using a credit card so that you have some fall-back protection if things go wrong—and simply not to use the coupons from Amsterdam or Dublin to London and vice-versa.

Strictly speaking, you are supposed to use all your flight coupons in proper sequence, but by tearing out the first coupon, the fact that you have not used it becomes undetectable. More adventurous travellers have also used the spare coupons between London and Dublin or Amsterdam on a separate holiday, pinning the original

coupon for the sector to London (now of course a return half of the journey) back into place with apparent impunity. Even without this bonus, savings on the official prices available for return scheduled flights out of London can be considerable, in spite of the extra mileage.

If none of these devices supplies a fare within your budget, you will need to look at charter flights—sometimes, in fact, they are the only way of reaching certain smaller airports near holiday resorts without flying to a big city and changing planes. They may also have the advantage of leaving from a provincial airport in Britain much closer to your home than, say, Gatwick or Heathrow.

Most of the major tour operators—such as Cosmos, Global and Thomson—sell off vacant seats on their package holiday charter flights, sometimes many months in advance for periods when they know demand will be small but their agreement with the airline requires them to keep the plane in the air. As with ITX fares, to keep within the rules, these charter seats can be offered only with accommodation and, as with ITX fares, it may exist only on paper. For Spain, for example, you are expected to provide your own accommodation (a relevant street map and a fertile imagination is all that is required), which you let to the operator for a nominal sum, and he in turn sub-lets it back to you at the same price. This farcical arrangement meets all the regulations and involves no risk whatsoever.

Only one country, Greece, has made a serious attempt to stop this method of getting round the rules by questioning travellers about their accommodation and in a few cases actually sending back those without plausible destinations. This action received a lot of adverse publicity while being of no apparent benefit to their own national airline so that it is unlikely to be repeated; but, in any case, cheap accommodation in Greece, especially the islands, is perfectly acceptable and frequently all that is available, so nothing is lost by arranging genuine places to stay and actually using them.

Most charters are operated on regular weekly schedules and, therefore, lengths of stay are possible only in seven-day periods, with a maximum stay of four weeks. The exception for lengths of stay are charters for special events, such as trade fairs, and such charters are a good way of getting to some major cities, which seem to have some kind of

convention almost every week.

Either way, you must keep to the dates you book and, if you miss a flight, you may well have to pay a scheduled fare home. It is important to remember that, on most charters, children's discounts are very small or simply not available, whereas on scheduled flights they can be as high as 50 per cent on tickets purchased well in

advance. The best family deal may, therefore, not be on a charter at all.

There is also an appreciable risk that, apart from the knock-on effect of delays on the previous operation involving the same aircraft, a charter flight will not take

place. If tour operators find they cannot fill or nearly fill an aircraft by a certain date, they may 'consolidate', jargon for cancelling a particular flight and putting their passengers on another, either one of their own, or one run by a different operator. They may decide to take this action in respect of your return leg because the flight out was poorly booked.

In this case they may not bother to contact you, or it may not be possible to do so. It is essential, therefore, a day early to ring the airport you will depart from for home to check that the arrangements still stand. Before you leave, make certain that you know which airline is handling your charter arrangements and what their holiday airport phone number is.

Charter flights do not necessarily involve older aircraft—indeed, in some cases, the emergence of new airlines has left the scheduled carriers behind in the purchase of the latest designs—but many of them do. These older aircraft are no less safe, but they are invariably noisier and frequently slower. Before booking it is prudent to discover what type of aircraft will be used, where it will refuel if it needs to, and how long the flight will take. Many charter flights take place late at night or early in the morning, with the result that you miss a night's sleep and also have to wait for your hotel room to be vacated at a time when you are most in need of it. Weigh up all these factors before deciding what is truly value for money.

As airlines and charter operators prefer to put bottoms on seats than to fly

with empty spaces (although some disastrous experiences in marketing strategy have shown that reducing prices can increase rather than reduce potential losses), the real bargains are to be had by the traveller prepared and able to risk a good deal of brinkmanship. Do not expect last-minute bargains at peak times—Christmas, Easter and during school holidays—but if you can leave at short notice outside those periods, last-minute discounts are frequently available. This requires a series of telephone calls to operators in the four or five days before departure, and a steady nerve.

Even riskier, but even more rewarding, is the standby ticket. On most routes passengers have to turn up at

the airport and hope that either the flight will not be full or that someone will not use their reservation.

However, in the autumn of 1983 some leading airlines showed their growing disenchantment with the system by giving up standby arrangements altogether on routes between the UK and USA. On certain routes where standby seats are still offered the combined cost of two of these tickets (the one out and the one back, bought separately) can be higher than a discount return bought in advance.

Where standby tickets do still exist at a worthwhile saving, that is on some long-haul routes, airlines may issue forecasts of the prospects of standby seats

Wise Words

Decide what you want from a flight and what inconveniences you are prepared to put up with.

Be prepared to do exhaustive comparative research.

Treat all quoted prices with initial suspicion and double-check them.

Bucket shops can offer valid bargains—just verify everything carefully and get it confirmed in writing. Put down only a small deposit and collect tickets in person.

Always look for the official validation stamp on tickets—a bucket shop's own stamp is not sufficient.

Insure against the need to cancel your ticket at the last moment.

When you purchase flight tickets alone, insure against the possibility of the carrier going bust.

available, ranging from 'poor' to 'good'. The more airlines that fly to your chosen destination, the better your chances of obtaining a seat. Airlines whose country of origin is not your departure or arrival point are the most likely to have seats available when the more obvious carriers are full. But during the summer, standby queues (usually at airline offices, not at airports, who have more than enough people to cope with already) can be long gruelling affairs, with the unappetising prospect of going through the whole nightmare again to find a seat home.

The availability of airline seats and fares fluctuates so much that not even the most skilful agents can keep up with all developments. To get a good bargain, shopping around and double-checking are, therefore, essential. But in your search for economy remember that, unless you are a traveller who revels in discomfort, the cheapest fare could result in a flight that would make you wish that you had stayed at home.

Nightmares

If you do not take the trouble to check that the bucket shop ticket you are purchasing is for a flight that actually exists, the consequences could be expensive. A Newcastle family bought tickets from a backstreet agent in Gateshead for a flight from Gatwick to Athens and, although the outgoing flight existed, the return one did not. After desperately trying to obtain seats on various other charter flights returning home, they eventually had to pay the full single scheduled fares for a British Airways flight back. The total cost was far in excess of what they would have paid for return scheduled tickets bought in advance, including connecting flights from Newcastle. Soon after they got home to Britain the bucket shop closed, without refunding any of their money.

Unless you are merely dropping off Aunt Agatha with a huge sigh of relief, the chances are that your main priority on reaching any UK airport will be to park your car. Do not be tempted to leave it unattended on a double yellow line, however briefly; security is now extremely tight and your car is virtually certain to be towed away. Recovering it will be tedious and extremely expensive. If, however, you are not travelling yourself, short term car park charges are reasonable for the first couple of hours. Birmingham, Bristol, Gatwick, Heathrow, Leeds/Bradford, Liverpool and Manchester airports all have separate car parks catering for short stays. At Manchester Airport, the covered car park offers reduced charges in winter, but it is often essential to book in advance for the long term car park. At some airports, especially Heathrow, National Car Parks and some local garages and hotels provide cheaper off-airport parking. They take you to the airport by minibus or coach and collect you on your return. At Heathrow, even when you can afford to use them, the short term car parks are very busy, especially at Terminal 1. If you really cannot get in there, Terminal 2 car park is within walkable distance from Terminal 1 and the route caters for luggage trolleys. However, one good tip is to ignore Car Park 1 at Terminal 1 and drive straight up the ramp to the overflow Car Park 1A. Once inside, take the down ramp. As everyone's instinct is to keep going up, the spaces of the two lower floors fill up last.

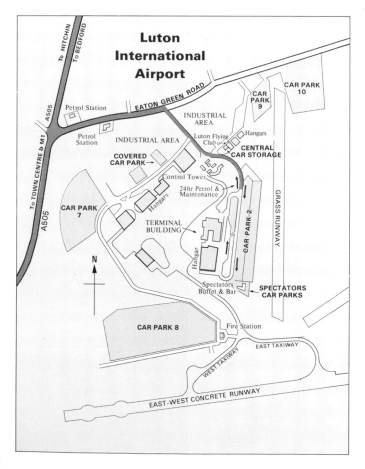

LUTON

Luton International Airport (Luton 36061)—mainly used by package-holiday tour operators, Luton Airport lies some two miles south-east of the centre of Luton and close to the M1, with access from junction 10 (3½ miles). Luton town is on the main line from St Pancras Station in London and the journey takes 28 minutes by fast train. Local bus and long distance coach services are also available, including the Green Line into the centre of London and a link with Heathrow and Gatwick Airports.

Car parking
On the airport There is limited undercover space and most of the accommodation is in open car parks run by the Borough

MANCHESTER

Manchester International Airport (061-437 5233)—the busiest UK airport outside Heathrow and Gatwick, Manchester Airport lies nine miles south of Manchester city centre. For private vehicles access to the airport is from junction 5 on the M56. The nearest railway station is Heald Green, about two miles

north-east of the airport with regular bus services. From here there are frequent trains to Piccadilly Station in Manchester and Crewe (via Wilmslow). Local bus and long distance coach services can be used from the airport.

Car parking
On the airport A variety of car parks is available—multi-storey, surface and perimeter, the latter with a free minibus shuttle service to the terminal building.

Off the airport Car storage near the airport is limited and it is advisable to book with the following garages in advance: Car Minder (061-436 5376), guaranteed covered parking space; Dial-a-Valet (061-865 1851), parking only is also available; Males Garages (061-437 3220), 300 yd from the airport terminal.

of Luton. Drivers should go first to the terminal building in order to unload passengers and luggage. There they will be informed which car park to use. They then drive to that car park and pay for the period over which they wish to leave their car. There is a free minibus service to and from the terminal building.

Off the airport Car storage space near the airport is limited, so booking is essential and it is advisable to give at least five weeks notice of requirement. The following garage is very close to the airport and has undercover storage facilities: Central Car Storage (Luton 26189 or 20957).

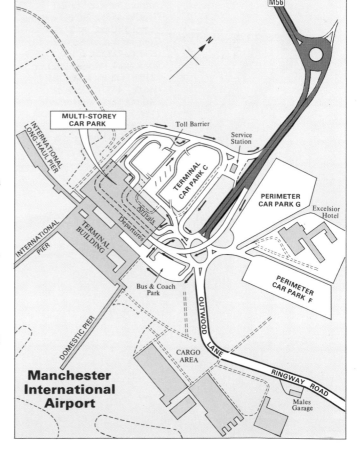

GATWICK

Gatwick Airport, London (Crawley 28822)—most of the major airlines operate from Gatwick Airport. It is also open to aircraft diverted from Heathrow, as well as the charter services of other airlines. Private vehicles can gain access from the M23 and A23 to Gatwick which has ample parking facilities for both short and long stays. The airport has its own British Rail station with frequent fast trains to Victoria Station in London. The journey takes 40 minutes. There is also a Green Line coach service to central London, local bus and long distance coach services elsewhere, and a coach link with Heathrow and Luton Airports, plus a helicopter service to Heathrow.

Car parking
On the airport An open-air and three multi-storey parks. *Off the airport:* Airport Parking (Copthorne 716466); Airport Service Station (Horley 4555); BCP Terminus Parking (Crawley 27164); Courtlands Car Service (Horley 71555); CTS Econopark (Horley 2021 or 72300); Gatwick Motors (Horley 4037); Gatwick Parking Service (Horley 71581); Lowfield Heath Service Station (Crawley 20347); E J Maynard & Sons (Crawley 25371 or 37465).

HEATHROW

Heathrow Airport, London (01-759 4321)—one of the world's busiest international airports, Heathrow lies sixteen miles west of London. The Piccadilly Line goes to Heathrow Central Station. Local bus and long distance coach services run into central London and elsewhere, including to Gatwick and Luton Airports. A helicopter service also links Heathrow with Gatwick Airport.

Car parking
On the airport Multi-storey short and long term parks. *Off the airport:* Airways Garage (01-759 9661); Chequers Airport Car Park (01-759 0212); Courtlands Car Services (Horley 71555); Cranford Hall Garage (01-759 9413, 9852 or 9555); Flyaway Car Storage (01-759 1567 or 2020); Kenning Car Hire (01-759 9701); National Car Parks (01-759 9878).

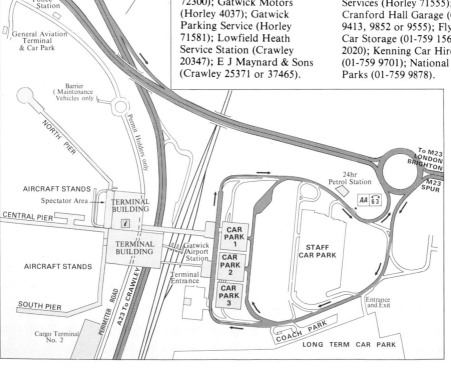

Gatwick Airport London

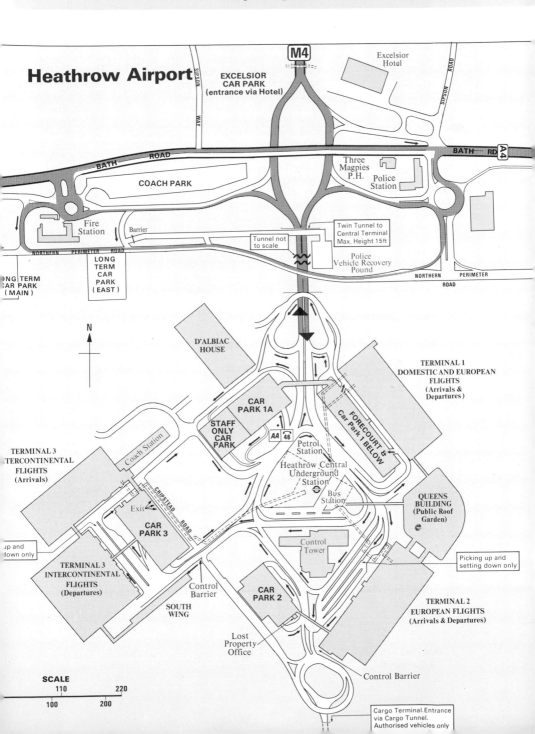

The costs of re-training airline crews and of carrying a huge range of aeroplane spares have been major factors in influencing companies to work towards having the smallest possible number of different aircraft making up their fleets. The principal beneficiaries of this trend have been the United States company, Boeing, whose 707, 727, 737, 747 and 757 aircraft now make up a substantial majority of the planes in service in the United Kingdom, both among scheduled and charter services.

For the uninitiated passenger, the most striking difference between aircraft types is undoubtedly width. The sheer size of wide-bodied planes, with anything up to ten seats across, is impressive. There are four basic designs of aircraft in this category, the Boeing 747, the McDonnell Douglas DC10, the Lockheed L-1011 Tristar, and the European Airbus A300. They hold between 300 and 450 passengers and are all subsonic.

The 747, nicknamed the Jumbo, was the first to enter service and remains the market leader—undoubtedly assisted by the unfortunate publicity surrounding the DC10, which suffered accidents eventually traced to faulty maintenance procedures. The 747 is unique in carrying an upper deck with the cockpit and a cabin behind that, which has now been stretched on the 747-300 series to increase its passenger capacity.

Although more and more airlines are using Boeing aircraft, an infinite number of seating arrangements, or configurations, are possible, particularly following the introduction of movable temporary cabin dividers to separate business and tourist class. Business travellers have also been wooed by airlines through improvements in seating (replacing the standard ten seats across by eight, seven or even six seats), with

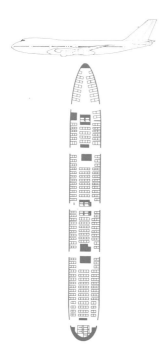

BOEING 747
450 passengers
15 cabin staff

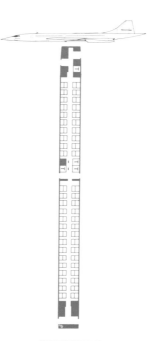

CONCORDE
128 passengers
6 cabin staff

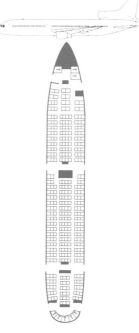

LOCKHEED L-1011 TriStar
256/400 passengers
12 cabin staff

TWA establishing a lead in business-class comfort by putting only six seats across its Ambassador Class. Other airlines, led by British Airways, have compromised on more flexible seating where a middle seat can be divided and 'shared' between the neighbouring passengers when there is room on a particular flight.

The 747 seems capable of any number of seating permutations, making it extremely difficult for even the most experienced traveller to select a favourable seat in advance, except by approaching the airline with whom he intends to fly and asking for a particular seat plan.

Before the 1973 oil crisis, when payloads were less critical, the upstairs cabin of the 747 was provided and designed for first-class passengers as a lounge where they could have drinks and in some circumstances take their meals. Later on in some airlines it became an elitist first-class section, carrying 'sleeperette' seats that could be reclined and were equipped with foot rests, so that passengers could stretch out fully and increase their chances of getting some sleep. These proved so popular that they soon had to be introduced in all the first-class sections, partly because the passengers most prepared to pay an extra premium to use them were also aware that the front of the aircraft was considerably quieter. On some aircraft, the upstairs cabin has become part of the business section—including the stretched version introduced in 1983 by Singapore Airlines—while on others such as the 747s of Japanese Airlines, cubicles with full-size (well, full-size for Japanese) beds have been introduced . . . probably the first planes to have sleeping accommodation since the Boeing 377 Stratocruiser of the early 1950s.

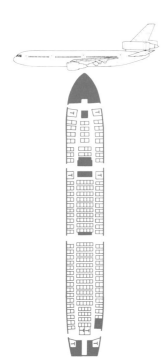

McDONNELL DOUGLAS DC-10
270/380 passengers
11 cabin staff

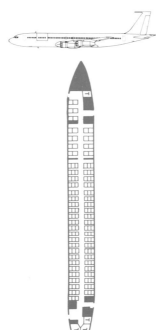

BOEING 707
135/219 passengers
6 cabin staff

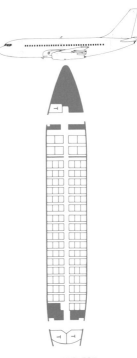

BOEING 737
115 passengers
4 cabin staff

Airline passengers get the flight they deserve. A harsh assessment, perhaps, but borne out by experience. Advance preparation and awareness can make all the difference between a miserable or a tolerable journey.

There will, of course, be degrees of discomfort. Most package holidaymakers on charter flights of, say, two and a half hours or less will survive the trip without too much difficulty, even if they make no effort to mitigate its worst features. For unprepared travellers, however, a longer flight can prove an experience they won't want to repeat.

The following advice, then, applies particularly to longer flights, but can be equally useful for shorter journeys, especially crowded charter flights.

First, find your seat. Seat numbers are often to be found in groups of three or more around the headrests or on the overhead luggage rack, in minute characters. The number usually indicates the row, a series of letters the seat; seat rows are almost always numbered from the front to the back of the plane. Passengers sit down in the wrong seats all the time, so do not be surprised if you think someone is in your seat; ask

PREPARE TO BE COMFORTABLE

the stewardess to sort it out.

Next, deposit your hand baggage in the overhead locker and any item that will not go in, despite any amount of pushing or shoving, under the seat in front of you. (Anti-social passengers sometimes get away with putting such luggage under their own seat, thereby inconveniencing other passengers instead of themselves, but you would not wish to do that, of course; so watch out for it happening to you.) Remove your coat or jacket, and loosen tight neckwear, putting discarded clothing in the overhead locker as well (if there is still room)—unless you can sweet talk one of the hostesses into hanging it up, a privilege usually reserved for first or business-class passengers.

Then adjust the air-vent knob above your seat: once you are sitting down and have

buckled yourself in, you will not be able to reach it. Now road-test your seat. Put your feet firmly on the floor and push. If it is at all loose, refuse to sit in it, because if there was an emergency the seat could become detached, and you, as well as your seat, would go flying round the cabin. Although this is an extremely remote possibility, sensible precautions can make all the difference between being a victim or a survivor. For the same reason, take some trouble in adjusting your seat belt, so that it does fit snugly, yet can be easily undone.

Try the buttons for the lights and for tilting your seat, if there are any. Bring down your folding meal tray. If something does not work, complain, because it may still be possible to move to another seat. After you are sure your fellow passengers are settled in the right seats, get out your personal survival kit for the flight. This should contain:

Magazines or books: even if you are not a prolific reader, boredom is likely to make you want something to look at.

Vacuum flask containing soft drink: dehydration is a common problem on aircraft, especially after drinking alcohol. Even first-class passengers rarely receive adequate service to avoid this problem, so having your own source of liquid is the best solution.

Slipperettes: as your feet invariably swell during the journey, taking off your shoes can make your journey more comfortable, even if you do have difficulty in putting them on again later. But for walking around or sleeping, a pair of slipperettes (they give them away in first-class on many airlines), or a second pair of socks are useful.

Eye mask, if you are planning to sleep, especially in the day time.

Ear plugs, or take the headphones from an up-market hi-fi set.

On longer flights you will be offered another means of blotting out the aircraft noise, or your neighbour's conversation; a headset on which you can receive a series of entertainments on different channels and hear the sound for the in-flight movie. On some airlines these headsets are provided free of charge; on others, you may be expected to pay a small fee.

Except when flights are delayed, most airlines have a set pattern of procedure on longer routes:

Drinks trolley: soft drinks and sometimes wine and beer free, others charged for.

Main meal: free except on Peoplexpress flights. Hot in first and business class and for all classes over long distance.

Film: a recent release, occasionally even a pre-release.

Sleep: lights out (apart from your own individual light) and blinds down.

Light meal: and on some airlines, hot towels to wake you up.

Duty-frees: sometimes by trolley or distribution of orders taken earlier.

Forms: for passengers not entering their own country; immigration and Customs for the USA, immigration only elsewhere.

As the trolley from which drinks, food and possibly duty-free goods are dispensed takes up all but a few inches of the gangway, going to the loo is a matter of skilful timing. The queue for the toilets will be the longest after the main meal, the film, if there is one, and the light meal. Passengers prepared to miss the first five minutes of the film or who can rouse themselves quickly after sleep, will be the least inconvenienced by the convenience. It is also worth remembering that, with so many people, the condition of the few lavatories deteriorates markedly during the flight.

All that you can reasonably rely on the loo providing at the start of the flight are toilet paper, and soap and paper towels. If you want to arrive refreshed, smelling pleasantly and looking presentable, you will need to bring your own deodorant, toothbrush plus paste and, for men, an electric shaver, which incidentally may operate at a slower speed than usual because of changes in voltage. Using these in the toilet will take some time, so you must be prepared to risk the wrath of those passengers in the queue behind you.

Always watch the demonstration of safety procedures, especially the location of the emergency exits. Make a note of the nearest, and the next nearest. Finally, listen to all the announcements.

Bad weather or some technical problem could force your aircraft to divert from its intended destination, or, improbable though it may seem, you could have inadvertently embarked on the wrong aircraft. Passengers booked on a domestic US flight once got halfway across the Atlantic before realising something was wrong!

Wise Words

What will you need on the flight and what can you store in the luggage locker or under the seat?

Road-test your seat. If it is loose or faulty, refuse to stay in it.

Take with you: reading matter, soft drink flask, slipperettes, eye mask, ear plugs.

Ensure that the conveniences don't inconvenience you.

Your plane has touched down. The stewardess is going through the motions of thanking you for travelling on Elastic Band Airways, while at the same time giving just the merest hint of being glad to be shot of you. She is also trying in vain to stop passengers from standing up and extracting their luggage from the lockers while the aircraft is still moving.

Do not stand up! Unless you are travelling on your own, remember that your package tour party goes at the pace of the rear legs of a centipede: the first cannot move until the rest is ready. If you are sticking with your tour party, your luggage will be in the hold with the rest. So there is no hurry.

Do not stand up! Let the rest of the passengers jostle each other in half-standing, half-sitting positions. Let them push and shove their way out. Wait until you can see the door the whole length of the aisle away. In the end you will either join the same passengers in the same airport bus or, if the aircraft is connected directly to the airport bays, form part of the same queue for immigration.

If you have an aisle seat (a middle seat means you have simply not read this book properly!) and the passengers inside are fidgeting, remind them that it will probably be ages before their luggage arrives, so they might as well stay put. If they still insist on getting up, then let them out, but don't be tempted to follow them. Just sit down again!

Immigration queues are a curse of modern air travel from

PATIENCE IS ITS OWN REWARD

which only super VIPs can escape. Be resigned to the fact that it can, and probably will, take time and there is really nothing you can do about it—especially if you have

several stopovers en route. Keep calm, stay polite, fill in the forms correctly . . . and keep an eye out for a staff shift change that might mean another counter opening up nearby which could save you half an hour in your present queue.

Except in the most inept airports, your luggage should be on the conveyor belt by the time you are actually admitted to the country you are visiting. All you need to know is the number of your flight and the letter abbreviation of the airline you have travelled with—the same combination you saw on departure.

Having found the correct conveyor belt, you need a luggage trolley. Murphy's Law dictates that either these are nowhere to be seen, or they are tucked away in long lines at the other end of the terminal. At some airports they are made as inaccessible as possible to keep the porters in business. If there are no trolleys to be seen, look for a likely opening where they might appear from, usually in huge convoys after someone has eventually gone to the trouble of rounding them up.

If you have a trolley, stake a claim to it by leaving some object of no value on it and position yourself next to the conveyor belt. Where you stand is irrelevant, because any saving in time would be extremely small and, remember, you are still travelling at the pace of the slowest member of your tour party. However, if you are too close to the point where suitcases appear, you may not have enough time to sort out the distinguishing marks on your bag from other similar ones. You may then have the frustrating experience of seeing it disappear again from view—temporarily, you hope.

Always take a good look at cases lying around near the conveyor belt. Passengers frequently take off the wrong bags, realise their mistake, and then leave them on the floor near the belt—sometimes because they don't care, but usually because there is no room to put them back on again. It is maddening to stand there, waiting for a suitcase which has been there all the time.

Except in the United States, where Customs require a separate form to be completed and search a great many bags, Customs abroad do not present any real problem for the visitor. Making it clear that you are foreign, by waving your passport around or speaking English in a loud voice, does sometimes help to speed you through—though, significantly, not in eastern Europe.

The local representative of your tour company will hopefully be waiting the other side of the barrier. This is where you need to achieve a tricky feat—if necessary, by dividing forces. Your objective is the seats near the front of the transfer coach door. This involves finding the coach in a hurry, but ensuring at the same time that your luggage is among the last to be placed in the space under the floor— usually accessible through a

hinged door in the side of the coach. This is essential if you want to be first off the coach and first up the steps of the hotel carrying your luggage.

Find out from the tour rep during the journey what happens at the hotel: whether bookings are made in individual names, or whether the reception desk has a list of clients appearing under the tour company block reservation.

Do not be tempted to leave your luggage to be delivered to your room: at worst it may be mislaid, at best it will arrive long after you want something out of it. Get to the reception desk first, if you can, obtain your room allocation, and take your cases up to your room.

Do not unpack. See why on page 126.

If you have succeeded in arriving without too much hassle, you need not be too complacent. You might have done better if you had not travelled on the package tour operator's coach at all. Although a few hotels might be so far from the airport that travelling there by taxi would be prohibitively expensive (a point you can check in advance with your tour operator), in most instances it will cost you little more than the price of two rounds of drinks if you and another couple you befriend on the trip share the bill. Then, with

luck, you will arrive at the hotel well ahead of the rest of the tour group.

The concept of spending money on a journey that is included in the tour price may be anathema to some, but everything depends on the price you put on your personal convenience. Starting a holiday off in style may influence the way you feel for the next fortnight.

Wise Words

Travelmanship requires you to think ahead, so the passenger who wants to arrive truly fresh and ready to relax will need to:

keep his baggage light and carry it himself

unless on a package tour, sit on the plane where he can be the first to disembark

reach immigration at the head of the queue

pass straight through Customs

use his own transport to the hotel

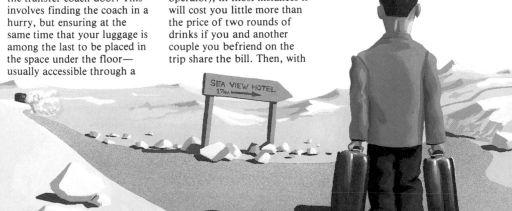

Neither travel agents nor British Rail seem to go out of their way to sell Continental rail travel. The commission on tickets is poor for the amount of work involved, the consequences of mistakes dire, and the queues at British Rail offices forbidding in the summer. Compared to road or air travel, it is an uphill struggle all the way for the potential rail passenger.

Self-help is vital. Few travel agents have real experts in this field and all you can usually expect from them is to look up the place you want to get to and quote the return fare. British Rail travel centres may be too busy to answer questions at peak periods. The solution to finding out what is available is to buy BR's cheap *Europe International Passenger Timetable*, issued twice-yearly, or the rather more expensive *Thomas Cook Continental Timetable*, issued monthly.

At first glance, the timetables look appallingly complicated. However, if you proceed methodically, they need not defeat you.

It is important to appreciate immediately that the British way of life conspires to make international rail travel particularly difficult. We do not believe in the 24-hour clock; we do not adopt the Continental version of summer time, or even change our clocks back for winter on the same day that they do; we do not run any trains at all on Christmas Day, or on Boxing Day except in years when the next day is a working day.

On the Continent, the

GOING BY RAIL

Let the train take the strain— while you watch the view and adjust to the idea that you are on holiday.

railways observe holidays with a rather greater degree of uniformity than churches. The following dates, therefore, should be avoided, as on these days the chances are that the journey times will be longer, and that restaurant and sleeper services will have been severely curtailed.

Austria—1, 6 Jan; EM; 1 May; AD; WM; CC; 15 Aug; 26 Oct; 1 Nov; 8, 25, 26 Dec

Belgium—1 Jan; EM; 1 May; AD; WM; 21 July; 15 Aug; 1, 11 Nov; 25 Dec

Denmark—1 Jan; MT; GF; EM; AD; WM; 25, 26 Dec

France—1 Jan; EM; 1 May; AD; WM; 14 July; 15 Aug; 1, 11 Nov; 25 Dec

Germany—1 Jan; GF; EM; 1 May; AD; WM; 17 June; 16 Nov; 25, 26 Dec

Italy—1 Jan; EM; 25 Apr; 1 May; 15 Aug; 1 Nov; 8, 25, 26 Dec

Netherlands—1 Jan; EM; 30 April; WM; 25, 26 Dec

Norway—1 Jan; 2, 8 April; MT; GF; EM; 1, 17 May; AD; WM; 25, 26 Dec

Sweden—1, 6 Jan; GF; EM; 1 May; AD; WM; 25, 25, 26 Dec

Switzerland—1, 2 Jan; GF; EM; AD; WM; 25, 26 Dec

UK—1 Jan; GF; EM; MDH; Spring BH; Aug BH; 25, 26 Dec

MT—Maundy Thursday
GF—Good Friday
EM—Easter Monday
MDH—May Day holiday
AD—Ascension Day
WM—Whit Monday
CC—Corpus Christi

Variable dates can be found in pocket diaries. On all other dates the full weekday service runs from Monday to Saturday, inclusive, with a restricted service on Sundays.

After the chaos of 1980, when, according to timetables issued for that year, trains entering Switzerland from Austria, France, Germany or Italy arrived before the Swiss said they had left, most Continental countries got together to standardise their summer time. For example, this was arranged to run from 25 March to 29 September in 1984 and from 31 March to 28 September in 1985 in all the following countries: Austria, Belgium, Czechoslovakia, Denmark, Finland, France, East and West Germany, Hungary, Italy, Luxembourg, Netherlands, Norway, Poland, Spain, Sweden, Switzerland and, somewhat belatedly, Yugoslavia.

Between those dates travellers to and from the UK could be confident that the time in western and central Europe would be one hour in advance, that is, 1am British time would be 2am on the other side of the Channel.

However, catch number one: between 30 September and 27 October 1984, and between 29 September and 26 October 1985—that is, until the British put their clocks back, UK and most Continental time would be the same.

Catch number two: because the Portuguese change their clocks on the same dates as the rest of western Europe, but are in the same time zone as the British (GMT winter, BST summer), for those same dates between the end of September

Dinner on the Orient Express—early elegance on rail

and the end of October, the Portuguese are an hour behind British time.

Countries further afield in Europe change their clocks on the same dates as western Europe, but remain an hour further ahead (usually two hours ahead of Britain), eg Bulgaria, Finland, Greece, Romania. The Turks have no summer time and are therefore two hours ahead of the British in summer, three hours in winter.

In the European part of the Soviet Union, including Moscow, summer time usually begins on 1 April and ends on 30 September. They are three hours ahead of BST in this period.

Having mastered the time zones, the next problem is the 24-hour clock. In the timetables each hour is numbered consecutively from

0 to 24, starting at midnight. A train arriving at midnight is shown as 24.00. A train leaving at midnight is shown as 0.00. Arrivals and departures between midnight and 1am are indicated in the same way, ie 0.01 to 0.59. One of the most common causes of travellers missing trains is misreading these times and arriving a day early or a day late.

Now comes the difficult bit: choosing a particular service to suit your requirements. When putting your journey together you will first have to master the intricacies of how the European rail system works. Just as London and Frankfurt are major gateway cities for air travellers with a multitude of connections in every direction, so the rail network has its own gateway cities.

They are Paris, Cologne and Basle (often passing through

Brussels en route). The fastest journey times from London, including the Channel crossing, are:

to Paris, 5 hours 25 minutes; from Paris, 5 hours 15 minutes

to Cologne, 7 hours 47 minutes; from Cologne, 7 hours 24 minutes

to Brussels, 5 hours 11 minutes; from Brussels, 4 hours 59 minutes

to Basle, 12 hours 19 minutes; from Basle, 11 hours 56 minutes

If you cannot find a timetable with a through train from London (usually Victoria, but occasionally Liverpool Street) to your destination, it should be possible to find a connection at Paris, Cologne or Basle.

Cologne and Basle present no problem in changing trains, but at Paris this can involve a journey across the centre between the Gare du Nord, the terminus for services from the Channel coast, and the Gare de Lyon, the most usual terminus for services to the

Nightmares

A British family travelling between Paris and Brussels caught sight of a station sign for Bergen when, they thought, they should have been entering Mons. They got off in confusion but, by the time they discovered that in bi-lingual Belgium Mons and Bergen were the same place, their train had left without them!

south-east or south. There are three alternatives to taxis:

Express buses operate between the two stations.

The RER—a fast suburban rail link. From the Gare du Nord, take line B2/B4 one stop to Châtelet-des-Halles, then take line A2/A4 one stop to the Gare de Lyon. In the reverse direction, take line A1 one stop to Châtelet-des-Halles, then line B3 one stop to the Gare du Nord.

The Metro—the Paris underground—is by far the cheapest, but is definitely to be avoided if you have a lot of luggage or need to travel during morning or evening rush hours.

However, because Paris, unlike London, does regularly operate trains right through the capital, it is possible to avoid this tedious journey between the termini altogether. Here are some examples of through services from

London and the Channel ports, although some operate during the summer only:

Calais-Paris-Nice

Calais-Basle-Innsbruck

Calais-Basle-Milan-Rome

Calais-Paris-Milan-Venice

Calais-Venice-Belgrade

Boulogne-Paris-Pisa-Rome-Naples

Calais-Paris-Narbonne-Port Bou

There are many other international through trains, some of them seasonal, with connections from London:

Ostend-Brussels-Cologne-Vienna

Ostend-Brussels-Cologne-Copenhagen

Hook of Holland-Hamburg-Copenhagen-Stockholm

Hook of Holland-Cologne-Munich

Ostend-Salzburg-Split

Ostend-Hanover-Berlin-Warsaw-Moscow (sleeping cars only)

There are connections to the Harwich-Hook of Holland ferry service from Manchester, Edinburgh, Glasgow and other major UK cities.

The importance of the through-train services (which are always subject to alteration) is that most passengers, already exhausted by having to carry luggage on and off the Channel ferry, are relieved of the need for any changes during the rest of the journey. This is especially welcome if they have to sit up all night in a second-class compartment.

It is perfectly possible to avoid carrying any luggage at all. You can register your baggage (at least 45 minutes before departure) through to

TICKETS

your Continental destination for a fee based on the distance to be travelled. There are, as you would expect, some snags. At peak times, your luggage may not travel on your train and could be delayed. Even at quiet periods, do not expect luggage carried by way of Barcelona, Lisbon, Madrid, Paris, Prague, Stockholm, Valencia, Vienna or Warsaw to arrive less than a day after you do—so carry something to get by. And, depending on your circumstances, the cost may not justify the convenience of travelling light.

If the cost of the rail trip is not critical, sleeping accommodation is also an attractive extravagance. Most long-distance trains running overnight offer a choice between couchettes and sleepers. Couchettes are simply (mixed sex) sleeping compartments with berths, four in first-class, six in second. Sheets, blankets and pillows are provided, but there are no private washing facilities.

Sleeping cars proper have washbasins with hot and cold water; newer coaches have air conditioning and, in Germany especially, some have a set of private showers.

With a first-class ticket, you may be offered the choice between a full single sleeper, a 'special' which is slightly smaller, or a large twin-bedded double. Except in Spain, which has four-berth sleepers on the Talgo trains (see later), second-class passengers are usually able to choose between a T2, for two people, with one bed above the other or two beds on the upper level; and a T3, for three people

with beds one above the other.

The availability of food and drink on trains varies from country to country, but there is a great distinction between first and second-class passengers, the latter being prevented from using a full restaurant car on some routes. Full waiter service is becoming increasingly rare, and many self-service restaurant cars are now in operation, especially in France, Germany and Italy. On some trains, buffet cars provide a small choice of hot dishes. On long-distance services, trolleys usually come round with (expensive) drinks and sandwiches, but it is unwise to rely on them.

It is also unwise to depend on your ticket being issued correctly, even with the increasing use of computers to make reservations. Understanding your own ticket is essential if you are to be certain it describes accurately the journey you intend to make. A mistake may be too late to rectify once you are on the Continent.

Almost all European railways now use the same kind of ticket, with coupons

similar in style to an airline ticket, self-carbonising and individually bound. Unlike most airline tickets, sometimes one rail ticket may be issued for several passengers travelling together for the outward and return journeys. Also, rarely, the actual travel day and time may not be specified, but tickets are normally valid for two months.

Reserved seats, couchettes or sleepers are recorded on separate tickets, together with their additional cost. Every ticket has spaces for not only the section of the journey for which the booking applies—if it is for a reserved seat, try to book for the whole way—but also (from left to right), the date of travel, time (on the 24-hour clock), class, number of the coach on the train, number of the train, and number of the seat, berth or compartment. Some people seem to spend half the journey walking up and down the corridors, looking for their seat, because they are unable to understand the Continental rail ticket. They are not alone: nor, apparently, do some travel agents.

Although fares from the UK to 300 destinations are shown in the *Continental Rail Fares* list, others have to be calculated from the frontiers of each country, with an 'add-on' to the final destination. Frontier point calculations vary according to the route and, even with sophisticated methods of computerisation, mistakes are common. A wise precaution is to check the calculation you have been given with the appropriate rail office in London, which will probably form part of, or work in close association with, its national tourist office. They may not, however, be able to make bookings for you other than for motorail services and certain tourist routes.

Some European rail networks offer special all-inclusive tickets with substantial reductions. 'Global price' tickets, which include sleepers and reserved seats, are available from London to southern Germany and Austria; to Paris (only via Le Havre, night service); from Paris to Barcelona, Madrid and Rome.

For passengers under 26 a Eurotrain or Transalpino ticket, valid for two months with flexible stopovers, can drastically cut the cost. The biggest bargain of all for the under 26 year olds is the Inter Rail pass, obtainable before leaving the UK, that provides unlimited rail travel for one month throughout Europe (except Bulgaria, Czechoslovakia, East Germany, Poland, Turkey and the USSR) and Morocco. And France has a *carte jeune*, obtainable from SNCF in

London and valid for the same age group, offering a 50 per cent discount on most journeys.

Sleeper services invariably have an attendant on each carriage, who will help you to find your compartment. Should you be double-booked, or apparently so, the golden rule is: stand your ground— even if others are already in possession of the compartment. Sleeping-car attendants have been known to

TOILET

take bribes to get people on to trains that are already full. If both you and the other party have what seem to be genuine tickets, the attendants will probably put one of you into a sleeper being held for someone further up the line, in the hope that they do not actually turn up.

Except in such circumstances, do not worry if the attendant disappears with your tickets, even overnight. This is quite normal practice on long-distance trains and, by leaving your passports with the attendant as well, you may well escape the discomfort of being woken up when the train crosses a frontier.

In France, even if you have an international coupon ticket, it is best to follow their national practice of date-stamping it. This is done at your departure point in France by inserting your ticket into an orange machine at the platform entrance, under a sign that usually reads *Compostez votre billet*. If you buy a ticket in France and fail

Wise Words

Avoid travelling on the Continent on certain national or religious holidays—see list.

Master the 24-hour clock and time zones, and you will master the intricacies of the Continental rail timetable.

Decide whether to send luggage separately.

Learn to decode the information on your rail tickets.

Do not travel without a ticket: heavy fines or surcharges apply.

Nightmares

Beware of the train that divides in the night, especially on the Continent, where the practice of detaching carriages along the route is quite commonplace. Prudent passengers will not stray too far from their compartment unless they are fully dressed and carrying money and their passport. One family travelling overnight by sleeper through France to Spain woke up to learn this the hard way: mother was missing. She had left her compartment to go to the loo in the middle of the night, had seen an engaged sign on the lavatory at the end of her carriage, and had walked further down the train to find an empty one. While she was, as they say, otherwise pre-occupied, the train reached a station and was split in two parts. The carriage she was in headed in the wrong direction, leaving her clad only in a nightie . . .

to date-stamp it, the ticket inspector is likely to charge you 20 per cent above the normal fare.

In Spain, passengers with international tickets who wish to break their journey have to get their tickets stamped at the station before continuing their journey. There is almost always a mad rush at ticket offices, because the one window selling the ticket you want is invariably open only 30 minutes before the train is due to depart.

If you buy a ticket more than two hours in advance of a train's departure, you must travel a minimum distance (or at least, pay for) 250km (155 miles) on the luxurious Talgo trains; 200km (125 miles) on Electrotrenes and TER trains, which usually have air conditioning; and 100km (75 miles) on express trains and Rapidos, which usually go long distances and overnight.

In Italy, train travel is cheap and therefore popular. Seat reservations are more or less essential for long journeys. Passengers travelling in groups on reduced price tickets sometimes run into trouble on the special fast Rapido services, as they can be asked to pay the full fare. Only holders of international coupon tickets are permitted to use the Rapido for short, intermediate journeys.

There is free access to the platforms at Italian stations, but if you choose not to buy a ticket before boarding, a fine is imposed by the ticket collector on the train.

In Germany, a much dimmer view is taken of travelling without first obtaining a ticket. If you do, you will be liable to pay double the fare. Long queues at ticket windows are in any case rare, because a large number of tickets can be obtained from automatic machines. Seat reservations are by computer, and the organisation is so sophisticated that, when changing trains at Cologne, Dortmund, Hanover, Mannheim or Würzburg, your carriage on the connecting train should be directly opposite the one on the train you are leaving. An information board *(Wagenstandanzeiger)* shows exactly where each carriage

will stop at the platform, so that you can position yourself before the train comes in.

In the Netherlands, ticket collectors also impose fines on passengers with incorrect or invalidated tickets, and the more you argue, the more the fine is increased . . . In Belgium, all ticket inspection is carried out on trains, and fines are frequently imposed on passengers with invalid tickets. However, the biggest potential problem in Belgium and the Netherlands are the electric trains which have different sections for different destinations; it is quite easy to sit in the wrong part of the train.

In Switzerland, any passenger boarding a train without a ticket is sold a single ticket with a surcharge—making the return journey substantially more expensive.

In Austria, there are some rather odd trains known as *Korridorzüge*. Corridor refers not to the trains but the portion of German or Italian territory that they cross, but where passengers are not allowed to get on or off, even when the train stops to deliver mail or newspapers.

In the Soviet Union, there are two classes of accommodation: soft class, with fully upholstered seats; and (you guessed it) hard class, with plastic or leather seats, converted to sleeping accommodation for overnight travel. Advance booking is necessary for every journey and travel within Russia is not particularly comfortable.

In contrast, if you are travelling across western Europe by day, the fastest and best trains are the Trans Europ Expresses, known as TEE. Started in 1957 with

New track had to be laid for the 170mph TGV, French Railways' crack express competing with air services

eight services, reaching in their heyday 37, but reduced from 27 to 22 in 1983, the TEE connect most Continental Common Market countries, along with Austria and Switzerland. The expresses are all first-class, with electric locomotives, air conditioning and full dining facilities. Perhaps the most famous is the Rheingold, serving Amsterdam-Cologne-Coblenz-Basle, with beautiful views of the Rhine valley.

Continental trains are extremely punctual. They are also, as a rule, very clean—and the glamorous expresses, very fast.

Faster, much faster, than the TEE are the TGV, the *Trains à Grand Vitesse*, with services between Paris, Lyon and Marseilles; and Paris, Geneva and Lausanne. At speeds of nearly 170mph (270kph) on entirely new track for much of this distance, in terms of time they are serious competitors to air services and much less inconvenient.

Each TGV has first and

second-class accommodation, a self-service restaurant and a bar; while for first-class passengers in some first-class coaches, meals are served at the passengers' own seats. There are supplements at busy times, but numbered seat reservations are essential on every train—automatic machines are available at stations for the use of anyone who has not booked in advance.

Finally, there is the Orient Express. Not the Venice-Simplon Orient Express, revived in 1982, that runs with vintage coaches from London to Folkestone and then from Boulogne to Venice, with certainly the most expensive train meals in the world. Rather, the genuine Agatha Christie article. The real Orient Express still leaves Paris daily, following the old route to Istanbul as far as Bucharest. It has first and second-class sleeping cars, a restaurant car in Hungary and Romania but, alas, not a Mata Hari in sight!

'Will I have to drive my car on to the motorail while the train is moving?' asked the elderly lady from Tunbridge Wells. 'Oui, madam,' said the French Railways official with a wicked glint in his eye, 'but do not derange yourself: we will slow it down specially for you to 60km an hour.'

They get a lot of questions like that in the London office of SNCF, French Railways, for motorail is nothing if it is not discreet—a connoisseur's way of travel whose supreme advantages seem to have escaped the attention of many. Fortunately, the instinctive British distrust of anything apparently involving some degree of technical skill, means that motorail (both here and abroad) has never quite reached the level of popularity of other modes of travel.

Motorail, a system where your vehicle is placed aboard a train and transported along with its occupants to another part of France, or to other holiday areas such as Italy, Spain or Portugal, is an eminently practical and sensible way to start and finish a trip. But no, you do not sit in your car all night, nor does the driver have to hurl his car aboard a moving train like some fairground stuntman.

In fact, unless you want to, you hardly ever have to drive your car on or off the train at all. This will be done for you by a team of drivers, frustrated racing drivers— some say, who pride themselves on being able to master just about every known make of car. They turn the roof-top parking lot at the big motorail centre in Paris into a mini grand prix circuit, so quickly do they load or unload their charges. (But don't worry, they've not written off a car yet!)

To make the most of your

THE BEST OF BOTH WORLDS

trip, all you need to worry about are several simple precautions. First, check your tickets. As motorail bookings are made by computer link with France, mistakes are extremely rare, but better safe now than sorry later. The actual train tickets are sometimes made out for all the people travelling and for both halves of the journey if you

The scenery is free, but you pay for 'training' your car

are coming back but, that apart, you should have a separate ticket for the sleeping berths and for the car in each direction. Check that the car ticket does have the destination on it you want, and that your sleeping berths are in the same compartment.

Next, if you have luggage on your roof-rack, make sure that it can be easily taken off when you arrive at the motorail departure point

because that is precisely what you will have to do. Practise stowing it in the car, leaving the driving seat clear, until you are quite sure it will go in. This may seem obvious enough, but SNCF have a substantial dossier on items from skis to grandfather clocks that could never be transferred from a roof-rack to the inside of a car.

Now study the map provided with your tickets, showing you where to take your car. Some places—for example, Boulogne, Paris, Fréjus—have special stations set apart from the main passenger stations, and they are not always easy to find. Look for a *Train Auto Couchettes* sign, the French motorail.

Join the queue, which at the Channel ports will be predominantly British and orderly, in Paris, predominantly French and probably not. Present your tickets, remembering that at this stage the officials will be most interested in the one for the car. An official will start making strange biro marks on it while walking around your vehicle. He is noting down any dents or scratches to prevent you from claiming that they happened on the journey. Have a look over his shoulder and query anything you do not believe is correct: has he marked down a muddy spot as a dent? The chances are that the improbable will happen, and your car will arrive with a muddy spot and a dent, too!

Another of the officials will give you a breakfast ticket for every paying passenger. As the French love children, he will usually give you an extra one for each small child, even if they are travelling free. Keep these with your other tickets, as you will need them later.

Unpack your roof-rack, if

you have one, stowing everything inside the car, lock all the doors except the driver's and leave the key in the ignition. Lower or unscrew the radio aerial, and watch your car being driven on to what looks like a series of car transporters connected together. There will be a good deal of clanking as the car is driven from ramp to ramp, but once made secure it is perfectly safe. The key will be left in the ignition and the driver's door sealed to protect your belongings.

Obviously it is common-sense to take your valuables with you on to the passenger carriages, which may already be linked to the car wagons, or parked elsewhere in the station . . . or they may be nowhere to be seen. If the passenger carriages are not in sight, do not start worrying. This means that the car wagons are going to be coupled to a regular passenger service, which will be along at the appointed time.

However short the wait or the distance to your carriage, do not be tempted to take more than the bare essentials on to the train. Even if you have a proper sleeping compartment rather than a couchette (which is simply a bed without private washing facilities), there is not really room for much more than a small bag per person.

Every sleeping car has an attendant who will show you the way to your compartment. He will also take away all your tickets, and probably your passports if you are crossing a border during the night, but never fear—he will

still be there with your papers in the morning.

He will also provide cold meals and a variety of drinks, but, as you would expect, at prices considerably higher than if you bought the items in a supermarket. The best bet is to dash to the nearest shops and buy all the ingredients of a picnic—some wine, French

bread, fruit, cheeses, pâté and the like—so that you immediately get into the right mood for your trip. Also buy mineral water, because you will be provided with only a limited amount of drinking water in your compartment. Restaurant meals are available on a few services, but it is best not to bank on their being there.

The size of your compartment varies according to the route and the price you pay. The most popular are known as T2s and T3s, second-class or tourist compartments with two or three berths. They are extremely well designed, but only an optimist would ask a really tall person to sleep in the top bunk of a T3. There is also a limit on the number of small children that can be squeezed into occupied bunks— one per bed, a rule allegedly introduced after a prolific mother tried to take advantage of the system!

Some compartments are designed so that you can hop into bed when you feel like it; in others, you have to wait for the attendant to come along and fold down the upper berths, a disadvantage countered by the fact that you have slightly more room to sit down.

If your free breakfast is to be served on the train, your attendant will take your vouchers and bring along trays in the morning, having asked the previous evening whether you want tea or coffee. On some routes, however, breakfast is served in

Wise Words

Check the details on your tickets when booking.

Make sure all your roof-rack luggage will fit inside your car.

Study the map that is with your tickets, showing the location of the motorail terminus.

Watch what the official inspecting your car lists as bodywork blemishes.

Take your valuables out of the car.

Buy overnight refreshments at shops in the terminus town.

driven the hundreds of miles overnight.

Motorail seems expensive, but that is because few people bother to calculate the true cost of driving the same distance and back. Such costs may include overnight stops with extra restaurant meals, petrol, oil and motorway tolls. The true difference in cost may be extremely small, especially if you have a sizeable car and intend to travel in peak season. Because the combined ferry and motorail ticket does not vary according to the size of the vehicle or the time of year, motorail can actually be cheaper than driving all the

way—and that calculation does not take into account wear and tear on the car and the driver.

Nor does the driver have to be too careful what he drinks, though a nocturnal visit to the loo at the end of the coach can involve some disagreeable acrobatics if he has been allotted the top bunk.

But nothing as spectacular, one hopes, as a former president of France who fell out of the Orient Express while answering a call of nature, clad only in his pyjamas. Cars may not join the train at 60km an hour, but passengers have been known to leave it.

the station restaurant and you use your vouchers there—no particular disadvantage in this, because it will take a few minutes to unload your car.

Vehicles are usually unloaded in the same order they were driven on. Do check for any damage from flying stones, especially to the windscreen, however remote the possibility. Your car will not be as spotlessly clean as you left it the night before, but nowhere near as dirty as it would have been if you had

Nightmares

Assume at your peril that every eventuality will be covered by your travel insurance while you are abroad. A loophole in the protection offered by Europ Assistance emerged for one motorail passenger after he discovered that he had been the victim of a theft less than 30 minutes

before his return departure from Nice. The thieves had whisked the briefcase containing his motorail tickets out of a locked boot. The driver had a Europ Assistance policy but found that it had no provision for circumstances where a car was drivable though the driver lacked but two critical ingredients: petrol for the return journey and the money to

purchase it. French Railways were sympathetic, but pointed out that the rules required any would-be motorail user to have a ticket and that their credit card limit was below the price of one for that journey. In sheer desperation the driver got round the problem by signing half a dozen Visa credit card vouchers and made his train in time.

If you cannot bear to be parted from your car, but hate the idea of driving it more than a few miles until you reach your destination, it is possible to have it carried by motorail as far as Algeciras (for the ferry to Tangier) or Villa San Giovanni (for the ferry to Sicily). This would involve you in at least two, and possibly three, separate motorail journeys but is perfectly feasible if you can stand the cost. With a few exceptions, West German and Austrian motorail services are the most expensive; the French are more costly at peak times, but cheaper in quiet periods; the Spanish and, more especially, the Italian services generally the cheapest. The most useful routes are from the Channel ports of Calais, Dieppe or Boulogne (which has its own modern terminal) and from 's-Hertogenbosch in the Netherlands.

MAIN MOTORAIL SERVICES

Calais–Nice. Calais–Narbonne. Boulogne–St Raphael. Boulogne–Brive–Narbonne. Boulogne–Milan. Boulogne–Avignon. Dieppe–Avignon. Paris–Madrid. Paris–Lisbon. Paris–Munich. 's-Hertogenbosch–Genoa. 's-Hertogenbosch–Ljubljana, Yugoslavia. Milan–Rome.

Milan–Naples–Villa San Giovanni. Genoa–Rome. Santander–Madrid. Bilbao–

Alicante. Madrid–Alicante. Madrid–Malaga. Madrid–Algeciras.

For Germany see
pages 108–109

D

L

NL

B

GB

Köln
Aachen
Eindhoven
Liège
Maastricht
Antwerpen
BRUSSELS
Namur
Charleroi
Valenciennes
Mons
Roubaix
Tourcoing
Gent
Oostende
Dunkerque
Calais
Boulogne
Hazebrouck
Béthune
Lille
Douai
Etaples
S–t Pol
Arras
Le Touquet
Abbeville
Le Tréport
Dieppe
Cambrai
Amiens
St. Quentin
Hirson
Tergnier
Laon
Compiègne
Fourmies
Aulnoye-Aymeries
Charleville-Mézières
Sedan
Longuyon
Verdun
Reims
Épernay
Châlons-sur-Marne
Vitry-le-François
Troyes
Chaumont
Bar-le-Duc
Toul
Vittel
Épinal
Gérardmer
Colmar
Kehl
Strasbourg
Saverne
Nancy
Metz
Thionville
Forbach
Saarbrücken
Trier
LUXEMBOURG
Arlon
Amsterdam
Utrecht
Haarlem
DEN HAAG
Hoek van Holland
Rotterdam
Fontainebleau
PARIS
Versailles
Chartres
Dreux
Rouen
Serquigny
Le Havre
Trouville
Deauville
Lisieux
Argentan
Alençon
Bagnoles de l'Orne
Brouze
Mézidon
Dives-Cabourg
Caen
Bayeux
St. Lô
Lison
Folligny
Coutances
Cherbourg
Granville
Avranches
Dol
Dinan
Dinard
St. Malo
Lamballe
St. Brieuc
Guingamp
Paimpol
Lannion
Plouaret
Morlaix
Roscoff
Landerneau
Brest

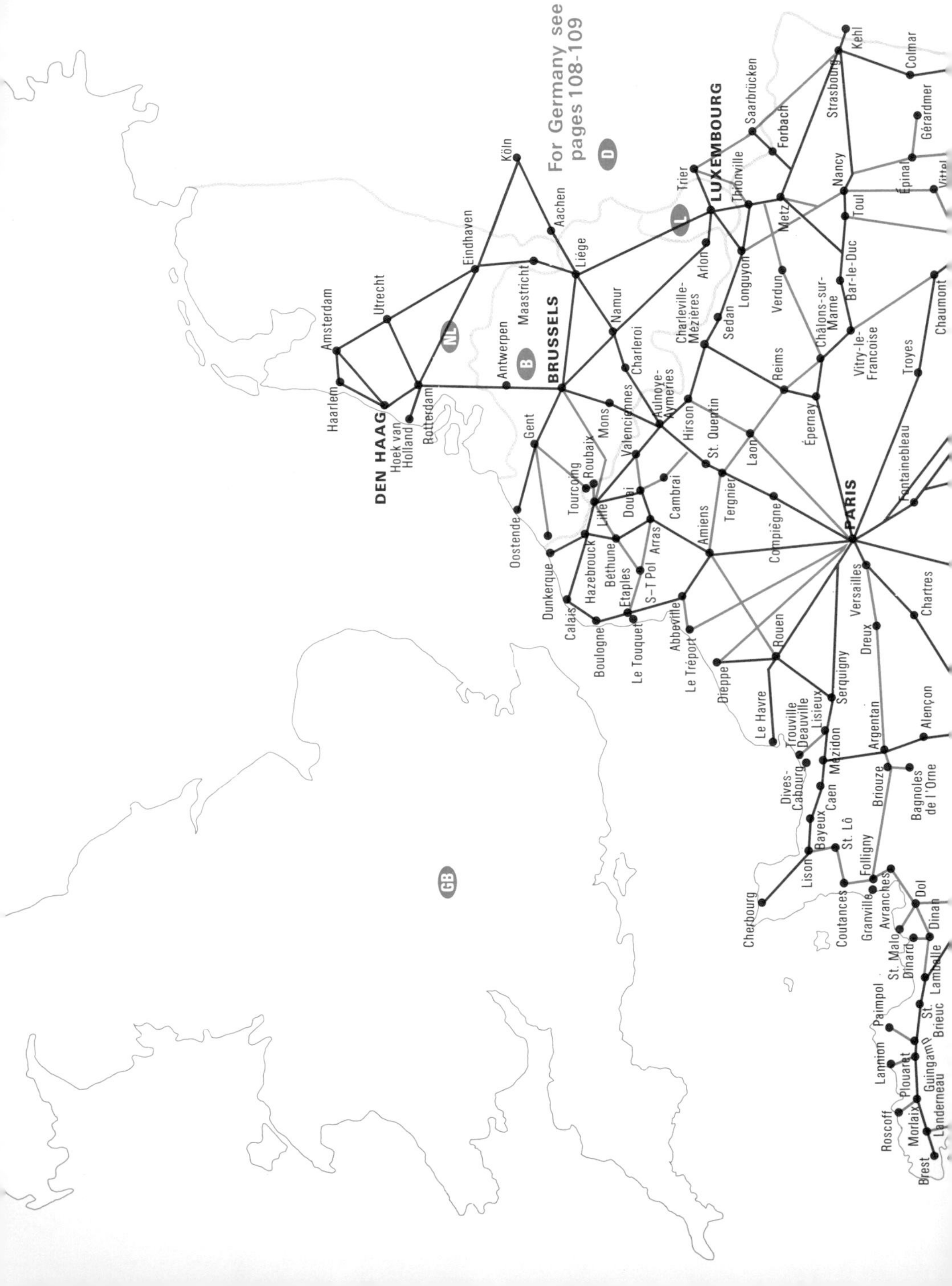

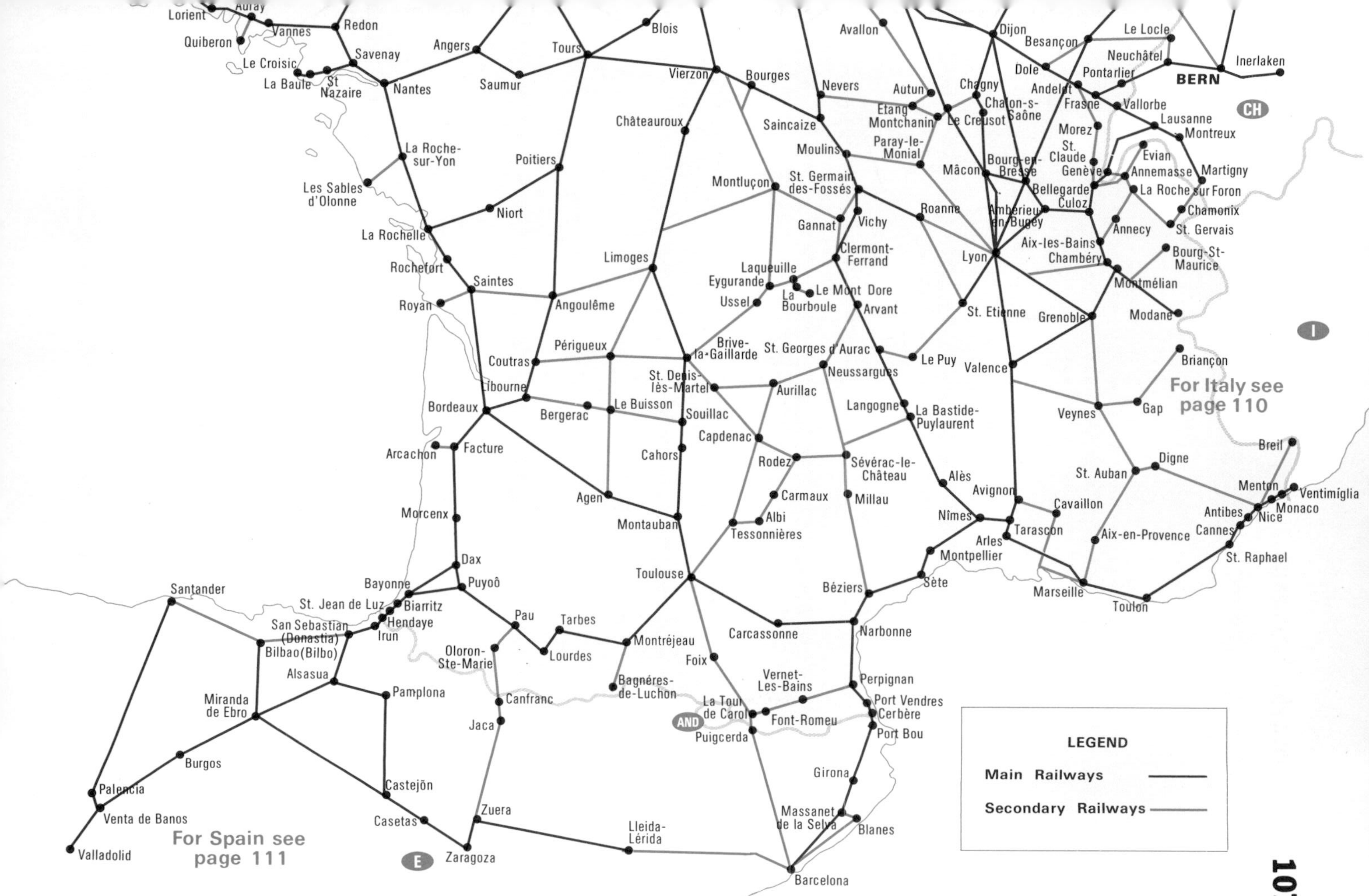

For Italy see
page 110

For Spain see
page 111

LEGEND

Main Railways

Secondary Railways

CH

BERN

Interlaken
Le Locle
Neuchâtel
Pontarlier
Vallorbe
Frasne
Andelot
Dole
Besançon
Dijon
Chagny
Chalon-s-Saône
Le Creusot
Autun
Avallon
Nevers
Saincaize
Moulins
Montluçon
Bourges
Vierzon
Blois
Châteauroux
Tours
Saumur
Angers
Nantes
Savenay
St Nazaire
La Baule
Le Croisic
Redon
Vannes
Auray
Quiberon
Lorient
Les Sables d'Olonne
La Roche-sur-Yon
Niort
Poitiers
La Rochelle
Rochefort
Royan
Saintes
Angoulême
Limoges
Périgueux
Coutras
Libourne
Bergerac
Bordeaux
Facture
Arcachon
Morcenx
Dax
Puyoô
Bayonne
Biarritz
Hendaye
Irun
St. Jean de Luz
San Sebastian (Donostia)
Bilbao (Bilbo)
Santander
Alsasua
Pamplona
Miranda de Ebro
Burgos
Palencia
Venta de Banos
Valladolid
Castejón
Casetas
Zaragoza
Zuera
Jaca
Canfranc
Oloron-Ste-Marie
Pau
Tarbes
Lourdes
Bagnères-de-Luchon
Montréjeau
Foix
La Tour de Carol
Puigcerda
AND
Font-Romeu
Vernet-Les-Bains
Perpignan
Port Vendres
Cerbère
Port Bou
Girona
Massanet de la Selva
Blanes
Barcelona
Lleida-Lérida
Toulouse
Montauban
Agen
Bergerac
Cahors
Le Buisson
St. Denis lès-Martel
Souillac
Capdenac
Brive-la-Gaillarde
Ussel
Eygurande
Laqueuille
Gannat
St. Germain des-Fossés
Vichy
Clermont-Ferrand
La Bourboule
Le Mont Dore
St. Georges d'Aurac
Arvant
Aurillac
Rodez
Carmaux
Albi
Tessonnières
Carcassonne
Narbonne
Béziers
Sète
Montpellier
Nîmes
Alès
La Bastide-Puylaurent
Langogne
Neussargues
Séverac-le-Château
Millau
Le Puy
St. Etienne
Roanne
Lyon
Valence
Montélimar
Avignon
Tarascon
Arles
Cavaillon
Marseille
Toulon
Aix-en-Provence
St. Auban
Digne
Veynes
Gap
Briançon
Modane
St. Gervais
La Roche sur Foron
Chamonix
Bourg-St-Maurice
Annecy
Aix-les-Bains
Chambéry
Grenoble
Culoz
Bellegarde
Genève
St. Claude
Morez
Ambérieu-en-Bugey
Bourg-en-Bresse
Mâcon
Amberieu
Etang Montchanin
Paray-le-Monial
Le Monial
Martigny
Montreux
Lausanne
Evian
Thonon
Annemasse
Montmélian
Breil
Menton
Ventimiglia
Monaco
Nice
Antibes
Cannes
St. Raphael
I
E

109

For Italy see page 110

For France see
pages 106-107

LEGEND

Main Railways

Secondary Railways

WIEN
Wiener Neustadt
Bruck an de Mur
Graz
Leoben
CS
Tabor
Gmünd
A
Linz
To Villach
Spittal
Chomutov
Karlovy Vary
Marianské Lázně
Plzeň
Česká Kubice
Wels
Passau
Salzburg
Berchtesgaden
Bischofshofen
Schwarzach St. Veit
PRAHA
Gutenfürst
Bad Brambach
Cheb
Wirsberg
Marktredwitz
Schwandorf
Furth Im Wald
Plattling
Landshut
Rosenheim
Freilassing
Bad Reichenhall
Kufstein
Zell-am-See
Wörgl
Innsbruck
Brenner / Brennero
Bolzano
Jena
Probstzella
Hof
Schirnding
Pegnitz
Regensburg
Ingolstadt
München
Weilheim
Murnau
Garmisch Partenkirchen
Mittenwald
Zugspitz
Saalfeld
Ludwigstadt
Coburg
Lichtenfels
Neuenmarkt
Bayreuth
Nürnberg
Domühl
Treuchtlingen
Donauwörth
Augsburg
Oberammergau
Kaufbeuren
Kempten
Füssen
Reutte
Sonthofen
Ehrwald
Landeck
Eisenach
Meiningen
Schweinfurt
Bamberg
Ansbach
Crailsheim
Aalen
Göppingen
Ulm
Buchloe
Memmingen
Immenstadt
Oberstdorf
Fulda
Giessen
Wetzlar
Limburg
Niederlahnstein
Gemünden
Aschaffenburg
Würzburg
Lauda
Bad Mergentheim
Schwäbisch Hall
Schwäbisch Gmünd
Herbertingen
Leutkirch
Lindau
Faldkirch
FL
Sargans
Buchs
Como
Frankfurt-am-Main
Frankfurt Flughafen
Mannheim
Heidelberg
Neckarelz
Heilbronn
Stuttgart
Tübingen
Horb
Ravensburg
Friedrichshafen
Konstanz
St Gallen
Milano
Betzdorf
Königswinter
Koblenz
Bingen
Main
Darmstadt
Ludwigshafen
Worms
Neustadt
Bruchsal
Pforzheim
Rottweil
Villingen
Tuttlingen
Singen
Thalwil
Schwyz
Como
Bellinzona
Lugano
Stresa
BONN
Bullay
Bad Kreuznach
Idar-Oberstein
Landau
Wörth
Karlsruhe
Rastatt
Baden-Baden
Appenweier
Eutingen
Freudenstadt
Hausach
Triberg
Donaueschingen
Neustadt
Schaffhausen
Waldshut
Zürich
Luzern
Göschenen
Locarno
Domodossola
Gerolstein
Wetzlar
Kaiserslautern
Homburg
Pirmasens
Kehl
Offenburg
Lahr
Freiburg
Müllheim
Mulhouse
Basel
Olten
Brig
Wasserbillig
Trier
Apach
Saarbrücken
Strasbourg
Colmar
Belfort
Biel
Neuchâtel
CH
BERN
Liège
Namur
B
L
LUXEMBOURG
Thionville
Metz
Nancy
F
Forbach
Lausanne
Genève
Martigny

For Italy see page 110

For France see
pages 106-107

110 Rail network: Italy

LEGEND

Main Railways ———

Secondary Railways ———

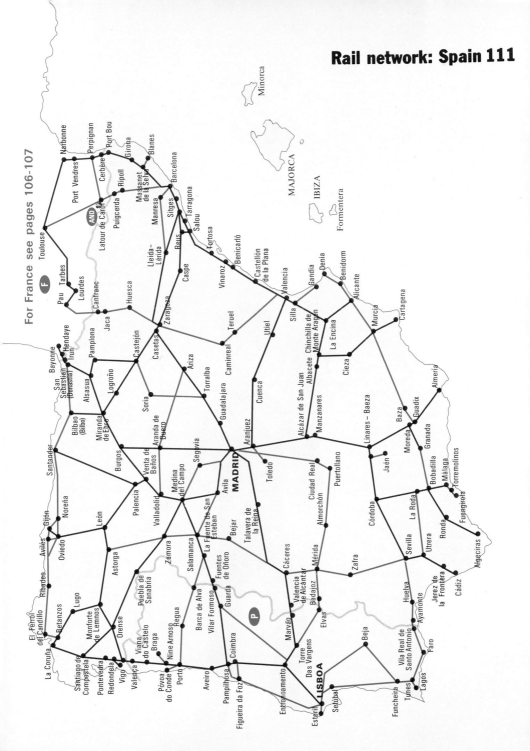

For France see pages 106-107

The first no-passport trip across the Channel—with the possible exception of the Scarlet Pimpernel's—came immediately after the Napoleonic wars, on 17 March 1816. The ship which made it was the 38-ton *Elise*, the route Newhaven–Le Havre, and the journey took seventeen hours in a storm. We know the passengers did not have passports, because in those days you could travel to France, Switzerland or Italy without one, and if you wanted to visit the Austro-Hungarian Empire, Thomas Cook would get you the necessary papers for three shillings, including a one shilling service charge.

With no formalities involved in crossing to the Continent, many seaside towns on the other side of the Channel caught the British enthusiasm for swimming and sun-bathing. Dieppe stopped using the seafront as the municipal rubbish dump, and was even honoured by a visit from a member of the French royal family, the Duchesse de Berri, who took a dip in 1824 accompanied by a white-gloved doctor who feared for her health. Boulogne was the first Continental resort to go in for rows of bathing huts *'à l'anglaise'*. Ostend in Belgium and Scheveningen in Holland became particularly popular for invalids, although, as a Dr Arthur Granville observed, the benefits of the seawater were offset by the considerable risk of being bored to death.

The number of British visitors quickly grew so large

GOING BY SEA

Ocean-going ships are a world of their own and offer a stylish escape from the reality of life ashore.

that in 1821 a Mr John Boyd of Dover started a regular commercial service to Calais. His cross-Channel steamer the *Rob Roy* had an average crossing time of two and three-quarter hours. Although improvement in boilers led to this time being steadily reduced, it was not until the SS *Empress* came on the scene in 1887 that crossing times of 50 minutes from berth to berth became possible, close to the Blue Riband records of the present Townsend Thoresen fleet.

There are pictures of aristocratic coaches being hoisted aboard these early vessels, but the first man to see the immense possibilities of a regular car ferry service was the founder of the Townsend Thoresen line, Captain Stuart Townsend. His ship, the *Artificer*, went into service in 1928. In those days every car was taken on board by a crane, even on the purpose-built ferry known as the *Autocarrier*, introduced by the old independent Southern Railway in 1930. It was not until 1946 that motorists were able to drive on and off a ferry called *The Forde*, on the Dover–Calais route; and the first purpose-built car ferry with this facility did not come into operation until 1952, when British Rail's *Lord Warden* began operations between Dover and Boulogne on 17 June.

The first hovercraft service began on the same route in 1968, which, together with the even faster jetfoil, extended the possibility of day trips and short breaks on the Continent, whether on foot, by coach or by car. Savings of around 25 per cent of the normal fare are possible by taking an 120-hour return, which allows five days on the Continent; and of roughly 50 per cent on 60-hour excursions. These have the

added benefit for British and Irish citizens of not requiring a passport.

All the passengers have to do is obtain an identification card from the ferry operator, which is stamped prior to departure. The cards must carry a passport-size photograph, which can cause problems if you forget to bring one with you in peak periods and have to join the queue at the booths available in most of the ferry termini. It is quite possible to miss the ferry of your choice because you are waiting to have your picture taken.

The 60-hour limit applies to time actually abroad, and does not include the crossing to and from England. The immigration authorities are usually understanding if your scheduled return departure time has to be extended because of some unforeseen delay in the arrival of your ferry. Similarly, ticket prices are based on the scheduled time of your return trip, irrespective of when the vessel actually sails.

Passengers usually have one or more of the following objects in mind in making a short excursion:

to buy some duty-free alcohol

and packs of cigarettes

to buy beer and/or wine in bulk abroad

to buy other Continental goods

to sample Continental cooking and wine

to see nearby places of interest

to drink as much duty-free alcohol as they can on the way over and the way back

Ferry operators would probably rather sail without people in the final category, but unfortunately they are usually mixed up with other less offensive passengers on the same coaches. However, serious problems are rare, and boisterous passengers are usually confined to early or mid-morning sailings outward bound on a Saturday, and the early evening return from the Continent on the same day.

The table overleaf shows how long you can expect a crossing to take between particular ports.
The longer crossings are obviously suitable only for stays of two days or longer. A crossing of more than four hours in each direction would make a day trip extremely

arduous. However, bear in mind that day cabins are available on most long sailings, and are comparatively cheap and rarely taken up. Being able to sleep, or at least to rest, on each of the journeys may make a much longer day acceptable. If you travel at night, thereby making the most of the sleeping time, you can sail quite long distances without really noticing it at all.

There are three key pieces of advice for the short sea voyage: take a car, if at all possible, take cash, take a calculator.

Take a car

Although having a car with you obviously costs a good deal more, it can transform a short Continental break. Without a car, you will constantly have belongings and shopping to carry from one form of transport to another, and it will severely limit what you can bring back. Why not share the cost with another family, even if it means a couple of people in the party travelling by train to and from the British port? They would still have the main advantage of the car once the destination is reached. Bear in mind, also, that the best beaches, the best restaurants and the best scenery may all be out of town and, better

still, out of reach of the day tripper without wheels.

Take cash

That is, take foreign currency, or at least buy it on the boat. You do not want to waste your precious time on shore queuing to change your money. Especially as, apart from the banks, you can expect a generally poor rate of exchange. This is a particular problem on Saturday trips, as in most of the Channel ports the banks are open from Monday to Friday, with occasional exceptions (one in St Malo). In Dieppe, however, they open Tuesday to Saturday and in Ostend they are additionally open on Saturday mornings.

Take a calculator

It is the only way to check instantly and effortlessly what things cost—especially, how the prices of duty-free alcohol on the boat compare with the prices in the shops. Expect the prices in the shops to be competitive and, for some items, cheaper, with the advantage that in the EEC you can take more home without paying duty. For further details, see pages 142–145.

Do not overlook the obvious. The weather does not mysteriously improve on the other side of the Channel. If it is cold and wet in England, it will probably be cold and wet on the Continent as well. Dress accordingly and make suitable plans where to go.

Do not expect to go shopping when Continental shops are traditionally shut. Apart from food shops early morning, few worthwhile shops are open on Sundays. A good many shops are also closed on Mondays, or at any rate closed for part of the day. There are also a number of public holidays in France when not only will few shops be open, but restaurants and hotels will be unpleasantly full. They include: 1 January, Easter Monday, 1 May, 8 May (not everywhere), Ascension Day, Whit Monday, 14 July, 15 August, 1 November, 11 November, Christmas Day.

Take out insurance. Even on a day trip, your car may be in collision with a French motorist, or worse (if he has no Green Card) with another British one. The risk of having to pay perhaps several hundred pounds in repairs is too great to take.

Travel insurance is also advisable as thieves haunt seaside resorts on both sides of the Channel and you could lose a lot of money. And if you are knocked down in a French street, you may not have the option of returning home for free treatment under the British Health Service. A trip abroad, however brief, will only go without a hitch so long as you prepare for it almost as though you were leaving Britain for good.

Wise Words

Always take a passport-size photograph for your ID card on short Continental trips when a passport is not required.

Change your money to foreign currency before you arrive on the Continent.

Carry a calculator.

Take a car if you can.

Selected Ferry Crossing Times (hours)

Route	Ferry	Hovercraft	Jetfoil
Dover–Calais	1¼*	35 min	—
Dover–Boulogne	1¾	40 min	—
Folkestone–Calais	1¾	—	—
Folkestone–Boulogne	1¾	—	—
Dover–Dunkerque	2¼	—	—
Ramsgate–Dunkerque	2½	—	—
Dover–Ostend	3½	—	1 hr 40 min

	Ferries only	
	Day	Night
Newhaven–Dieppe	4	—
Dover–Zeebrugge	4¼	—
Folkestone–Ostend	4¼	—
Weymouth–Cherbourg	4-4½	4½
Portsmouth–Cherbourg	4½	6½
Felixstowe–Zeebrugge	5	8
Portsmouth–Le Havre	5½	—
Plymouth–Roscoff	6	6
Southampton–Le Havre	7	7
Sheerness–Vlissingen	7	8½
Gt Yarmouth–Scheveningen**	8	—
Portsmouth–St Malo	9	9
Hull–Rotterdam	14	14
Hull–Zeebrugge	15	15
Newcastle–Esbjerg	20	20
Harwich–Hook of Holland	6¼	7½
Harwich–Esbjerg	20	20
Harwich–Hamburg	20	20
Newcastle–Bremerhaven	21	21
Newcastle-Bergen-Stavanger***	18-20½	18-20½
Harwich–Gothenburg	23	23
Plymouth–Santander	24	24

*Townsend Thoresen; Sealink takes 1½ hr

**mainly freight service

***summer only

According to old salts, life on the ocean wave in a luxury liner is not what it was: there are too many one-class ships for a start, and hardly anyone dresses for dinner. Cruise ships, after all, being a microcosm of society, have to respond to its changing patterns.

When the price of oil soared in 1973, the cruising business underwent some fundamental reorganisation. From then on, operating the ship at its most economical speed became of paramount importance. As a consequence, most cruise ships reduced the distance they intended to travel by cutting out one or two ports of call, or called at places closer together, or stayed in one geographical area and flew passengers back and forth to a nearby airport.

Though ships that call at a fresh destination every day are rare, their itinerary would be virtually impossible by any other combination of transport, let alone in the relaxed atmosphere where you take your hotel with you to view different scenery each dawn. Ships are, in fact, floating hotels—some of their owners acknowledge the fact to the extent of describing their pursers as hotel managers. The larger ships are more like floating cities, such as the *QE2* with a population above 3,000 and enough power to supply her home port of Southampton. The *QE2* has a cinema, swimming pools, chapel, an abundance of shops and a surgery.

There are three main types of cruise:

round-the-world

return trip to a British port

fly cruises

Long-distance sea travel for pleasure was started by the

RELAX IN CIVILIZED COMPANY

Peninsular and Oriental Steam Navigation Company, the P&O of today, in 1842, when passengers could sail from Southampton to Alexandria, admittedly only by changing ships twice, at Gibraltar and what was then Constantinople (Istanbul). Those were the days when the better-off passengers overcame the lack of air conditioning by going port out and starboard home—the cooler side for cabins in the fierce sun. It was not until 1881 that the first round-the-world cruise took place, in the SS *Ceylon*.

Round-the-world cruises are for people with a lot of money. The Inland Revenue is widely reputed to put one of its younger officers on board (steerage, of course, and not much chance of fiddling his expenses) to seek out businessmen who have not declared their profits and are busy spending them. All the major cruise operators are used to bookings being made in cash and equally large sums being deposited with the purser to cover extravagant entertainment on board.

Cruises are also for people with patience. The novelty soon wears off for most travellers, who find even a varied and unlimited quantity of food monotonous, and conversation with their fellow passengers hard to sustain over a long period of incarceration on board. On cruises lasting three months or more it is not unusual for people who were bosom pals after a fortnight to be barely speaking to each other at the end.

Dining arrangements are therefore of great importance when choosing a cruise, even a short one. Even when travelling with your best friends, if you can avoid hurting their feelings, arrange not to eat dinner with them every night.

If you have the option of selecting a table before you get on board, choose a small one where you can be on your own, though you may have to give up a sea view in doing so. If bookings are made after you board, leave unpacking

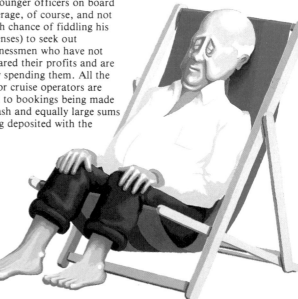

until later and make a beeline for the reservations desk; or pick one member of the party to stand in the queue.

Cruise lines offer one important advantage over a hotel: they provide detailed plans of accommodation, so that you can see the disadvantages of any particular cabin. Having eliminated the cabins you cannot afford, check for snags on those you can. Is the disco below or the cinema above? Is it near the kitchen? Is it near the engines? Does it have its own shower and toilet? Although air conditioning has made being in inside cabins much more tolerable, they can

Tea being served on board the luxury liner Duchess of Bedford on its maiden voyage in 1931

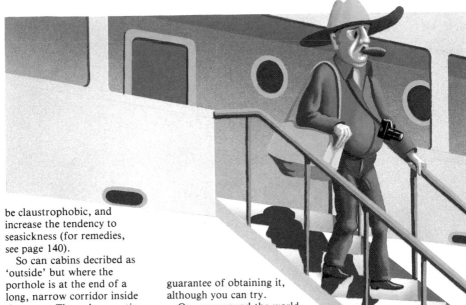

be claustrophobic, and increase the tendency to seasickness (for remedies, see page 140).

So can cabins decribed as 'outside' but where the porthole is at the end of a long, narrow corridor inside the room. The only exceptions are perhaps the 'court' cabins invented by P&O, each of which has a large corner window (with a blind to ensure privacy) which in turn looks on to the sea through a small courtyard and a larger window still, in the ship's side.

Deciding what is actually the best cabin in your price category is, of course, no

Nightmares

When cruising, be certain you know all the departure times and be there beforehand. One couple who made the sailing from Southampton with just two minutes to spare, were less fortunate at Tangier and literally missed the boat. Four ports, six flights and £1,200 each worse off, they caught up with their ship at Dubrovnik.

guarantee of obtaining it, although you can try.

On many round-the-world cruises it is possible to do this by booking a particular two or three-week section, but then you have relinquished the one great advantage of cruising from, and to, a British port: the ability to take as much luggage as you want and, within reason, to bring back huge souvenirs by the dozen.

Against that, flying to and from your particular embarkation point does reduce the chance of sailing into bad weather. Even if you consider yourself a good sailor, the Bay of Biscay, less than a day out of Southampton, can be rough in summer and provide seas of awe-inspiring proportions in winter. Four or five days of bad weather with the deck space restricted and sick bags everywhere, is depressing enough on the outward voyage, a positive anti-climax on the return.

Fly cruises also largely eliminate the potentially

unproductive 'sea days' and substantially increase the number of places you can see in a fortnight. Among the more popular starting points are Venice, Piraeus (the port of Athens), Miami, Los Angeles or San Francisco, and Vancouver. Expect a high percentage of Americans on cruises out of US ports and be prepared for a veritable traffic jam of cruise liners in the glacier bays of Alaska.

If you want to sail out of British ports such as Southampton or Tilbury, then ports of call are rather limited on a fortnight's cruise. In summer, expect a variety of

Mediterranean or Scandinavian ports; in winter, the Atlantic islands such as the Canaries, Madeira, or Portugal, North America, and the Atlantic coast of Spain. You will need at least three weeks free to reach the Caribbean, and even then the actual stay will be only a little longer than the journey there and back.

Cruises are ideal for two categories of traveller: those who want (or need) to relax completely, and those on their own. It is quite possible to do absolutely nothing on a cruise once you have unpacked your luggage, other than to eat, drink and sleep. Phone calls from the office, even in this age of high technology, are still likely to frustrate even the most persistent person trying to reach you. You need never see a British newspaper throughout the voyage.

For the unaccompanied passenger, cruises provide a heaven-sent opportunity to meet other people without

Wise Words

When booking your cabin, check:

is there a disco below?

is there a cinema above?

is it near the kitchen?

is it near the engines?

does it have its own shower/toilet?

appearing to want to. Every ship has numerous activities which single people are encouraged to join, and once your cabin steward and, preferably, the purser knows that you are alone, he will probably want to include you on the invitation list whenever ship's officers give parties.

Drinks are the largest (apart from tips, possibly the only) item of additional expenditure on board ship. As a rule, alcohol is significantly cheaper than in, say, a UK hotel, but not so cheap that you can

splash out on exotic cocktails every night and not wince at the final account. The more you drink, the more likely you are to have to visit the ship's doctor, who, not being an employee of the National Health Service, will present you with a bill. Serious illness should be covered by your normal travel insurance.

An invitation to the captain's table may depend on how much clout you have as a passenger, so if you work for some influential organisation, and being seen on the 'top' table is important to your morale, make sure that the shipping company becomes aware of your connections before you sail. If the romantic spirit of the voyage takes you, and you have designs on a fellow passenger, it is worth remembering that you cannot be married at sea. The captain is legally empowered to conduct only burials or christenings, which may not be exactly what you had in mind.

CRUISING ON THE HIGH SEAS

Life on the ocean waves can be a wonderfully relaxing way of seeing the world. Here is a selection of some of the more popular cruises which start from our home ports (in italics).

SCANDINAVIAN/ BALTIC CRUISES

June – Royal Viking
Southampton, Bergen, Arendal, Oslo, Leningrad, Helsinki, Stockholm, Copenhagen, ✈ *London*

June – P&O Cruises
Southampton, Hardangerfjord, North Cape, Narvik, Andalsnes, Bergen, Oslo, *Southampton*

June – CTC Cruises
Tilbury, Ulvik, Eidfjord, Bergen, Hellesylt, Geiranger, Trondheim, Loen, Olden, Stavanger, Rotterdam, *Tilbury*

September – CTC Cruises
Hull, Kristiansand, Copenhagen, Riga, Leningrad, Helsinki, Stockholm, Aarhus, *Hull*

LONG CRUISES

June/July – P&O Princess
Southampton, Madeira, Martinique, Barbados, Grenadines, Dominica, Vigo, *Southampton*

August – Cunard
Southampton, New York, Quebec, Saguenay River, Newport, New York, *Southampton*

December/January – Cunard
Christmas cruise:
Southampton, New York, Port Everglades, Freeport, St Thomas, Martinique, Barbados, Grenada, Caracas, Curaçao, Port Everglades, New York, ✈ *London*

December/January – P&O Princess
Christmas cruise:
Southampton, Bermuda, San Juan, Antigua, Martinique, Barbados, Madeira, *Southampton*

January/April – P&O Princess
World cruise:
Southampton, Tenerife, Bermuda, Port Everglades, Nassau, Montego Bay, Balboa, Acapulco, San Francisco, Honolulu, Papeete, Sydney, Honiara, Manila, Hong Kong, Singapore, Colombo, Djibouti, Safaga, Suez Canal, Port Said, Athens, Tangier, *Southampton*

NORTH CAPE
NARVIK
TRONDHEIM
HELLESYLT ANDALSNES
GEIRANGER
OLDEN LOEN
BERGEN ULVIK
EIDFJORD
HARDANGERFJORD
HELSINKI
LENINGRAD
OSLO
STOCKHOLM
STAVANGER
ARENDAL
KRISTIANSAND
RIGA
AARHUS
COPENHAGEN
HULL
TILBURY
SOUTHAMPTON
ROTTERDAM

HONIARA

SYDNEY

MANILA

HONG KONG

SINGAPORE

COLOMBO

PORT SAID

DJIBOUTI

ATHENS

SUEZ CANAL

SAFAGA

TANGIER

SOUTHAMPTON

VIGO

MADEIRA

TENERIFE

MARTINIQUE

GRENADINES

SAN JUAN

ST THOMAS

ANTIGUA

DOMINICA

BARBADOS

GRENADA

SAGUENAY
RIVER

NEWPORT

BERMUDA

QUEBEC

NEW YORK

NASSAU

FREEPORT

CURACAO

PORT
EVERGLADES

MONTEGO
BAY

BALBOA

CARACAS

ACAPULCO

SAN FRANCISCO

HONOLULU

PAPEETE

122 Cruise ports

When choosing a cruise from all the variety of tempting brochures, note the stops where landing by tender is indicated, because waiting for it can often be a tedious business. The best cruises make the most of sailing time after midnight, when you leave one port of call as you fall asleep and wake up on the way to the next exciting place.

February/March – CTC Cruises
Tilbury, Lisbon, Gibraltar, Casablanca, Las Palmas, Tenerife, Madeira, Vigo, *Tilbury*

April/May – P&O Cruises
Southampton, Malaga, Messina, Vólos, Istanbul, Limassol, Haifa, Piraeus, Gibraltar, *Southampton*

April/May – P&O Princess
Southampton, Gibraltar, Palma, Alexandria, Kos, Izmir, Thera, Piraeus, ✈ *London*

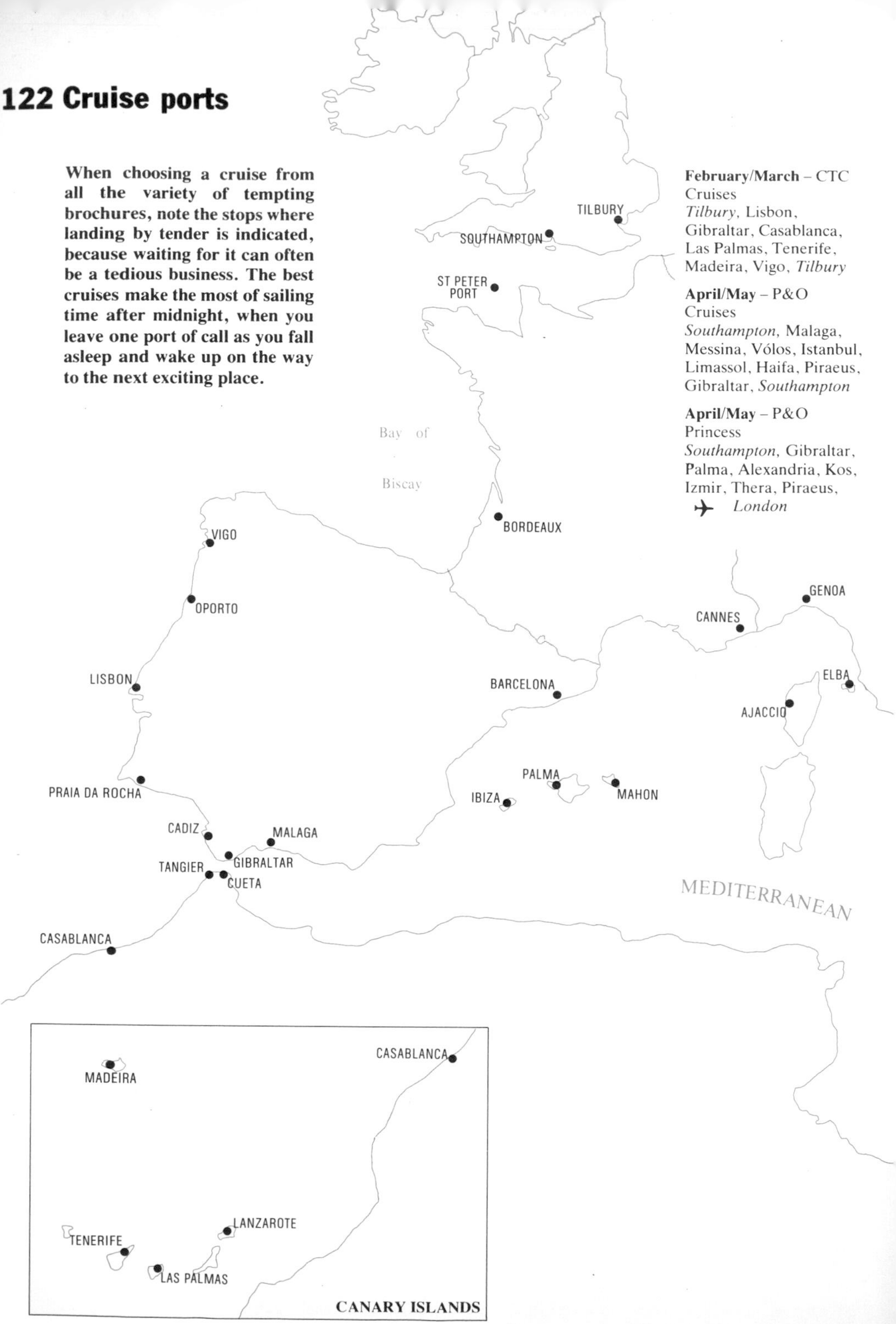

TILBURY
SOUTHAMPTON
ST PETER PORT

Bay of Biscay

BORDEAUX

VIGO
OPORTO
LISBON
PRAIA DA ROCHA
CADIZ
MALAGA
TANGIER
GIBRALTAR
CUETA
CASABLANCA

BARCELONA
PALMA
IBIZA
MAHON

GENOA
CANNES
ELBA
AJACCIO

MEDITERRANEAN

MADEIRA
CASABLANCA
LANZAROTE
TENERIFE
LAS PALMAS

CANARY ISLANDS

May – P&O Cruises
Southampton, Gibraltar,
Barcelona, Cannes,
Elba, Naples, Palma,
Southampton

May/June – P&O Cruises
Southampton, Lisbon,
Praia da Rocha, Tenerife,
Las Palmas, Madeira,
Vigo, *Southampton*

June – P&O Cruises
Southampton, Gibraltar,
Dubrovnik, Corfu,
Messina, Palma,
Southampton

July/August – P&O
Cruises
Southampton, Gibraltar,
Palermo, Loutraki,
Corfu, Palma,
Southampton

August/September –
Royal Viking
Southampton, St Peter
Port, Bordeaux, Vigo,
Lisbon, Gibraltar,
Valletta, Piraeus,
(✈ *London* or
continue to) Varna,
Odessa, Yalta, Istanbul,
Kusadasi, Patmos,
Mykonos, Rhodes,
Heraklion, Piraeus,
✈ *London*

August/September –
Norwegian American
Southampton, Bordeaux,
Oporto, Lisbon,
Casablanca, Cadiz,
Gibraltar, Ceuta, Mahon,
Genoa,
(✈ *London* or
continue to) Piraeus,
Mudanya, Varna, Yalta,
Constanza, Istanbul,
Mykonos, Heraklion,
Valletta, Genoa,
✈ *London*

September/October –
Cunard
Southampton, Ibiza,
Barcelona, Ajaccio,
Naples, Palermo,
Gibraltar, Lisbon,
Southampton

December/January –
CTC Cruises
Christmas cruise:
Tilbury, Rotterdam,
Lisbon, Tangier,
Lanzarote, Tenerife,
Madeira, *Tilbury*

124 Cruise lines regard shore excursions with mixed feelings. On the one hand, they provide a marvellous excuse for getting rid of most of the passengers for the day, giving the crew some time off, and also cutting down on the cost of meals. On the other, they are a big administrative headache and draw a disproportionate amount of complaints.

In order to keep those complaints to a minimum, the shipping companies try to hire the best available local firm to run their shore excursions. It is significant, however, that they are still not confident enough to accept liability for shore arrangements, even though exclusion clauses are probably not worth the paper they are printed on.

Nonetheless, cruise lines try to persuade passengers to book early for excursions. Advance bookings often deliver a bigger profit and reduce the administrative problems on board ship when there is a rush to go on tomorrow's trip.

Unless you are one of that curious band of passengers who likes to sail from port to port without ever leaving the ship, you will urgently want to study the list of excursions on offer. The itineraries are usually given in some detail.

If you do not fancy a particular programme and want to succumb to a latent sense of adventure, approach another couple and persuade them to join you on a little independent excursion of your own. The trip may not turn out to be as easy as following the herd, but it is likely to be a lot more fun.

When the ship docks, and the other passengers troop off to the waiting coaches, look around for that other means of transport which is virtually guaranteed to be in search of

TRY AN INDEPENDENT ADVENTURE

some promising passengers: the posse of local taxis. They may not exactly meet the minimum standards for British hackney carriages, but that adds to the sense of occasion.

The taxi driver will greet you as a long-lost brother or sister when he discovers that far from wanting a short ride into town, you want to book him for a complete tour. You will soon wipe that smile off his face by haggling over the price. (Jot down all figures to avoid disputes later.)

Outside European ports, expect the taxi driver's first price to be at least double what he is prepared to accept. Remembering that you have still to pay for lunch on top of the fare, aim to get the taxi for slightly less than the price of two cruise excursion fares. As it is the attraction of going it alone which lured you away from the official excursion, do not begrudge the extra effort involved in making the driver understand the number of places he is supposed to visit. Then neatly reverse the order in the excursion booklet.

Why? Because you do not want to risk being in the same tourist spot at the same time as the coach passengers when the object was to get away from them. Agree in writing on a time when the taxi will bring you back to the port, as while the ship may wait for a whole coachload of passengers, it could well leave three or four of them behind

rather than miss the tide.

A word of warning. Stick carefully to the itinerary you have chosen, and make sure that someone on board ship knows the places you intend to visit. Leave a note of the driver's registration number and his name, if he will give it. It is improbable that he is going to whisk you off to some mugger's paradise, but better safe than sorry. Remember to take your passport even if it was not required for the excursion: if you become stranded, better with the correct documents than without.

With luck, you will arrive back at the boat having had a much better time than anyone on the official trip, and probably at less cost— provided you do not part with any money in advance.

Pay at the end with exactly the right money, because in these circumstances, taxi drivers never have change. His complaints about the deal will follow you all the way to the gang plank but, if you look back, the chances are you will catch on his face the suspicion of a smile in recognition of a kindred spirit!

Wise Words

Team up with others and plan independent excursions.

Keep all negotiations with local taxi drivers on paper.

Stick meticulously to the itinerary you have chosen.

Leave a note of the taxi driver's number and name on board ship, and tell someone where you are going.

Pay the driver with exactly the right money.

STAYING THERE

Hotel, villa or campsite,
the fantastic nightlife
is on your doorstep –
but is it all you expected?

If you want the best deal at a big hotel, walk in off the street. Not only will they be prepared to offer you a discount, but you will have favoured 'independent traveller' status, instead of being a mere statistic on a package tour.

Be discreet. Do not expect the receptionist to have the authority to agree a discount, or the hotel to thank you for asking at the top of your voice while dozens of package tourists are clamouring for their keys. Ask to see the duty manager to discuss 'an arrangement'.

Do not be put off by the fact that it is the height of the season. Many managers have a

BE DISCREET AND GET A BARGAIN

more. It follows that someone arriving on spec and prepared to pay cash can easily negotiate a 20 per cent discount, and sometimes as

difficult in Stuttgart), have you got one without standing on the chest of drawers? If you were promised a double bed, does yours look as if it has come apart in the middle (French and Italian hotels seem to have far more genuine double beds than Spain)? Are there enough pillows (look in the wardrobe for extras)? Do all the lights work? If there is any, does the air conditioning work, and is it noisy?

Does the room have all the information you might need about the hotel's amenities? Can you find the order forms for breakfast in your room, laundry lists, instructions on using the phone (but more advice later)? If you have a bathroom attached, is there any hot water (but do let it run

Basil Fawlty obsession with obtaining 100 per cent occupancy, and will go to almost any lengths, including dragging likely looking foreigners in off the street, to fill the last room.

Understand the margins. Most hotels give eight per cent commission to an airline or travel agent that makes a reservation for a client. If the booking is made through a central handling agency, a further small commission may be involved there. Finally, the customer may elect to pay by credit card, which could cost the hotel up to seven per cent

much as 50 per cent if they are prepared to haggle. Never admit that you intend to stay only one night, as a hotel makes its smallest profit from someone taking only bed and breakfast.

Watch out that the hotel does not in the end have the last laugh. Rooms left empty may be next to the lift shaft or the night club. Before you unpack, run a rigorous check on your surroundings; that applies irrespective of whether you are a package holidaymaker or in off the street. If you were promised a view of the sea (admittedly

a while before you give up all hope!)? Does the shower work properly? Does the toilet flush? Is there toilet paper and a bar of soap? Are the sheets clean and freshly laundered—in fact, have they really changed the sheets since the last occupant? If you are not sure, this is the moment to decide that you want a different room.

Unless you can't discover the route to the nearest fire exit, you need not automatically reject any room above the height of a fire engine's turntable ladder—that is, about the sixth floor upwards—but it is not an excessive sign of paranoia to walk all the way down the fire escape staircase to see if you can in fact escape into the street. Some hotels abroad are notorious fire risks, and hotel fires can be horrific. Remember, your safety comes first (see page 146).

Depending on their size, hotels usually provide some, if not all, the following:

one or more bars, including one by the swimming pool

one or more restaurants

foyer shops

laundry service

breakfast in your room

direct-dial telephones

a room fridge stocked with bottles and cans

The bar is vital to a hotel's profits. Invariably it has a huge mark-up on drinks per measure compared to the price of a bottle in a supermarket. Small bowls of salty peanuts are thoughtfully provided to keep the guests thirsty.

The pool is often artistically shaped so that serious swimming is impossible. The diving board may delight a few Olympic medallists but looks frighteningly high for the novice. As a consequence, most would-be swimmers and divers are trapped in their poolside seats, kept awake by

canned music, under (hopefully) the glare of the sun. All they can do is drink. The more alcohol they have the less advisable it is for them to swim and the less likely they are to notice if the measures are short, the drinks are watered down, the bills exaggerated.

In most instances, holiday-makers on package tours receive neither the choice nor the quality of restaurant meals available to the independent traveller. But at least what they are getting is included in the price. All the hotelier can do to boost his income is inflate the cost of wine, and this he often does, sometimes by as much as four times the price of a bottle. But much of his staff's attention will be on the independent client, with the promise of bigger tips at the end of the meal. You will be offered tempting dishes from the à la carte menu, which may multiply the cost of lunch or dinner several times, once each course, vegetables and coffee have been charged separately and local taxes added.

The foyer is likely to be crammed with shops, in which prices are proportionately higher because the hotel

concession charge has to be met out of the profits. However, most of the customers will be foreigners, handling an unfamiliar currency, and ignorant of the local going rate.

Despite the cost, there may, of course, be good reasons why you still want to drink, eat and shop in the hotel. You may be tired; the pool may be particularly agreeable; you may be looking for company. More often than not, however, finding where the locals drink, eat and shop, will add to your enjoyment and provide better value. Of course, saving money by having coffee in a Paris side street at a bargain price, could sometimes mean you are missing the point of the trip by not experiencing café life on the Champs Elysées.

Breakfast in the local café is almost certain to be superior to, and cheaper than, the one offered in the hotel. If breakfast is not included, and you can be bothered, then eat out. Sometimes it may cost you less for a full breakfast round the corner than for the extras you order in your room, as the mark-up on items such as orange juice or a boiled egg can be enormous. This is another way hotels can boost their profits, tempting clients

with breakfast menu cards which you hang on your doorknob overnight.

The laundry service is another potential money-spinner. If you have travelled light, you may well regard the laundry bill a small price to pay for the convenience of keeping all your luggage with you in the cabin on the plane. However, it is a bill that can be reduced by simple measures. Take soap powder with you, or buy some, and wash any light items in the basin. Have suits and dresses pressed, not cleaned. Unless you need something in three hours' time, never elect for the express service, which will probably differ from the ordinary service only in the red marks on your bill.

Hotels have spent a lot of money in installing automatic telephones over the past few years, and they are looking to their customers to recover the cost. Many hotels add a huge percentage to the cost of calls. The solution: make a quick call and ask to be rung back; call 'collect' to transfer the charges (you may still be stung for a service charge, but it is

certain to be cheaper); or use a public phone in the foyer. Provided you know the basic code for international calls (see page 189), making calls back to Britain or elsewhere is relatively simple, and after a few days on holiday you will probably have a pocketful of local small change to put to good use.

The refrigerator bar in your room, commonplace in first-class hotels, is a trap. Not only will its prices be high, but it sits there, tempting you, 24 hours a day. The hotel will keep it restocked, and may even stop you putting your own drink inside and using that. Be brave; bring your own duty-free bottles into the hotel and freeze

your own ice to freshen your drinks, using bottled water (for safety). That way you can have drinks on the balcony at a fraction of the hotel price.

Recognise that the objective of the hotel is to keep you reliant on its services as much as possible. The more you use them, the more you spend. From the owner's point of view, the ideal hotel must be one situated miles from anywhere with no alternative distractions.

If you are caught in such a situation, hire a car. This isn't extravagant if you take into account what you save on drinks, meals and taxis, and

(see page 189)

Wise Words

Walk in off the street if you want to try a hotel for discount rates.

Beware the rooms the hotels fill up last. They may be noisy.

Bring your own drinks—hotel bars and room fridges are expensive traps.

Watch the laundry bills.

Eat out whenever possible.

Avoid phoning from your room—charges are steep.

Check all bills and settle them the night before you leave.

Pay cash whenever it is convenient.

using a local firm should keep the cost down.

The most independent clients are those with their own transport. If they do not like a hotel, they can easily move on. If they are uncomfortable in big hotels, or consider that the discount they have been offered is not large enough, they can settle for a family hotel off the beaten track, where discounts may be unheard of but the food can be famous.

Do not make the mistake of waiting to settle your bill on the day of departure. You may have to queue, and you will not have a proper chance to check it. Ask for your bill the previous evening when the reception desk is quiet, and go through it with a fine toothcomb. Take a calculator, query anything you are remotely uneasy about and ask to see the original voucher if it is something you are alleged to have signed for. Whether by accident or design, hotels frequently make mistakes, and hardly ever in your favour.

After you have settled up, perhaps making a last attempt at a discount for cash if you had intended to use a credit card, pay cash for the remainder of your stay to avoid the morning queue. In fact, throughout your stay, paying cash as you go along can avoid a lot of argument later, though it may be less convenient at the time. Otherwise, take a notebook to the bar or restaurant and put down each item ostentatiously. Insist on itemised bills for everything more complicated than a couple of beers. The word will soon get around the staff that you are not a customer to be trifled with.

A story-book inn built in the traditional Swiss style

Simple whitewashed walls set the scene for typically Swiss restaurant cuisine

Nightmares

At the peak of the holiday season in Spain the margin of time between one group leaving and the next arriving is so slender that often the latest arrivals are left waiting in the transfer bus or the hotel foyer. Nearly all the hotels overbook then help each other out on a reciprocal basis. As a consequence, quite a large percentage of holidaymakers spend some, if not all, their time in a different hotel to the one in which they were booked. One man in Lloret del Mar, disliking his alternative hotel intensely, hit on a novel way of making a nuisance of himself: he threw his bed out of the window into the swimming pool. He was found a room at his original hotel the very same afternoon.

130 One thing is absolutely certain: whatever a taste of the local nightlife costs, it will not have been worth it. This is where the largest profits are made in the tourist industry, and where most travellers lose their money and sometimes even their virtue. Without sounding pious, the only sensible advice is: forget it. Stay at the hotel. Ring home. Read a book. Go to bed early, and on your own.

Not convinced? Well, let us say you have already done your preliminary homework, and you are in Paris, or Hamburg, or Munich, or Amsterdam, or Bangkok, or Tokyo specifically for the nightlife. You are going to sample it if it kills you.

It could well do. A large percentage of tourists are robbed wandering alone in a 'red light' district. Do not go on your own; avoid public transport after dark; do not get drunk. In other words, do not present yourself as a target to a potential mugger.

Be inconspicuous. Do not dress well: a well-dressed visitor is thought likely to have a well-filled wallet. In fact, do not carry a wallet at all, or your passport (although your International Driving Permit with its photograph and date of birth may be useful if you are called on to identify yourself or establish your age), or more than one credit card. Take only the amount of cash you are prepared to spend. Put one sizeable note in your shoe, so if the ungodly take everything, you still have the taxi fare back to the hotel.

Cut out the middlemen. Your friendly hotel porter is a middleman who will steer you in the direction of one night club or floor show, in return for a substantial commission. Booking agencies are middlemen. They may make

FOLLOW THE RULES . . . AND HAVE FUN

fifteen to 20 per cent on the price of your admission ticket. Try to get round them and cut your own costs in the process.

Take Paris as an example. Among the shows generally regarded as worth seeing are:

Bal du Moulin Rouge

Les Folies Bergères

Le Lido

L'Alcazar

Crazy Horse Saloon

Go in person, during the day. Their prices are usually open to negotiation if you do it discreetly, rather than at the top of your voice at the head of a queue of Japanese tourists. The logic is that if you pay cash, they have avoided commission to hotels, porters or credit card companies. Five per cent off is frequently possible, more on a quiet night.

Do not get carried away. You and your party have come to see the show, not to eat or drink. For a good meal, go to a restaurant before or after. Drink only what is compulsory —probably half a bottle of mediocre champagne per person. Do not be tempted to order more drinks: you do not want to afford it.

Not risqué enough for you?

Now you are on dangerous territory. Advance planning is essential. Still avoid the hall porter. Ask the barman, who probably is not on any commission, for his view on what is value for money and make it clear that if he is proved correct, you will give him a big tip tomorrow.

Study a map. Give the taxi driver the full address and follow the route ostentatiously all the way. Not only may he take you the long way round, but he may suggest other, he claims, superior places. Do not believe him. If he stops without explanation and disappears inside what looks like a club, he is probably negotiating his commission. Have nothing to do with his plans.

Let us say that you have selected Homme & Femme, our fictitious name for a pair of night clubs in adjacent houses, with, it is claimed, escape doors linking the two to cover the disagreeable possibility of the arrival of the police. Each will have a floor show which is free. Free, that is, provided you buy some extremely expensive drinks. The only way you will keep your bill within bounds is to sit at the bar (thereby avoiding tips to the waiter) and drink something like beer or lemonade.

Boys and girls will appear, depending on your sex and inclinations, with the immediate object of encouraging you to buy them drinks. They want you to sit at a table and order champagne. Decline. It will cost you an arm and a leg.

In many clubs the drink will also almost certainly not be champagne. The pop of a cork behind the scenes may be coming out of the same rigged bottle all evening: what you get will be sparkling white wine. If you order something else, there may be next to no alcohol in it at all—just a taste on the rim of the glass. Or the hugely expensive bottle of prime Scotch that you have been persuaded to buy has been assembled the previous evening from 20 leftovers of a much more indifferent variety.

You are leaving. If you are unlucky, you will be waylaid by a con artist posing as a policeman. You have paid with counterfeit notes, he will claim. You protest, but, of course, you cannot be certain; like everyone else, you have trouble sorting out your change, let alone spotting a counterfeit note. But the 'detective' is sympathetic. If you pay again, he says, nothing will be done and he will give you a receipt for the counterfeit money. You have just been taken by one of the oldest tricks in the book.

You can get a glimpse of the oldest profession for nothing if you are cautious and discreet. In Hamburg, walk down one of the alleys off the Reeperbahn

Wise Words

Do not go out alone.

Beware of public transport after dark.

Do not drink too much.

Do not dress too well, or carry your wallet and passport.

Negotiate night club prices in person.

Save tips by sitting at the club bar, not a table.

where the prostitutes sit in shop windows, offering them-selves for sale. In Bangkok, step into a massage parlour off the Patpong Road, and watch the Japanese businessmen selecting their companions for the evening through a spyhole in the wood. Earlier, they have left their golf clubs in special lock-ups at Bangkok Airport, having told their wives they are off on a golfing holiday.

Back in Tokyo, even the Japanese find the nightlife

expensive. It is probably the costliest exercise in the world. At a night club with a cabaret you will have to pay a substantial cover charge, plus 35 per cent service and taxes. Multiply all that with the size of your party and the number of your drinks, and you will definitely need a calculator (Japanese, of course) to work out the total bill.

It is dawn in the Rembrandtsplein of Amsterdam, or in Munich's Schwabing district, and the public transport is already running. Do not be tempted. The muggers' night does not end until rush hour. If you have done your homework well, you know what your taxi fare should be, even allowing for the extra night charge. If the taxi driver tries to charge more, refuse to pay, and if he is persistent, go into the hotel and tell the night porter to call the police. With a bit of luck you will get a free ride, which is more than could be said for the rest of the evening.

Never mind. It was worth it, wasn't it? Keep taking the tablets.

This chapter carries an official warning to women. Unless you are careful, a self-catering holiday could be described as one in which your kitchen, and especially your cooker, is less than miraculously transferred from the UK to a foreign destination. You may spend your time doing as much cooking, shopping and housework as you do at home, and be expected to look on it as a holiday. So, before you leave, discuss exactly how the work will be divided among everyone present and how often you will eat out.

Nevertheless, self-catering has many advantages over staying in a hotel. It can be cheaper, or, to be more precise, you can obtain more for the same amount of money as, if you can afford it, the temptation to rent a really luxurious villa will be considerable. You can relax, free from restrictions and the need to deal with strangers. You can get up when you like, wear what you like, make as much noise as you want and let the children run free without worrying who they are bothering. You can more easily use your own things, like a portable sound system with tapes, or the children's larger toys.

You can eat what you

DO THINGS YOUR WAY

like and where you like. It obviously makes more of a holiday if you can manage to eat out at least once a day and sampling a whole series of tempting restaurants is much more pleasant than queuing at the same hotel dining room every night. If you start to run out of money, or tire of the local food, you can shop for the ingredients and cook in the local style or as you would at home.

If you want, you can get right away from it all. Many villas are situated well off the beaten track, a long way from other holidaymakers and resorts, and even out of sight of the locals.

There are four broad

categories of self-catering accommodation: individual villas; gîtes; apartment blocks; static caravans. Villas come at the top of the range and may include a cook and other full-time staff to look after a large party. These can be expensive to rent, but not unreasonably so in relation to the quality of the accommodation, which will often include bedrooms with en suite bathrooms, or even whole suites; and a large swimming pool. Teaming up with another family or some friends can make sound economic sense, reducing the price per person to what you can afford.

The more expensive villas are those with a private swimming pool, an asset that is more common in France than it is in Spain or Italy where sometimes, even if there is a pool, the water will not be available to fill it. Of course, some villas are small and simple and do not have any staff: to meet all requirements, there is a huge range of properties and prices available.

Gîtes are a French institution, although this type of accommodation is found in other countries as well. Gîtes de France offer thousands of properties all over the country that are almost all rural and

offer only basic amenities. Even the most comfortable would be little better than a two-star hotel. They are, however, modestly priced and usually owned by someone in the local community or, indeed, the community itself (of which, like it or not, you instantly become a part).

Contact Gîtes de France, at 178 Piccadilly, London W1V 0AL, to obtain a membership form. The small membership fee entitles you to the official handbook (with around 2,000 entries), a booking service, and special price rates on some Channel crossings.

Apartment blocks, sometimes standing on their own but more often in holiday villages, have communal facilities such as a swimming pool, a launderette, a snack bar and a supermarket. Unlike villas and gîtes, you may be able to reach them by public transport and do without a car, if you intend to stay in one centre. However, you have lost a major asset: outside your apartment, you can expect little or no privacy.

Because a car is essential for a great many self-catering properties, many families do drive from the UK. Even then it is possible to obtain a package deal, more precisely a discount on the ferry price in return for booking both the crossing and the accommodation through the same company. If you want to be mobile during your holiday, but don't want to drive long distances, an alternative is to book a package by air which includes hire car from the arrival airport.

The respective advantages of going by road or by air (with the exception of motorail, going by rail is neither convenient nor conspicuously cheaper) are that road is nearly always cheaper and you can take more stuff for your self-catering holiday, while air is nearly always less arduous. If you are taking children much may depend on whether you can obtain substantial discounts for them. Up to two years old, they normally travel free, provided that they do not occupy a seat. Under twelve, discounts can vary between ten per cent at peak school holiday times, to 100 per cent (that is, free) on a limited number of weeks when the tour operator expects to have difficulty in filling his accommodation.

Many of the smaller companies who offer self-catering accommodation do not go out of their way to sell through travel agents, thus avoiding paying out a commission on sales. If you rent from them you will forfeit

the protection of an inclusive holiday purchased through an ABTA travel agent anyway, so you may then feel inclined to cut out the middle-man altogether and to do a deal directly with whoever is the owner.

In the first year this may not be easy, because you will be uncertain what you are getting for your money and whether or not you particularly like the villa's situation. However, if you intend to go back, approaching the owner direct may pay dividends, because the chances are he, too, would like to avoid paying part of his rent to a third party. If, as is quite likely, he proves to be an absentee landlord, by hunting around you may find the odd bill addressed to him or, failing that, discover who he is by asking in a local shop. Leaving him a note may result in obtaining a quite startling discount, because the level of

mark-up can be huge—30, 40, even 50 per cent.

However, renting direct from British owners who advertise in UK newspapers may not always be the bargain one might suppose. These owners may have to pay to advertise quite frequently to fill a whole season, and they often have an inflated view of their villa's value.

The cost of self-catering accommodation varies enormously in the course of a season, far more than in hotels. This is because the Continental customer, often a businessman with his family, has little choice about when he can take his holiday. His company or his clients go away in late July or throughout August, and accordingly so must he. Avoiding this period can have a dramatic effect on the price, with villas costing as much as 40 per cent less in

May than they do in August.

Outside this July–August period, it is quite possible to go on spec. This is not as risky as it sounds because, particularly outside the really fashionable areas, few properties are let continuously. Let us suppose you want a gîte. First, choose the area of France in which you want to stay, then put up at the local one or two-star hotel for a few nights, and go hunting. You may have the official English gîtes handbook; if not, ask at the local tourist information office, town hall or one of the local shops. It will be very bad luck indeed if you are not fixed up in a few hours, and probably at a much better price than if you had tried to book in London.

However you book, make sure that you understand exactly what is included in the price. In some cases you may be expected to pay extra for gas, electricity, cleaning, even for water, and you may be asked for a deposit to cover these charges and possible breakages. Do read the inventory carefully, as the owner or his representative do not always go through it meticulously after each visitor, and you could end up paying for an expensive dish which the previous occupant failed to admit breaking.

Some companies will include an assortment of food for when you arrive—particularly useful if you expect to reach your destination after the shops are shut. However, according to your tastes, there will be a number of items it would be wise to bring from Britain, where they are either much more easily obtainable or a good deal cheaper.

HP Sauce—indeed any bottle of sauce, as the British practice of pouring such sauce on food is regarded as positively barbaric.

Chunky marmalade—you can buy any number of jams to eat with your bread but outside large cities real marmalade is almost unobtainable.

Baked beans—these are not to be found in any sauce acceptable to British children.

Tea—expensive and horrible, or simply horribly expensive.

Chocolate—the cheap assembly line variety and other British sweets are all very expensive on the Continent.

Breakfast cereals—simply not eaten in many countries.

Spreads such as Marmite or peanut butter.

Dried milk—fresh milk may be difficult to obtain.

There are two other ways of obtaining self-catering accommodation: exchange and time-share. Doing a home exchange with another family can be fraught with difficulty, and result in bitter recrimination and regrets. However, an organisation called Home Exchange International, with offices in London, Los Angeles and Paris, claim to have reduced the risk of this by matching families carefully and insisting on impeccable references and insurance cover. The attractions of living rent-free in California or various parts of France are certainly considerable, and leaving your house occupied eliminates much of the risk of a burglary.

Time-share is a scheme by which people buy the right to live in a property for a specific number of weeks each year, and sometimes exchange their weeks with owners of other time-share properties on a year-to-year basis. Many purchasers seem to have come unstuck with this arrangement, finding unexpectedly high maintenance charges, disputes over ownership of the overall property, inadequate property insurance, difficulties with local utilities. Against that, other people have obtained a marvellous, almost inflation-proof bargain that could give

them a cheap holiday for the rest of their lives. If you are tempted, use a specialist company based in the UK that will guarantee to overcome any problems and has insurance to back it up.

If any of your self-catering holiday arrangements would involve sharing with another family or friends, think carefully before committing yourselves. Do you really know what they are like? Can you stand being with them 24 hours a day? Or, for that matter, can they stand being with you and your children! Many potentially marvellous villa holidays have been ruined because of disputes over the food kitty, over who is to have the car, over trivial matters blown out of all proportion. Even in the most harmonious of sharing arrangements, an element of competition may creep in to everything from how many lengths of the pool the various children can swim to who can cook the best gourmet meal. This is the time when you really find out who your friends are.

Continental sites for camping or static caravanning are generally much better than in Britain, but in the summer months, especially during July and August, they are also much more crowded. Even the best sites deteriorate with excessive use, when the basic facilities often cannot cope. Overflowing effluent around site lavatories is a sign to move on, and move quickly.

France and the Republic of Ireland are the most popular overseas countries in which to have a static caravan holiday. A majority of these well-equipped homes sleep six in bunk beds and are certainly not cramped. Some have their own showers and many are connected to both gas and electricity main supplies. The sites offer a wide range of facilities, permanent toilets, a launderette, a self-service shop, sometimes a television room and a children's playground.

Whether camping or caravanning, in order to take advantage of the best sites, you require an International Camping Carnet (see page 9). In the summer season if you intend to stay anywhere for a significant

EVERYTHING YOU WANT ON TAP

period, say, more than two nights, advance booking is almost essential. But how? Even if you enclose an International Reply Coupon with your reservation letter, the chances are you will not get a reply. The organisers of popular sites are either too busy to engage in correspondence or simply do not bother, knowing they will be turning people away all the summer. In those circumstances, the best you can hope for is that your booking is recorded. The only usual exceptions will be reservations made by the Caravan Club for members under their Advance Booking Service. However, a north-eastern company, Romanport of Middlesbrough, will make

bookings for you provided that you give them at least a month's notice.

It is a wise precaution, whether or not you book in advance, to arrive by about 2pm, if only because your booking will at best simply guarantee you space to camp and not a particular pitch. The most attractive ones will obviously be taken first. If you do arrive late, you may have to stop the first night in an unattractive late-night arrival area; most Continental sites close altogether at 11pm until 7am.

This means that even after you are settled in your camp, if you go out for the evening and you arrive back after 11pm, you will have to leave your car outside the gates and walk to your outfit, which may well be a long way away.

Radios, portable televisions, record players and allied equipment are all expected to be turned off after 10pm, when visitors are requested to be quiet.

Even the smallest site should have hot and cold showers and proper toilets available, which is why you may have trouble trying to dispose of the contents of your own chemical toilet.

Unwanted holes in your tent could, however, provide a more pressing problem. Erecting the tent at least a week before you leave is a sensible thing to do, so that all points of stress—where guy-ropes are attached and where the tent poles come into contact with the fabric—are carefully inspected. Leaving it out in the rain will help to test whether it is waterproof.

If you are travelling to a static caravan, make certain in advance exactly what is provided and what you need to take for the holiday.

For either camping or caravanning a list of items, some essential, some optional, should be drawn up both when packing and when checking what has been packed. This list is useful, too, if Customs require one at a frontier.

Here is a suggested alphabetical list of what *not* to leave behind:

Get to your camp site by early afternoon—particularly if it is as popular as Lauterbrunnen, near Interlaken, in Switzerland

adaptor, plug
air mattresses and pump
all-purpose knife
ashtray, if you smoke
bottle opener, corkscrew, tin opener
breakfast cereals
bucket (large and square) to double as a basin
camera and films (to prove you are crazy enough to make the trip)
camping clothes (hard-wearing, nothing fancy)
camp stove and fuel
carving knife
casserole dish (if you are cooking seriously)
clock
clothesrack, clothesline, and pegs
cutlery, cooking utensils
dishcloth, scouring pad, tea towels
documents (page 6–9 and 62)
dustpan, brush
egg cups
egg whisk
electric light bulbs, extension cable
face cloth

first-aid kit
folding chairs, table
food containers
frying pan, saucepans
gum boots
icebox, portable
insect repellant
jugs
kettle
matches, lighter
mosquito nets
picnic table
pillows, pillowcases
plastic bags, for litter
plates, cups, saucers, bowls
pressure cooker
radio/cassette player
razor, blades, or new batteries
refuse bin
rope
screwtop sugar jar
shoe cleaning kit
shopping bags
sleeping bags
soap, soap powder
string
swimming caps (mandatory at some sites)
teapot, teabags
tent, tent poles, tent pegs, mallet
tent-tidy
toilet paper
toothbrush, toothpaste
torch, batteries, bulbs
towels
tow-rope
trays

tumblers
washing-up bowl, liquid
water carrier
water-purifying tablets
wheel chocks
windshield
wine glasses (to make the journey—and the inconvenience—worthwhile)

Although off-site camping is not permitted in the Netherlands, Portugal and Yugoslavia, subject to various national and local restrictions, casual camping is allowed elsewhere. However, camping by the roadside is not advised and is positively illegal in several Continental countries. If you camp in isolated areas, you may have visitors in the night, on two or four legs, with alarming consequences.

2 PINTS TODAY PLEASE

138 Travelling with children requires great forethought and patience. It is essential to think through the journey in every detail, to make sure your baby or child can cope with what you are planning to do and, wherever possible, to have a flexible and unhurried timetable. If you don't do this, a journey can turn into a nightmare for everyone involved. It may actually be kinder to the children to leave them with someone they know and love. However, taking your children by the most suitable means of transport on an appropriate holiday can be very rewarding and great fun, especially as, on the Continent, children are invariably welcome everywhere.

If you have the option, always take babies by car, and

ALL THE FAMILY ARE WELCOME

preferably not before they are immunised against diphtheria, whooping cough and tetanus, usually at three months. A car is desirable because of the number of items needed, possibly including carrycot and bedding, disposable nappies (in France, these are

good and easily obtainable), clothes, feeding bottles, steriliser, baby foods, toys, sunshade, tissues and lots of empty plastic bags.

Small babies should be secured in their carrycot with the pop-on cover and then, on the Continent, the carrycot *must* be put on the rear seat and restrained with a proper harness, correctly bolted to the anchorage points provided.

Disposable nappies solve one end of a baby's requirements during a journey. Feeding is another matter. Even if you are breastfeeding you will probably need sterilised bottles containing cooled, boiled water or juice and these are best stored in a coolbox. If your baby has formula milk, some means of mixing is necessary, unless you carry made-up bottles in a coolbox.

There is no merit in serving milk or baby food warm. It is simpler and prevents possible bacterial spoilage if sterilised milk and food are stored, then served, cool. With this in mind it is useful early in a baby's life to accustom it to taking food and drink at various temperatures. If warm nourishment is required, either take a vacuum flask or two of hot, boiled water for mixing the formula or a heater that plugs into the cigarette lighter socket (if you have one) and takes made-up bottles or jars and cans of food. In order to avoid keeping a hungry baby waiting and howling in desperation, heating and cooling will require extra careful timing.

Travel by train may require a retinue of porters at every

station. Also, private, clean and convenient places to breast-feed and change infants are few and far between. The only conspicuous exception is Sweden, where most trains have special compartments for mothers with young children. Motorail is in many ways an ideal method of travelling in that you can reserve a sleeping compartment with private washing facilities. However, larger carrycots may be difficult to accommodate—they cannot be left on the train seats overnight in case of a sudden stop.

Air travel, particularly because of the risk of delay, notably on charter flights, can be a nightmare with babies or very young children. Most reputable airlines, however, do go to considerable lengths to make things easier. Carrycots are provided, or passengers may be permitted to bring their own, so long as they are collapsible and no more than 30in (76cm) long, 16in (41cm) wide and 8in (20cm) deep. The baby cannot be left in the carrycot during take-off, landing or whenever the pilot expects turbulence, when it must be strapped into the infant seat belts provided.

Although, outside the USA, a baby carried free has no baggage allowance, a carrycot, blankets, bottles and food will always be allowed free, provided they weigh under 10kg (22lb). Carrying a steriliser should not be necessary, unless you need one at your destination, as virtually every aircraft has facilities. Some airlines carry formula milk, baby foods and disposable nappies—check with your travel agent.

Cots provided by the hotel at your destination should be subject to a rigorous safety check. Make certain that all the assembly screws are secure and that there are no protruding fittings on which the baby's clothing could be caught. If there are any flaking or peeling pictures inside the cot, remove them. Ensure that the cot is deep enough to stop your baby climbing out, and that any gap between the mattress base and the bottom rail is too small for him to trap his hand or foot or even head. Check that the wire mesh supporting the mattress is free from holes and that the mattress is thick enough not to slip out of the side of the cot.

Once a child who travels in a car has outgrown·a carrycot, at nine months, or earlier if he is strong enough to sit for long periods of time, he must be strapped into a child safety seat. Pick one with a BSI Kite Mark. These seats must be held with the correct floor-mounted restraints. Most seats can be equipped with deep-edged trays for food and toys—even if a good deal of both end up on the car seat or the floor.

The older a child becomes, the less prepared he is to sit still for long periods, so expect the three to six year old to become increasingly irritable, unless you can travel by night. Be prepared to make frequent stops, as often as once an hour, to relieve bladder and boredom, and be prepared to give the child a lot of attention, singing songs and playing games. Take some of the useful low-priced books that are available with any number of games for childen in confined spaces. If your car has a cassette deck, playing tapes with stories and songs

Nightmares

Because parents are relaxed on holiday, they may be less vigilant and minor mishaps are more likely to happen to children. But prompt and simple action will usually sort these out.

Wounds To avoid cuts and grazes becoming infected, always wash thoroughly under tepid running water. To remove grit, soak the area for half an hour then gently lift out the pieces with moistened cotton wool. Wounds heal best when exposed to the open air; if this is not possible, tape gauze over them.

Eyes A foreign body on the inner edge of the eyelid can be gently picked off with the moist rolled corner of a clean handkerchief. For something on the eyeball itself, use a twist of damp cotton wool.

Sprains Apply cold compresses for half an hour to reduce the swelling. Then use thick pads held with an elastic bandage to support the wrenched ligament. Bandage firmly but not too tightly.

Stings With a bee sting, first get the sting out with tweezers or a needle sterilised in boiling water, then wash the area under cold running water. Apply Hydroderm ointment sparingly: give children over twelve an antihistamine tablet, aged three to twelve give half a tablet. Antihistamine may also reduce swelling following insect bites.

allows adults to relax or concentrate on the road.

As your children grow older, you can involve them in the preparations for the journey and, if travelling by car, in the planning of the route and even in the actual navigation (with an occasional check to make certain you are not travelling south-west into the Sahara). At least this will stop most six to eleven year olds from beating each other over the head. If it doesn't, separate the children, not by putting one in the front (which is dangerous, not to mention illegal), but by placing a big bag or suitcase on the middle of the back seat.

From the age of twelve, children will become increasingly unenthusiastic about the prospect of holidaying with their parents. Consultations on where the holiday should be and what kind of holiday, where to stop on the way for a meal or a night's rest, may make them feel that they are being treated as adults so that they respond accordingly. If not, allowing them to do their own thing as far as is possible without risking their personal safety, is probably the only answer.

Many children become irritable or fractious simply because they do not feel well. Travel sickness is especially common among the fives to fifteens. Hyoscine-based tablets act very quickly, and can even take effect when a child has actually started to be sick. The most effective remedies, however, are steady driving, open windows and frequent stops. Antihistamine tablets take longer to have an effect but last longer, and have the advantage of causing drowsiness.

Wise Words

Match the method of transport to a child's age.

Plan the journey carefully and list every requirement.

Make allowances for possible delays.

Involve older children in the preparations and map reading and ask them what they want to do.

Carry a child's travel sickness remedy and other suitable medicines.

On planes, give children plenty to drink.

Check hotel cots carefully.

Take infants and children with you to foreign restaurants.

Seasickness can be tackled in the same way, although it is worth remembering that the centre of a ship is invariably moving less than the rest, and that standing on deck in the fresh air is often helpful. Always be sure that any drugs you give are suitable for children, and do not exceed the correct dosage for their age.

Children seem less likely to suffer from jetlag than adults, and sleep more easily during a flight. However, they suffer even more from dehydration, and should be given frequent soft drinks. If their ears go funny during a flight, persuade them to yawn or swallow to ease the pressure. Babies often solve this problem for themselves by screaming.

Food, especially for young children, can be a real problem, but often with no real dead-lines to meet on holiday until the last day, you can afford to take a more relaxed atti-tude should meals take longer than usual. Children may well not appreciate the menu in a gourmet restaurant, but they will be expected, welcome and catered for—either with small portions of their own or an extra plate so that you can feed them from your own for nothing. Continental children are not naturally better behaved than British ones; they are simply used to eating out and regard it as a perk, not a pain. The best way to make children relax abroad is not to remind them how much it costs, but per-suade them, and at the same time your-selves, that living abroad is no big deal.

HOW TO COPE

B & B NO VACANCIES

Avoiding mishaps
is one thing –
but when trouble strikes,
who's there to help?

142 The opportunity to bring home alcohol, tobacco and other goods, free of excise duty and Value Added Tax, is regarded as an inalienable right by most holidaymakers. Yet until recently it had no basis in law, and there were strong moves afoot within the EEC, itself on the way to becoming an excise-free zone, to abolish duty-free concessions altogether. It was something of a surprise, therefore, when in the summer of 1983 the EEC came out in favour of traditional duty-free

KNOWING WHERE TO STOCK UP

shops and proposed fresh legislation to guarantee their existence until at least the end of 1987. They also laid down a scale of increases in the value of goods bought in local shops that could be brought home duty-free. There was also encouraging news for wine drinkers, with a proposed increase in the amount that could be purchased in local shops and taken home tax-free, from four to six litres.

Powerful voices within the travel industry had argued that the consequences of abolishing duty-free goods within the EEC would be not only disgruntled holidaymakers, but a huge rise in airport taxes

and in airline and ferry company fares. This is because all these organisations unashamedly make substantial profits from duty-free sales, making it essential for the traveller to judge the options carefully before he can be sure of obtaining a real bargain.

The prices charged for duty-free goods vary so much from organisation to organisation and from month to month, that it is impossible to be certain in advance where the best buys are to be found. The only exceptions to this are airports trying to attract additional business who subsidise their duty-free sales as a promotional exercise: the most notable examples are

Schiphol in Amsterdam and Changi in Singapore. If you are flying to either destination, or changing planes there, this is the place to buy.

Singapore Airport also has the comparatively rare convenience of a duty-free shop to which you have access on arrival, so there is no reason to carry bottles or cartons with you. Or rather, there is even less reason than elsewhere to join the hordes of tourists who clink their way across frontiers, oblivious to the fact that their burden may be pointless.

As most British airports' duty-free prices are inclined to be expensive, there is usually little point in buying duty-free goods on your way out with the intention of carrying them all the way back, a surprisingly common practice among British holidaymakers. The prices at most foreign airports will be no more expensive, and in many cases substantially lower—although sometimes the duty-free shop may be closed if you depart at an unsociable hour.

The prices on airlines will sometimes be slightly below those at British airports, but the choice will be much more limited, and bottle sizes invariably half litre or less. There is also the infuriating possibility that the trolley will not have the particular item you wanted by the time it reaches your seat, or, in turbulence, that no duty-free goods are offered at all.

Occasionally, there is a similar risk on hovercraft, although Hoverspeed do cover this contingency by providing duty-free shops at their terminals on both sides of the Channel. The other ferry companies, however, no longer always have to compete with a duty-free outlet at the ports: in some places you have to buy on board if you intend to buy duty-free goods at all.

This matter of where and when to buy is not as self-evident as it might appear. On the Continent, the prices in the shops, especially in supermarkets, even (as they will be) duty-paid, can be either the same or cheaper than duty-free prices on ferries, on airlines or at airports.

Some comparisons of duty-free with shop prices:

Austria Cointreau cheaper than duty-free; gin, rum, vodka, whisky about the same as duty-free prices; cognac and cigarettes dearer than duty-free.

Belgium Cointreau cheaper; other spirits only slightly dearer; cigarettes the same as duty-free.

France Cointreau cheaper; gin and vodka the same; wine much better value than in duty-free shops.

Germany (West) Cognac, gin, vodka cheaper; others the same as duty-free.

Greece Cognac cheaper, but 'star' classification is different: a 5-star brandy is only average. Bar prices are cheap so there may not be much point in taking duty-free alcohol.

Italy Spirits and liqueurs substantially cheaper than duty-free; cigarettes the same as duty-free.

Netherlands Cointreau, cognac, gin slightly cheaper than duty-free—unless you are travelling through Amsterdam Schiphol airport.

Portugal Duty-free usually cheaper, except for vodka and locally made gin. Shop prices

Duty-frees at journey's end cause passengers—and Customs officials—hours of anguish

vary considerably.

Scandinavia All duty-free prices are much cheaper, enormously so in Norway. If you intend to bring your own, note that you are allowed to take only a standard (75cl) bottle of spirits into Denmark and Norway, a 1 litre bottle into Finland and Sweden (provided that you are aged 20 or over; under that you are allowed no alcohol at all).

Spain Cointreau, rum, vodka much cheaper; gin and whisky the same; cigarettes the same; cognac dearer than duty-free.

Yugoslavia Locally made spirits very cheap; internationally known brands dearer than duty-free.

Of course, you have to shop around: every city and resort has shops with prices well above the average, especially in fashionable districts. Inflation and changes in the value of currencies may alter the emphasis in one or two cases. However, with the exception of Scandinavia, the message is clear: taking your duty-free drink with you, unless you intend to stay in an

expensive hotel, is more trouble than it is worth.

With shop prices matching or beating duty-free prices, it is nearly always to your advantage to buy in EEC countries rather than on your way home, because the allowances are higher (see table overleaf).

'Other goods' include bottled beer, usually much cheaper abroad. A limit of 50 litres per person was imposed after groups of young men began importing into Britain beer by the van load, a loophole that had previously escaped the authorities. For similar reasons the personal allowance for mechanical lighters was restricted to 25.

You cannot buy some goods in the same category duty-free and others within the EEC and obtain the higher allowance. For example, if you buy a bottle of scotch on the ferry, you will be allowed only two bottles of wine free of duty, even if you bought them in a French supermarket. However, you can devote the whole of your alcohol allowance to wine, and bring in all seven litres as still wine, provided that it is bought in local shops in the EEC. Bottles mainly come in 70 and 75cl sizes, but Customs officers normally ignore this distinction and allow ten per person duty-free. By reading Customs Notice No 1, acquaint yourself with what other imports are restricted or prohibited.

Her Majesty's Customs and Excise is a much maligned organisation. It is not really staffed, as Ian Fleming is once supposed to have remarked, 'only by normal members of the Gestapo going about their duties'. Secretly, they want to

		Goods bought duty-free or outside the EEC	Goods bought in local shops in the EEC
	Tobacco		
	cigarettes	200	300
or	cigars	50	75
	cigarillos	100	150
	tobacco	250gm	400gm
	Alcohol		
	spirits, liqueurs	1 litre	1½ litres
or	fortified wine	2 litres	3
or	sparkling wine	2	3
and	still wine	2	4*

passengers under seventeen are not entitled to tobacco and drinks allowances

Perfume	60cc	90cc
Other goods	£28 worth	£120 worth**

*6 litres proposed by EEC

**increases proposed by EEC—1984: £170; 1985: £195; 1986: £220; 1987: £244

NOTHING TO

be loved and, if treated with humanity, will relax some of the rules, albeit slightly, in your favour. Do not get their backs up by:

surreptitious cheating (such as opening seven packets of cigarettes and smoking one from each)

blatant cheating (such as bringing an extra bottle of booze for baby)

aggressive packing (if you cannot get a case undone or out of the boot, you will stay there until you do)

not producing a list (if you claim you do not know what you have got, you could have to empty everything out)

having no money (if you have duty to pay, your goods stay with Customs until you do)

above all, do not be tempted to smuggle—the penalties, delays, inconvenience and embarrassment will be out of all proportion to any potential financial gain.

Customs officers have almost unlimited powers. They can arrest you, refuse your duty-free concessions, confiscate your car or your suitcases and take both apart without putting back the contents or paying for the damage. Your insurance policy is unlikely to cover such a contingency either, although if you are innocent you might obtain redress by complaining to the ombudsman through your MP.

Such a grim scenario happily does not affect most travellers. Most run into trouble through exceeding, accidentally or deliberately, their duty-free allowances. If the Customs officer discovers this, they are likely to charge

you the appropriate excise duty plus VAT on both the duty and the cost of the goods down to the last penny.

If you declare goods correctly over your duty-free limit, the same Customs officer is likely to round down the amount of, say, still wine, to a convenient figure and not to enquire too closely whether you have bought supermarket plonk or a rare and prized vintage in calculating VAT.

Customs officers have their greatest discretion when calculating duty on items other than drink and cigarettes. They price items out of a huge book that covers, for example, virtually every make of camera, tape recorder and watch, so there is little point in asking a Singapore shopkeeper to give you a spurious invoice for a much lower figure.

If you have declared everything, they may be in a generous mood and decide that the camera you purchased three weeks ago at the start of your stay abroad is already secondhand, and

Wise Words

There is little point in buying duty-free goods to bring home again when flying out from a British airport. Prices at foreign airports will usually be cheaper.

Airline prices sometimes undercut airport prices, but the choice is limited and supplies short.

Except when visiting Scandinavia, the prices of alcohol and cigarettes in the local shops may match or beat duty-free prices.

Smuggling is not worth the risk—the duty is often not that high.

Have regard for the powers, discretion and instinct of Customs officers.

difficulty at Customs on your return. (Of course, if you smuggled it in last time, this could prove rather difficult.)

An increasing number of ports and airports are now divided into red and green channels—the green being for passengers with nothing to declare above their duty-free allowances. They will be allowed to drive or walk through without hindrance, unless a Customs officer makes a spot check. They work by instinct, but if you want to reduce the risk of delay, then avoid:
scruffy luggage, especially tied with string
long hair on men: unkempt hair on women
jeans
seeming in a hurry
loud conversation

charge you duty accordingly.

Many travellers are tempted to smuggle valuable items because they have not taken the trouble to find out exactly what the duty will be. In fact, it is under nine per cent for a cine camera and under eight per cent for a tape recorder, plus VAT. If you have bought an expensive item of this nature in the UK and intend taking it abroad, it is prudent to carry some proof of purchase with you to avoid

And when driving, if you have any of the following, you could be given a hard time:
sports car with a good-looking partner
expensive car carrying four male passengers
caravan or trailer

The most likely group to pass quickly beneath the Customs officer's gaze is the family in a car that has seen better days, with two children in the back, one of whom is having a temper tantrum. It takes a brave man to ask if *they* have anything to declare.

Nightmares

A Yorkshire family returning from a package tour in Majorca, where they had already suffered from overbooking and bad weather, were stopped in the green channel at Leeds-Bradford Airport. The Customs officer discovered that they had one litre of spirits too many and this, for the husband, was the final straw. He disposed of the extra bottle by breaking it on the officer's desk, whereupon its contents went all over the officer's uniform. As a result he was fined for attempting to evade Customs duty, attempting to destroy the evidence, and assaulting a Customs officer—the end of a not quite perfect holiday.

The most common holiday disasters happen back at home. Returning to find that you have been robbed can do more to ruin a trip than any series of mishaps abroad, especially as you may be left with a nagging fear that it is going to happen again.

The most effective discouragement for would-be burglars is to give the appearance of still being there. Persuade a trusted relative to stay, or buy a series of timers that switch the lights on and off or do the same for the radio and TV; never pull curtains or lower blinds.

In stopping the milk and newspapers, do it personally, rather than by leaving out notes that could be read

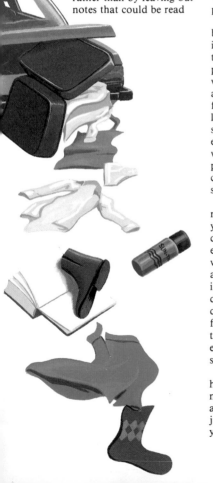

THINK AHEAD — AND SAVE THE DAY

by someone else. Persuade a neighbour to park in your drive rather than their own while you are away—and pray that they are not burgled instead, or you will never hear the last of it! Check that your house contents insurance is sufficient to cover all your valuables and that you have paid the current premium.

Your house could catch fire, but at least you would not be in it. The same might not be true of your hotel. Fire precautions in foreign hotels vary from the adequate to the appalling. Never take anything for granted, especially the local fire brigade, which in some countries may take an eternity to reach the fire, and will almost certainly not possess a turntable ladder capable of stretching above the sixth floor.

The higher your room, the more vital it is to memorise your route (by counting the doors) to at least two fire exists, and to test that they work. That means descending at speed and trying the door into the street. If you arrive in daylight, test it again at night; doors are frequently locked for security reasons. If at any time you find the emergency exit barred, arrange to stay somewhere else.

The odds against a fire in a hotel where you are staying may seem absurdly remote but are never high enough to justify being unprepared. How you act may make the

difference between death and survival. Do not try to leave your room without dressing adequately, as the time you lose in putting on your clothes should be weighed against the extent to which you are protected from heat and broken glass.

Before you open the door, feel the walls; if they are hot, act with extreme caution. Never leave without your key: if your route down is blocked by smoke or debris, your room may be the safest place. Going up to the roof may help to get you away from the heat but put you in greater danger later, although few modern buildings are ever completely gutted.

In a fire, never use a lift. If you are trapped in your room, ring reception, or if there is no answer and the telephone is still working, ring the emergency services (the number is usually at the front of the local phone directory). Telling someone exactly where you are can be crucial.

Put the plugs in the washbasin and bath, turn on all the taps, and leave them on. The wetter the room is, the slower it will burn. If it is not too heavy, lift the mattress into the bath and saturate it; then stack it against the door and keep it wet. Soak towels and sheets, wave them around the room to catch any fumes. Then pack them into cracks around the door to keep out the smoke. Do the same with the ventilation system. If the outside window will open, try to bring fresher air into the room, but be prepared to close it in a hurry if conditions outside are actually worse. Wrap a wet towel around your mouth and nose and remember that the freshest air is closest to the floor. Far more people die from the effect of smoke than of flames, and these measures have already increased your chances of survival.

If you are reading this chapter with a growing sense of scepticism and a feeling that it cannot happen to you, then be warned: hotel fires are not confined to American skyscrapers. They occur in Europe with frightening regularity. In May 1983, more than 40 tourists died in a fire when a butane gas burner exploded in the first-floor restaurant of the Hotel Washington in Istanbul, a hotel with only six storeys.

Fires on ship are comparatively rare, but not so rare that precautions can be safely ignored. The basic rules are: always take the lifeboat drill seriously and know the escape route to your boat. Never assume that the alarm bell has gone off by mistake and so wander around looking for confirmation that there really is an emergency. Do, however, take time to dress warmly: dying from exposure in an open boat is only marginally preferable to going down with the ship, and generally speaking, can be avoided.

Aircraft fires usually follow a crash, which is an extremely rare occurrence in itself—so rare that you could fly continuously for the rest of your life, never touching down except to change planes, and still be considerably safer than in your own home.

Your survival in an air crash depends on being in the right part of the plane, and that is completely unpredictable. In theory, you will be safer sitting right at the front or right at the back in an aircraft with underwing engines, and in the forward cabin of a plane with rear engines—well clear of the fuel tanks.

Never sit in a seat that does not feel securely mounted, and sit, if possible, with your back to the nose of the plane, however awkward this may seem in the opening stages of the flight. If you cannot actually sit in a row with an emergency exit, make sure that you know exactly where it and others are.

In an emergency there may or may not be time for the cabin crew to show you how to tuck yourself into the safest position for impact, of course, still wearing your seat belt. Expect more than one severe jolt, but when you are reasonably certain that the crash is over get out fast, and when you are clear of the plane keep running. Many people who survive the initial impact have died in the resulting confusion before the rescue services could arrive.

As with hotel fires, smoke can kill as easily as flames, especially as few airlines have overcome the safety problems involved in the use of cellular or foam plastics in aircraft furnishings. They are resistant to fire, but once they ignite, they produce a highly poisonous atmosphere. Although oxygen masks drop down from the overhead lockers in an emergency, the impact of a crash could well cut the oxygen supply, and in any case you have to abandon your oxygen when you try to leave the plane.

When escaping, never attempt to take any belongings with you: there have been stories of passengers sliding down emergency shutes clutching their bottles of duty-free alcohol, which is rather like carrying your own personal bomb.

Air crashes may be remote, but air turbulence is not. The pilot may have little warning, and in any case can do little to prevent his aircraft dropping several hundred feet like a stone. There have been fatal injuries to passengers who hit the ceiling under such circumstances, making it prudent to wear your seat belt for as much of the journey as possible. Especially as a court decision in 1983 made it extremely unlikely that passengers outside the USA could successfully claim any substantial damages for injuries sustained in this way, whether the pilot gave any warning to passengers or not.

Injuries can result from

more common occurrences on holiday: road accidents (see page 49), hotel accidents and beach accidents. An insurance policy (see pages 22 and 49) that provides both an emergency telephone service and private medical treatment is a wise precaution everywhere, and essential if you are travelling outside northern and western Europe.

Health problems can arise from quite simple causes, and can be minimised by sensible preventive measures (see page 23). If a sun tan is important, use protective creams and remember that if you make a miscalculation a week of agony may ruin your trip. Do not make the mistake of believing that because you do not feel hot the sun is not burning you. That applies to being out on a dull day or in a breeze, bathing, or climbing, because clouds shield only part of the sun's rays, water can increase their effect, and at high altitude the sun can penetrate the atmosphere more easily. If you do burn, reducing the temperature of the affected skin is probably the best remedy—by applying cold water, or calamine lotion, or a freezing spray.

Snatch-and-run street robberies are an everyday occurrence in some cities. Pickpockets often work in pairs: one removes your wallet and passes it instantly to an accomplice in case you should notice what is happening and grab him.

The only sure way to prevent the attention of these crooks is to leave most of your money and credit cards in the hotel safe, and carry what you need for the immediate trip in an inside zipped-up pocket. Women holidaymakers are particularly vulnerable because they may not have any safe pockets. The straps of their handbag can be cut or the bag simply snatched. Juvenile thieves riding motorbikes are a native hazard in Italy, and small children in North Africa and South America are often used to take most of the risks, on the assumption that you would be reluctant to have them arrested, even if they should be caught.

It is better not to do any catching yourself. The superficial attraction of catching a thief in the act quickly turns to regret should you be delayed abroad by a court hearing at which your property will probably be needed as evidence. Also, thieves can turn nasty if faced with the prospect of arrest and perhaps a prison sentence.

When confronted by thieves who threaten you with a weapon, the only sensible advice must be: give in gracefully. You do not wish to end up in hospital, or for someone else to collect the death benefit on your insurance.

To reduce the chances of being attacked and robbed, stay alert to your surroundings. Back alleys and old quarters off the tourist track, even when unsalubrious, exert a fascination for visitors (see page 130) but, unless you are in a sizeable group, don't let your curiosity and enthusiasm for 'local colour' carry you away. Women need to pay particular attention to their personal safety, especially in societies where unaccompanied females are regarded as fair game.

Thieves thrive on distraction, and holidaymakers or travellers are easily distracted. The moral is, concentrate on protecting your belongings. Do not:

go in jolly groups to the bank when changing your money

leave your luggage lying about at airports, even for an instant

carry your wallet sticking out of your back pocket

leave your hotel door unlocked, let alone ajar

use the 'please clean my room' sign, announcing that you have gone out

hide valuables in a room—thieves are expert at finding them

leave your room key at reception, because thieves may bluff their way into collecting it at busy times

If you are robbed, do not expect the local police (or even the tourist police, a special department set up in many resort areas simply to deal with foreign visitors) to show more than a passing interest. As with burglary in Great Britain, stealing from tourists is a disagreeable statistic without apparent remedy. The best you can hope for is a written acknowledgement that

Wise Words

Treat the threat of a hotel fire seriously, and become familiar with the emergency exits and sensible precautions.

Learn the disaster drill for ships and aircraft.

Beware of pickpockets and muggers, or of getting into a public-spirited fracas.

Nightmares

Should you be unlucky enough to be staying in a country that falls victim to a coup, the only advice is to keep as low a profile as possible, stay close to your hotel, make sure that the British Embassy or Consulate know where you are, and obey all instructions— especially from men carrying guns. The odds against such an experience are enormous, but this did not prevent one group of British tourists in the summer of 1982 from finding themselves in two separate attempted *coups d'état*. The first week of their two-centre holiday, in Nairobi, was spent under curfew after a revolution failed; the second, in the Seychelles, was spent confined to their hotel grounds after an attempt to overthrow that government. Their brochure described the tour as 'an adventure holiday with a difference'.

you have been to see them, which you can pass on to your insurers (see pages 10 and 21).

If you are really unlucky or really foolish, the police may have some reason for arresting you. Although the powers of arrest of British police have increased over the years, in the UK it is still comparatively rare for innocent citizens, or those who have committed some minor offence, to end up behind bars.

The disagreeable truth is that in many countries arrest merely on suspicion is quite commonplace. So be aware, but keep the risk in proportion. Try to make sure that someone knows quickly that you have

been arrested, and where you are. The nearest British embassy or consulate will usually intervene, if grudgingly at weekends, and will certainly

know of local lawyers to act on your behalf. Expect your passport to be taken away as a matter of course, even if you are allowed to return to your hotel.

By the time you have been wrongly arrested, suffered simultaneously from sunburn and diarrhoea, had your pocket picked, been mugged or molested, survived an air crash and escaped a hotel fire, you may wonder whether a holiday at home would be better next time.

However, preparing for the worst is the most likely way of preventing it.

When James Garner played an unorthodox detective in the American television series *The Rockford Files*, he carried a portable printing press in his car, so that he could produce in a matter of seconds any business card appropriate to his investigation.

Taking a printing press with you on holiday would be a little drastic, but there is a lot to be said for the basic concept: that you should present yourself in the best possible light for the occasion.

It is a fact of life that the people who complain successfully are invariably the most articulate, the most literate . . . and the best dressed. Therefore, by all means wear comfortable and preferably lightweight clothes for travelling, but look smart. If you are female, wear a stylish dress. If you are male, wear a jacket and tie—you can always take them off later. Scruffy travellers in jeans do not always receive the sympathy—or attention—they may deserve. By all means carry a personal card, even if you do not have a business. Personal cards make it easier for desk clerks to remember

DRESS FOR THE PART

your name. Print your telephone number in full to imply that you regularly receive calls from abroad. Start with 44 (the UK code), leaving out the zero on your area code. For example a London number, 01-383-0000, would be shown as 44 1 383 0000. Carry a small notebook to write down copious detailed observations. Notebooks make a petty tyrant nervous, and usually more responsive. If they offend, insist they tell you their name, and write it down.

If you do not receive the kind of response you think is reasonable, take the matter higher. Everyone has a superior to whom problems can be referred, either on the spot or contactable by telephone. Get to know who that person is, and speak to them personally.

If you are in a queue, stay in it. Other people behind you may become irritated, but an angry queue will eventually work in your favour. When you get attention you'll probably be dealt with more quickly to avoid raising tempers even higher. Try to sound confident. Stay calm; be polite, but firm. Antagonising the people you are dealing with rarely persuades them to work hard on your behalf.

Airlines, ferry companies and hotels all suffer from 'no-shows', that is people who

have booked flights or passages or rooms and do not turn up as promised. Because many such bookings are by telephone or are for flexible tickets—tickets that can be used for later journeys without financial penalty—travellers can and do change their plans with impunity. As a result, the travel companies form a judgement on the extent to which they can overbook without finding themselves with more people than places. Sometimes they get it wrong.

If you have a guaranteed airline seat—indicated by the letters 'OK' on your airline ticket—the airline is not legally obliged to carry you, but it must arrange alternative transportation at no extra cost. They may be reluctant to switch you to another airline, even if that is the next flight, because it will lose them revenue; in that case, ask to see the station manager of the airline on which you were due to travel, and complain.

If you are travelling on a full-fare scheduled airline ticket, the Association of European Airlines, to which most western European countries belong, lay down a scale of 'denied boarding' compensation. It is 50 per cent of the one-way fare of the flight sector involved, if a change of flight results in your arriving more than four hours later within Europe or more than six hours later elsewhere. The scale may be reduced to 25 per cent if you are travelling at a discounted rate on a scheduled airline. You are, of course, free to pursue a higher claim with the airline involved.

On American airlines compensation can be much higher—the full fare of the sector involved, or double the full fare if, on an international flight, you arrive on an alternative flight more than four hours after your original schedule. For this reason US airlines, especially, tend to offer financial inducements for volunteers to accept a later flight if one of their flights is overbooked.

If you are overbooked on a flight that forms part of a package tour, then you may be better advised to concentrate your efforts on the tour operator's representative. This particularly applies if you are booked on a charter flight, because the airline may not have another aircraft going to the same destination for as much as a week, and they are unlikely to do much to sort out a mistake which is probably down to the company who chartered their flight.

But you could reasonably insist on the airline contacting the tour operator if, as may be the case at a foreign airport, they have no representative on the spot. You could also ask them to advise you on what other airlines have flights to your exact destination, or at least back to the UK, and see if they have any seats available. If all this fails, you would be perfectly justified in making use of the emergency telephone service provided by your travel insurers (now you see why you need it—see pages 22 and 49).

It is still quite possible, however, that you will be involved in additional accommodation expenses, in extreme circumstances possibly even scheduled flight tickets home, so carry a credit card for just such an eventuality and claim back later.

If you appear to be a difficult (though still polite)

normal events of peak holiday travel—aircraft with technical problems, striking air traffic controllers, or straightforward congestion in the air—may also make you eligible for some kind of compensation on your travel insurance, but frequently not until 24 hours have elapsed. In the meantime, your demands on the airline and/or tour operator may quite reasonably escalate. After a delay of:

one hour—ask them to telex the airport where you are due to arrive to get a message to anyone expecting you, either at the airport itself, or at your office or home

two hours—if they haven't already offered them, ask for vouchers for you and your party to have a cafeteria snack

three hours—ask for vouchers for a full meal, hot breakfast, lunch or dinner, whatever is appropriate

four hours—insist on a hotel room nearby where you can rest and take a shower, and get them to pay for the transport there and back, too

If some of your luggage goes missing on arrival after your flight, it is vital that you complete some formalities before leaving the airport.

First, tell the airline that carried you that your luggage has gone astray, or, if that airline's business is handled by another carrier at the foreign destination (a common practice for smaller operators), tell them. While still at the airport, complete a Property Irregularity Report (known as PIR) on which you will have to describe your bags in some detail and insert the baggage claim tags number. Baggage tags are clipped to your flight

ticket when you check in, so keep them handy, and do not make the mistake of parting with them.

Second, ask the airline or their handlers what their daily compensation rate is for emergency purchases while your cases are lost. Some airlines may not have any such rate at all; others, instead of an allowance, may offer passengers an emergency bag containing, for example, toilet articles.

Third, after 24 hours go out and buy whatever you reasonably need and go on adding to it throughout your holiday if your luggage still has not turned up. Keep all the receipts carefully as they will form part of any claim you make.

Fourth, write to the airline immediately, even if you are waiting for another flight and it is quite inconvenient. Claims not notified within a few days may not be accepted.

Fifth, if you do intend to claim against the airline, ask them for a claim form and make certain that you fill it in and return it within three weeks of the loss.

Compensation from airlines is usually based on the weight of your baggage, so you may be better advised to make a claim under your travel insurance, where you will be paid according to its value.

If your luggage is damaged, you can reasonably expect the airline to assist you with emergency repairs to get the contents to your hotel, or to provide an alternative temporary container. Airlines sometimes repair luggage in their own workshops, or offer vouchers for repairs to be done by specific companies; or they may offer compensation based on their assessment of the current value of your suitcase. In every instance, however, it is vital to report the damage immediately you reclaim your luggage.

If you are going by ferry and it is overbooked, try to insist on being transferred to the next sailing, even if it is with another company. If you make enough fuss, the staff may even decide to leave someone else behind instead. Beware, especially, of going through passport control on a kind of standby basis, because if you are not put on the sailing you were supposed to be booked on, it will be much more difficult to change your tickets.

If you are overbooked at your hotel, and you made the booking yourself or directly through a travel agent, you will have to fight your own battle. If the hotel admit that they are expecting you but simply have no room, then ask to see the manager and demand that he arranges alternative accommodation in a hotel of at least equivalent standard and with similar amenities (it is no good being moved from a two-star hotel on the beach to a four-star in the centre of town if a beach holiday is what you wanted).

If the hotel is more expensive, make them promise, in writing, either to pay your bill or refund the difference before you leave the resort. Make them pay for your transport to the new hotel, and back again if they find room for you later in your holiday.

If the hotel deny having accepted your booking, then you will be wise to be in a position to produce confirmation—either a letter to you or a message to your travel agent. Booking solely by telephone at short notice leads to most misunderstandings and leaves you in the weakest position when problems occur.

If the hotel have no room for you, and accommodation is part of your package tour, it is the responsibility of the tour operator to find an alternative. Make it clear to their representative that you want a hotel with similar amenities and that if the tour company do not find something entirely suitable, you intend to sue (see pages 14 and 153).

If you appear to be a difficult (though still polite) customer, the tour operator is more likely to pull out all the stops to meet your requirements. However, be cautious in accepting an upgrading to a much more expensive hotel, even at no extra basic cost. Firstly, extras such as drinks or non-set meals may be much more expensive, and secondly you may not like the people who can afford to go there in the first place.

Try to find out from the tour operator's representative exactly when the company became aware that you could not stay in the original hotel. Some tour operators have been known to keep back information from their clients for days or even weeks in the hope that once they have reached the resort (or even a different one) they will feel too insecure to make a fuss. If you find out this was the case it may add to the substance of your complaint later.

Write a letter to the tour company immediately, complaining about the inconvenience, but make it brief. Hand it to their representative, and get a receipt.

If you are moved to a more expensive hotel, keep receipts for all your extra bills as they may prove part of your claim for compensation later. If your original hotel is near enough, pay them a visit and compare bar or food prices.

You may have other, slightly less serious, problems concerning your hotel. If there is something wrong with your hotel room (see page 126), discovering it before you unpack gives you a better chance of being moved to a more suitable room.

Direct any complaints to the hotel manager and if that does not result in satisfaction, insist that he contacts the tour operator's representative. If the problem concerns the standard of food or the amenities, and is not or cannot be put right (such as the swimming pool not having been built yet), make a note of the rep's explanation, exchange addresses with other dissatisfied clients in the hotel, and take photographs, where appropriate, to support your complaint.

If you made the booking yourself, and your cause for dissatisfaction relates to the means by which you reached your destination (for example, you were given a cold meal rather than the hot one you had been promised on an aircraft; or there was no cabin available on your ferry despite the fact that you had booked one; or the coach broke down) you will have to complain to the operating company.

But if you made the booking through a travel agent, as long as he is a member of the Association of British Travel Agents, then the

ABTA Code of Conduct obliges him to handle a complaint on your behalf (see page 12). However, a few of the less diligent agents will simply pass on your letter of complaint and accept without demure the operating company's explanation, so you may be better advised to deal with the matter yourself.

Invariably, the agent will claim that as he is acting on behalf of someone else—the airline, the hotel, or the tour operator—your contract is with them and he is not liable if things go wrong. The law, however, does require him to take reasonable care, to check your travel documents, and to provide the correct information about your holiday. If he promises you amenities (such as a children's pool, for example) not supported in the operator's brochure, he could well be held liable for inducing you to take out a holiday you would not otherwise have accepted.

In most cases, your point of attack will be the tour operator—it is he who has taken most of your money, and you unquestionably have a contract with him. First, read the booking conditions that appeared either in the brochure from which you selected your holiday (see page 16), or on the booking form you completed later. In some cases these will appear highly complicated, in small print that is difficult to read, and suggest that you have no claim against the tour operator. This will be because the tour company is trying to rely on the law of agency, suggesting that in booking hotels and aircraft and arranging local transport and excursions, they cannot be held responsible for negligence by the 'principals' —the owners or operators of hotels, aircraft, coaches and the like.

Do not be put off. The Unfair Contract Terms Act has tipped the balance of the law in your favour. Whatever the tour operator says in his brochure, he is responsible for providing you with the kind and standard of holiday you were led to expect. If, as he may allege, some other party is to blame for what went wrong, unless it is an aspect of your holiday, say car hire, for which he could not reasonably be held responsible (and says as much in his booking conditions), it is up to the tour operator to compensate you and seek his own redress afterwards.

It is always worthwhile checking the booking conditions in case the tour operator is one of a few holiday companies that make a commitment in certain circumstances—such as a change of hotel or resort— which may save you a good deal of argument.

Write to the tour operator as soon as possible. Address your letter to the customer services manager. Keep a copy. Always date your letter, as it may well be the first of many. Be reasonable, and be relevant. Resist the temptation to include every possible niggling complaint to supplement your principal grievances.

Expect to dig in for a long fight. Tour companies are not great believers in the old adage that 'he who gives generously, gives twice'. They will respond with sympathetic noises, but rarely an offer of money. When they do make an offer, you may well think it derisory.

If you feel you are getting nowhere, write to the managing director of the company (ring up first and ask what his name is). Make it clear that at the very least you will be going through the ABTA conciliation and arbitration service, if the company is an ABTA member, as most are; and that at worst you may sue. Pressure from the top may result in an improved offer, or if not that, then in a faster response to your complaint.

Form a view on what you honestly believe would be a reasonable offer of compensation, taking into account to what extent your

Wise Words

Travel in smart clothes.

When you are at the head of a queue and something goes wrong, stay there until you get satisfaction.

In the case of a substantial delay, demand meals and accommodation.

If an airline lose your luggage, buy what you need until it turns up, and claim compensation.

If you are overbooked at a hotel, insist on being provided with the right kind of alternative.

When complaining to tour operators, do not be misled by limited booking conditions that have no force in law.

Use the free ABTA arbitration service.

Take out a separate insurance to cover your legal expenses.

holiday really was spoilt. Mark any letter in which you name this figure 'without prejudice', so that you can ask for more later if you have to go to court.

If you cannot reach agreement with the tour operator, write to the Association of British Travel Agents at 55 Newman Street, London W1P 4AH, enclosing full details of your complaint and copies of all correspondence. If you do not have ready access to a photocopier, many public libraries offer a service for a small fee.

If the ABTA conciliation service (which is free) does not produce the response you want

from the tour company, you can opt for the independent arbitration scheme run by the Chartered Institute of Arbitrators. ABTA tour operators are bound to accept arbitration decisions under this scheme, which has very modest costs, provided that arbitration is based on documents alone and you resist the temptation to put in a personal appearance.

If you are dealing with a non-ABTA operator, or do not want to risk arbitration, then your only recourse is the courts. The small claims procedure of the County Court will keep your costs to a minimum and is relatively informal, allowing you to conduct your own case. But a great many claims involving more than one person are likely to constitute too large a case to be considered there.

In that event, you would have to take out proceedings in the County Court, a daunting and expensive prospect even if the case were to be settled before getting into court, as many are.

It is possible to insure yourself and your family against just such a contingency, covering yourself against the costs of going to law, win or lose. The DAS Legal Expenses Insurance Company, based in Bristol; Legal Benefits, part of the Legal Protection Group; and Family Legal Expenses Insurance, a consortium of the Sun Alliance, Eagle Star, General Accident, Provincial and Royal Insurance companies, all offer policies for an annual premium that otherwise could easily be swallowed up by the cost of one solicitor's letter.

Unless they suspect that you

are a professional complainer —someone who makes a habit of reducing the cost of the annual holiday by some pretext or other—most companies will eventually offer reasonable compensation if your claim has any real substance, rather than risk the attendant publicity of court proceedings.

They could offer a substantial reduction on another holiday, which may cost them less than a financial settlement and be worth more to you. Unless you are convinced that any holiday with this particular company is certain to be an unmitigated disaster, you may feel inclined to be compensated in kind. They will probably look after you rather better next time.

Nightmares

Sometimes it is hotel owners who have cause to do the complaining. In dry months, water in, for example, Italy, Greece and Malta, can be rationed and taps turned off at the mains during the night. For one British holidaymaker in Sorrento, this had a spectacular effect after he had returned to his hotel following a not altogether alcohol-free party. He turned on his tap in vain to get a drink of water, and went to bed, leaving the tap open and the plug in the washbasin. Early in the morning, while he slept heavily, the water came back on, filled his basin, flooded the bathroom, made its way down the corridor and eventually cascaded down the stairs to the reception hall.

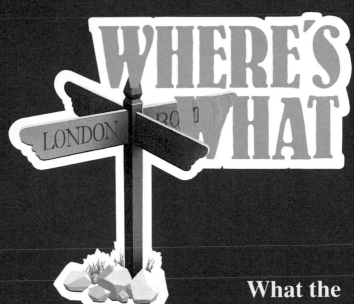

WHERE'S WHAT

What the guide books won't tell you – see Europe through fresh eyes

AUSTRIA

INNSBRUCK

The patronage of Empress Maria Theresa and Emperor Maximilian did much to maintain Innsbruck's position of power and prosperity in the 18th century. Its most famous street, Maria-Theresienstrasse, is named after her and the romanesque Triumphal Arch was built for her in 1767. The breadth of this street, with trams running down the centre and majestic buildings overshadowed by the Alps behind, helps to create one of the most compelling views in Europe. You can go by cable car or cable railway to obtain an even more striking panorama, but do wrap up well: it can be bitterly cold at several thousand feet above sea level. On a clear day, you may be able to see the sun glinting on the famous Goldenes Dachl (Golden Roof), which is actually heavily gilded copper, and covers the ornate stone balcony of a gothic-style house. It is to be found in the pedestrian area of the Old Quarter, whose windows overhang so far in the narrowest streets that they touch when opened. Real coffee and delicious cakes tempt many a passer-by to sit at the table of outdoor cafés, but if these are too crowded you can make your way to rival establishments on the banks of the River Inn.

Air Airport is at Kranebitten, three miles (4.8km) west.

SALZBURG

Wolfgang Amadeus Mozart was born here in 1756, and fine music is part of Salzburg's sustained appeal, with its annual festival probably the best in

Europe. If you do not want to hear Mozart's works played here, at least go to his birthplace, an old middle-class house turned into a museum. You can see his clavichord, and some delightful tiny models that Mozart used to plan the settings for his operas. Of course, Salzburg was one of the great cities of Europe long before the Mozart family settled there. Ruled by prince-archbishops, its Hohensalzburg Fortress, built in the 11th century and rising 400ft (122m) above the town, was regarded as impregnable

Salzburg, birthplace of Mozart, is a great musical centre

Horses go through their paces at Vienna's Spanish Riding School

even after the invention of powerful siege guns. It is certainly the largest completely preserved fortress of its kind on the Continent, well worth the demanding climb to reach it if there is a queue at the funicular. Otherwise, simply stroll around the old city streets that spread out from the Residenz, a 17th-century palace the bishops built when they judged there was no longer any need to retreat to the draughty castle. If you can time your arrival at the palace for 11am or 6pm (7am is another option usually ignored by tourists), the Glockenspiel bells, all 35 of them, chime out in concert.

Air Salzburg-Maxglan Airport is three miles (4.8km) west.

VIENNA

The golden age of the Austro-Hungarian Empire, broken up after the First World War, has never been completely extinguished in what many would argue remains the cultural centre of Europe. By nibbling a two-tiered cake at one of Vienna's delightful coffee-houses, strolling along car-free and carefree boulevards past exquisite shops, or absorbing superb views at almost every corner, it is simplicity itself to recall the times of Mozart and of the Strausses whose music lingers on, played by tiny orchestras to accompany your meal at fashionable restaurants. See how the other half lived at the Schönbrunn Palace, with its beautiful apartments, its vast grounds designed to perfection, its collection of coaches that provided the Hapsburgs' personal taxi service. If the Hofburg, their Imperial Palace, becomes too much for you, sneak off to the Spanish Riding School and watch the training. You still need a ticket, but it is cheaper than the evening performances and you get a much better idea of the patience and perseverance that goes into their musical programme.

Air Vienna-Schwechat Airport is eleven miles (17.7km) east.

BELGIUM

BRUGES

A city of wealth and elegance since the 15th century, with access to the sea until the river silted up, forcing the good burghers to create their own sea port of Zeebrugge. Its churches and historic buildings contain priceless works of art —especially the Groeninge Museum, with masterpieces by Hieronymus Bosch, Jan van Eyck and Memling. Memling also has a museum all to himself with, for the less squeamish, a display of medieval pharmacy. A sense of the period lives on in the Beguinage, a sanctuary run by

Benedictine nuns. Bruges is not, like Amsterdam, famous for its canals, but it has a whole network of them, overshadowed by tall, gabled houses. The narrow streets make exploration on foot essential and, at peak periods, even that can be an ordeal because of the hordes of other visitors. The city remains famous for a product that also goes back many centuries, handmade lace.

BRUSSELS

Except when the bureaucrats and their documents are carted off in bulk to Strasbourg, Brussels is the centre of the European Economic Community—making the city, already relatively expensive, now hideously so. Brussels boasts some of the best restaurants in Europe, but the price of your meal will not dent your budget, it will demolish it altogether. However, even in Brussels it is possible to walk and view places beautiful and places curious without risking bankruptcy. At its heart is one

of the most exquisite squares in Europe, the Grand' Place. Surrounded by 17th-century guild houses, vying with one another in flamboyant decor, the square is dominated by the Hôtel de Ville, the town hall with a gothic structure of quite majestic proportions. For the suicidally energetic, there are 420 steps to the summit of the tower. Not far away is the Manneken-Pis, the famous bronze statue of a boy answering a call of nature. Then there is the Scottish connection, L'Église du Finistère, with its wooden statue of Our Lady of Aberdeen. Its original owner was an 11th-century bishop of Aberdeen—a contemporary of Macbeth, for his sins.

Air Brussels Airport is eleven miles (17.7km) north-east.

LIÈGE

The struggle for independence in the Low Countries meant that one trade flourished for

A quiet corner of the canal network in Bruges

centuries—weapons. Liège became famous for its guns and, on a modest scale, still is —but nowadays only those made for hunting and fishing. When the Walloons were trying to eject the Spanish, Liège made flintlock firearms by the thousand; many of them can be seen in the Armourer's Museum, along with examples of the evolving techniques of the gunsmith. If you are fortunate, you may catch another visual expression of old traditions in the puppet shows in the Rue Féronstrée, with a cast of local heroes from memorable moments in the city's history. Liège is also an ideal centre for exploring the River Meuse, a kind of second division Loire, with less magnificent but equally intriguing châteaux. If you go out for the day, keep the children quiet with a bag of *couques*, gingerbread cakes that need sharp young teeth to break them.

CYPRUS

A divided island in every sense. Since 1974, when Turkey occupied the northern part of the island, it has had a frontier running across the middle of the capital, Nicosia. The political situation permitting, tourists from the south can visit the other side of the city, but neither the Greek nor Turkish Cypriot authorities encourage it. The traditional seaside resorts of Kyrenia and Famagusta are in the Turkish part of the island, but the Turks have not made the most of them. There are no direct flights from the UK; visitors must travel via Turkey. In contrast, the Greek hoteliers who lost everything during the Turkish takeover have rebuilt in the south, with Limassol, Larnaca and Ayia Napa the busiest resorts. The island still has echoes of its

British past: vehicles drive on the left and distances are measured in miles. However, visitors who take a holiday in the Turkish north should note that if evidence of their visit appears in their passports, they may well subsequently be refused entry to the south.

Air In the Greek section, the international airport is three miles (4.8km) south of Larnaca: in the Turkish section, Ercan (Tymbou) Airport is eight miles (12.8km) east of Nicosia.

CZECHO-SLOVAKIA

PRAGUE

The birthplace of Franz Kafka, whose literary efforts became unconscious predictions of political perils to come. *The Trial*, in which the nature of the crime eludes the accused, and *The Castle*, with the remoteness of those in authority, could just as well have been written in the days of Dubcek, and the ill-fated Prague Spring of 1968. Kafka lived in a street known as Zlatá Ulička or Golden Lane, which in earlier times was where the alchemists claimed to have turned lead into gold. One of them, an Englishman named Edward Kelley, practised black magic in pursuit of his trade in the 16th century—somehow what one would have expected in the mysterious city of Prague, one-time capital of Bohemia, a country whose position on a European map few would have been easily able to fix precisely. This remoteness was fortunate as the city was out of the range of Allied bombers in the war, and over-run by

On the beach at Larnaca, one of the largest and best-known resorts in the southern port of Cyprus

the Russians too quickly to suffer much damage. Prague's remarkable skyline of gleaming spires, a kind of fourth-dimensional Oxford, survived unscathed. So too did the Wallenstein Palace, a baroque masterpiece, and Hradcany Palace, a rather sinister castle. When, in 1618, the Czechs first tried to resist oppression in the days of Hapsburg domination (thereby starting the Thirty Years' War) the famous Defenestration of Prague took place here: two government officials were thrown out of a window in the Hradcany. Prisoners still fall out of windows, but then history has a curious habit of repeating itself.

Air Ruzyně Airport is nine miles (15km) west.

DENMARK

COPENHAGEN

Both Hamlet and Hans Christian Andersen have unintentionally done a good deal for Danish tourism, with Copenhagen receiving most of the benefit. However, the truth is that Copenhagen simply does not compare with a great many cities in Europe when it comes to historic landmarks. Of the best, the Amalienborg Palace is the home of the Danish royal family, who understandably are not keen on the idea of holidaymakers traipsing through their sitting-room, though a few museum apartments are open to the public. Christiansborg Palace, where parliament sits, usually has conducted tours only once a day, and none at all in July. The Little Mermaid, a small bronze statue commemorating an Andersen fairy tale and overlooking the harbour, requires a largely uninteresting

At the Tivoli, Copenhagen's popular amusement park

boat trip just to get a glimpse of it. What rescues Copenhagen from mediocrity is the Tivoli Gardens, even though it is open only during the summer months. The Tivoli is far from being the largest pleasure park in the world, but it is probably the only one where you can be on a roller-coaster one minute and listening to an open-air

Hans Andersen's Little Mermaid, watching over Copenhagen

symphony concert the next. It has an amazing range of entertainments with food to match, everything from hamburger stalls to delightful, romantic restaurants among the fairy lights. For family entertainment, the Tivoli is impossible to beat. Otherwise, take a trip out of town to see the 16th-century castle at Elsinore, the setting for *Hamlet*; or try the hydrofoil across the sound to sample the deceptively quiet Swedish town of Malmö.

Air Kastrup Airport is six miles (9.6km) south-east.

Rail Central Station.

FRANCE

AIX-LES-BAINS

Rheumatic Romans, appreciating the advantages of its thermal waters, built the baths and you can see their remains (the baths not the Romans) within the spa buildings of the still famous health resort. It stands on Lac du Bourget, the largest lake in France, and the town itself, all subdued elegance, is sometimes a relief from the crowded lakeside. Dr Faure's Museum has a roomful of Impressionist paintings worthy of any gallery in Europe, with works by Cézanne, Pissarro and Renoir, and two rooms of Rodin sculptures and watercolours that somehow escaped the Rodin Museum in Paris. If you do not lose your shirt at the casino, the lake offers some relatively expensive trips to Sierroz Gorge and Hautecombe Abbey, where the Gregorian monks are on public view and usually in good voice at Sunday mass.

A hair-raising road clings precariously to the cliff-side at Chambotte, near Aix-les-Bains

ARLES

A public expenditure cut in the 12th century all but ruined Arles' monument to posterity. The townspeople incorporated into their fortifications the huge Roman arena where second division gladiators and lions (the best had been sent to Rome) slogged it out for the benefit of the citizens of what was then the capital of Roman Gaul. The Emperor Constantine came here intermittently to escape the summer heat of his capital. He might well have approved of the principal modern spectacle offered in the arena each summer, a kind of bloodless bullfight. Arles recovered its status as a religious centre in the middle ages, and the Church of St Triophime offers a testament to the exquisite decorations of the period. However, Arles' most famous resident was the painter Van Gogh, who produced many of his famous works in the town and in the surrounding countryside of the Camargue. A pity that few of the townsfolk of the day bought any of the pictures.

AVIGNON

The city owes its fame to a medieval struggle for power in the 14th century, when Pope Clement V escaped the King of France by moving the papal seat lock, stock and bible to the Vatican enclave of Avignon. That may explain why successive popes created the Palais des Papes as a forbidding fortress, without windows so that no assassin's arrow could fly through, and why the city contains a massive surviving network of battlements and towers. Ironically, as so much has stayed complete, the Pont d'Avignon of the nursery rhyme (actually the Pont St Bénézet) is not. Only four of the original 22 arches remain and the bridge ends suddenly partway out in the Rhône. If the local inhabitants ever did dance on it in a ring, then the chances are some of them ended up in the river, as the bridge is scarcely wide enough for a carnival.

BIARRITZ

Where Bertie dallied, and his mother Queen Victoria arrived to put a stop to it, and European monarchs stayed as part of an aristocratic grand tour. The facades are still the same, and the surf still pounds the shores on a windy day in a way no other Continental resort would ever survive, but the visitors now are far less upper-class and much less British. Even the English colony has taken flight, preferring inland Pau, so that the Anglican church is graced by an English minister only on the occasional Sunday. None of this is really apparent, of course, if you stroll along the promenade with its marvellous displays of flowers, or rent a little beach hut on the sandy shore. But the shops, my dear, the shops: more Californian surfin' than *haute couture*, more brash knick-knacks for successful gamblers than presents for a lady. Gamblers? There are two casinos—vying with one another for bad taste and your money—which will clean you out of what the hotels and restaurants have left. Over-priced, over-sexed, and over there: Queen Victoria would not have been at all amused.

Once-fashionable Biarritz and one of its casinos

BORDEAUX

The city was a possession of the English crown for 300 years, including the turbulent times of the Black Prince when England and France fought for that old-fashioned concept: no, not chivalry—territory. Not that there is much to show for English rule: the old buildings were largely pulled down to make room for the 18th-century quarter which includes the Esplanade of Quinconces. This claims to be the largest square in Europe—an irrelevant statistic until you are looking for someone in it. The English connection seems even more ironic because the cornerstone of Bordeaux's prosperity, the wine trade, first flourished in that era, making the duty slapped on at Dover these days

all the more unpalatable. Drink it cheaply while you can, as the best sights to see here are Médoc, Graves and St Emilion, and you can have your fill of them without stirring from your table.

BOURGES

If there is one consistent thread through French history, it is the way treasurers of the king managed to salt away enough of the loot to build themselves a little country retreat that would not seem out of place in the Gardens of Versailles. Jacques Coeur was one of them: his palace—by no means an over-generous description—was built on the remains of the town wall and used royal labour as well as municipal bricks. Monsieur

Coeur was treasurer to Charles VII, who, when times were hard in the 15th century, made Bourges, which lies south of Orléans, his capital. Squeezed as he was between the English and the Burgundians, he had nowhere else left until Joan of Arc (or some suitable last-minute replacement) was burned at the stake, so turning the balance in his favour. Today Bourges is a quiet provincial town with only the beautiful Cathedral of St Étienne as a reminder of its prestigious past. You can see the cathedral for miles and, if the angle of the sun is right, catch an astonishing view of the stained-glass windows—dazzlingly beautiful. Fed by waters of the Auron and the Yèvre, the Garden of Prés-Fichaux has colour and symmetry worth travelling many miles to see.

The west front of the cathedral at Bourges—an outstanding example of 12th-century romanesque architecture

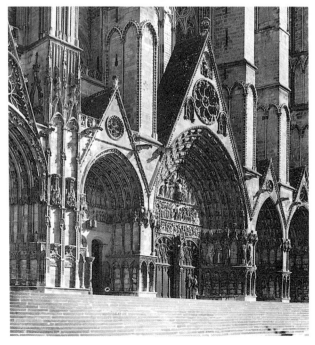

Cannes—even going on the beach is expensive

CANNES

Ostentatious luxury is the order of the day, with luxurious hotels cheek by jowl along the tree-lined Boulevard de la Croisette, where the menu card probably cost more to produce than most of us spend on an entire lunch. These palatial residences are matched only by the private villas in Cannes' hinterland, from where the really rich and the really famous rarely venture out: everything, and everyone, comes to them. Whether Lord Brougham, induced to spend a winter in the tiny fishing village by rumours of plague up ahead near Nice, ever imagined the transformation he was about to stimulate seems exceedingly doubtful; we have a lot to blame him for. Even the fishermen are jammed into a tiny section of the harbour, where the yachts and the dues (or should it be the

over-dues, for this is the town of extended credit) are equally breathtaking. If you are agile enough to cross the main road, a kind of continuous rehearsal for the French Grand Prix, you can relax on one of the private beaches, where deck chair, umbrella, air mattress and beach boy or girl are yours . . . at a price. If the sun tan oil runs out, try a boat trip to the Île-St-Marguerite where the Man in the Iron Mask is said to have been imprisoned. Presumably he could not pay for lunch.
PS In May, Cannes plays host to the International Film Festival, with its hangers-on and, in the case of the hopeful starlets, its hangers-out. Unless you fancy yourself as a late entry for the world gate-crashing championship, drive on.

CARCASSONNE

If you wonder how the fortress walls of Carcassonne survived in perfect condition

after a couple of medieval sieges in which lumps of rock were hurled at them from giant catapults, the answer is they didn't: what the siege engines could not achieve on their own, the underprivileged completed, working like termite ants to acquire material for their own homes. By the end of the Wars of Religion, Carcassonne's 13th-century fortifications were in utter ruin, and rescued fom oblivion only by Viollet-le-Duc, a 19th-century architect of some distinction and no little determination. He rebuilt the walls, cutting a few historical corners, but no matter: the result is a kind of medieval Disneyworld, with a double line of defences rising above the Garonne Valley. There are nearly two miles of fortifications, offering a memorable walk. Although the fortress is in itself a town of some considerable size, it is so swamped with tourists at high season that queues are common: queues to park, queues to visit, queues for the loo. Try a wet day in November.

CHAMONIX

Actually called Chamonix-Mont Blanc, it is below the highest peak in the Alps (15,771ft/4,807m). The town is at 3,402ft (1,037m), and is not one place but a whole collection of villages. Signposts in the area are confusing until you appreciate that nearly everything is expressed in terms of heights rather than distances. Chamonix is also the hub of a mechanical monstrosity, all cable cars and cog wheel trains getting in the way of a view that, quite literally, takes your breath away. Nevertheless, the skiing conditions are among the best in the world, the instructors all look like young Omar Sharifs (and don't play much bridge), and the kit alone can require you to bring along your bank manager. Once you climb above the cable car termini, however, there are some marvellous walks on offer in summer, past frozen snow and Alpine flowers. You must, however, succumb once to auto-mation—take the super de luxe cable cars, the *téléphériques*, to the Aiguille de Midi. This is among the highest, most spectacular rides in the world, giving an unsurpassed view of Mont Blanc. Dress warmly, and take sandwiches, for the quality of the food at the top does not match its price.

Hounds and huntsman in front of the château at Chantilly

CHANTILLY

Forget the châteaux of the Loire: Chantilly, with its sumptuous furnishings, paintings, and unsurpassed library of early books, overshadows them all. Its stables would have discouraged even Hercules, accommodating as they did at one time more than 240 horses and innumerable hounds. Hunting was the passion of the owners, the Condé family, close cousins of Louis XIV, who turned the entire place into a frenzy by arriving one day unannounced. Throwing together a quick supper might have been rather easier had the King not brought with him his personal entourage of several thousand, all of whom also expected a lavish meal. Vatel, the Condé's chef, reputed to be the finest in France, summoned supplies from miles around, and almost pulled off the meal of a lifetime. But when he heard that the fish he was expecting to cook for the meal's dénouement had not arrived, he retired to his room and committed suicide. He was actually a little premature, as the fish had arrived after all.

Rail On a direct line from the Gare du Nord in Paris. Avoid race days in June, when the château is shut, and Sundays, when it is overflowing with visitors.

CHARTRES

The town council had a more sensitive political barometer than the foreign ministers of Europe for, when each of the two world wars began, they dismantled the windows of their Notre Dame Cathedral and stored them until the end of hostilities. This was no ordinary feat: in all there are 3,000 sq yd (2,742 sq m) of pieces, marvellous shades of blue dating back to the 13th century and providing a whole spectrum of medium and dark blues in changing light. With the glass restored, Chartres Cathedral has survived intact, since it was rebuilt, prodigiously, in 30 years following a disastrous fire in 1194. The stimulus for this labour of love was the recovery from the fire of what is supposed to be the veil of the Virgin Mary, worn by her at the birth of Christ. The veil is still preserved in the Chapel of St Piat. Although the cathedral *is* Chartres, the town's steep, narrow streets are worth a walk before you depart.

A patient craftsman restoring the priceless stained glass in Chartres Cathedral

DEAUVILLE

Their first promenade was made of wood, apparently because the shifting sands defied attempts at a more permanent construction, but that was Deauville's one notch below perfection—at least that is how the architects of the town viewed it. The rest is still all stylised architecture and broad avenues, inspired by the Duc de Morny when he visited the obscure village on its site back in 1866. The British had a hand in it somewhere, if only because our seaside resorts were much visited by the French aristocracy in the days when you could travel without a passport across most of Europe, and they borrowed our bathing huts for *bains de mer*. However, unlike the better-known resorts on the end of one or other cross-Channel ferry service, Deauville has made no concession to modern economics. It caters unashamedly for the rich, it is a jet-set resort not for those who fly in them, but for those who own one. Its background of yachts and racing and gambling make it a photographer's delight for the latest Parisian fashions; and a place where a mistress and her master can start a scandal with an innocuous little stroll. Elegance and luxury are there for the taking, at a price, but it is cheaper on the outside looking in.

DIJON

The giant kitchen in the palace of the Dukes of Burgundy would suggest that the dukes eat well in this gastronomic centre, acknowledged as such even in a country where cooking is a fiercely competitive art. In the days when Burgundy was an independent kingdom, a kind of knight hopping about the chessboard of Europe, it was a centre of progressive thinking, imaginative justice and truly creative art. Not that the dukes, from Charles the Bald to Charles the Bold, looked much further than the *droit du seigneur* for their pleasures. Still, the prosperity and security they defended helped in their turn to preserve the delightful streets of a medieval city, with so many grand houses that the tourist office has an index of their erstwhile owners. The gothic church of Notre Dame houses in its tower the remarkable Horloge à Jacquemart, the clock and bell appropriated as part of the spoils by Philip the Hardy in 1382 after he beat the Flemish and wanted his citizens to have an audible reminder of his prowess. Avoid hotel rooms in its proximity, for it strikes every quarter of an hour.

DINAN

Not to be confused with the pretentious resort of Dinard, Dinan is a medieval city that rarely heard the tramp of soldiers and is remarkably well preserved for that very reason. The old quarter, perched high above the River Rance, is enclosed by castle walls 14th-century in origin. From the ramparts, the view of the Brittany coast is second to none. After a passing shudder at the castle dungeon, appreciate the English Garden on the terrace, high above a gothic bridge. In the cobblestone streets of the old town, the houses hug one another, providing shelter for outdoor traders through the ages—although these traders once also proved a ready target for the contents of chamber-pots. On market days, Thursdays and Saturdays, stalls are crammed end-to-end in the Place des Merciers, with local craftsmen offering the fruits of their labours.

FONTAINEBLEAU

French kings first took up residence in the Forest of Fontainebleau in the 12th century, long before they moved to Versailles. If the palace seems to lack an impression of symmetry, the impulsive additions of various monarchs may explain it. François I did the most to turn it from a fortified château into a renaissance palace, importing Italian artists to

Deauville—a consistently fashionable resort which the rich have made their own for over a century

transform the interior with a host of mosaics and paintings. But much of the truly pretentious decor was the work of Napoleon I, who lived here in the closing years of his rule. The Cour des Adieux was the scene of his impassioned, if temporary, departure for Elba in 1814. The surrounding forest is magnificent, replete with splendid walks, and on its edge is the village of Barbizon, the home of some of the most famous French painters, including Millet and Rousseau. Their houses are worth a visit, if you can find somewhere to park away from the hideous double lines.

Rail Fontainebleau is on a direct line from Paris— 45-minutes from the Gare de Lyon.

GRENOBLE

The gateway to the Alps, although its sci-fi cable car, fully encased in clear plastic, would seem more in place on a moon station. Actually, the car takes you in three minutes flat to the Bastille, an ideal vantage point for absorbing the magnificent range of Grande-Chartreuse Mountains, and an imperious view of the city. You then have a choice of athletic pursuits, including a downward route to the Parc Guy-Pape through tunnels, over bridges, around sinuous paths and into echoing caves. Or you could go upwards, tackling the mountains themselves, on well-marked trails not dangerous in themselves but mighty impressive to anyone left down below. Either way, you end with a drink on the outdoor terrace where, with a lump or two of ice and a dash of liqueur you can reproduce the Chartreuse Mountains in a glass.

Rail Place de la Gare.

La Rochelle's picturesque town hall, founded in the 13th century

LA ROCHELLE

Elegant arcaded streets and brightly coloured boats bobbing up and down in a harbour dominated by medieval towers, make it all too easy to overlook the desperation of La Rochelle's struggle to survive during the French Wars of Religion. The city was virtually torn down stone by stone by Cardinal Richelieu in the 17th century, after a long siege in which the protestant defenders were decimated by starvation and disease. Encouraged by England, who saw the commerical advantages of keeping La Rochelle as an independent port, the city had become a major stronghold of the Huguenots, where they could be safe from religious persecution in a predominantly catholic France. Until, that is, Richelieu persuaded Louis XIII to let loose his army, including his crack regiments of musketeers, an event recalled by Alexander Dumas in his epic account of the adventures of three of them.

LOCHES

A pleasant little town situated on the Indre River, south of Tours, with the ruins of its royal château rising high above. Richard the Lionheart stormed and took it in 1194, one of his more useless exploits even by his royal standards, for the château was soon back in French hands and turned into a prison. The inmates were confined to damp dungeons (well preserved for today's visitors) until the reign of Louis XI, who did nothing to improve their lot. Good King Louis hit on the idea of dangling cages from the dungeon roofs in which prisoners could only sit, or lie, so were condemned to permanent agonies. In June 1429, Joan of Arc visited the Logis Royal to persuade the indecisive Charles VII to go to Reims to be crowned and so re-establish the legitimacy of his rule. The mistress of Charles, Agnès Sorel, lived in the castle and gave lavish gifts to the local clergy in order to be buried on consecrated ground. She got her wish, but after Charles's death, the clerics protested to the new king, Louis XI, and asked him to remove Agnès's remains to the castle. By all means, said the king, provided her gifts go with her. Both stayed.

LOURDES

Nearly five million pilgrims visit Lourdes every year, including the old and the sick in the hope that dipping themselves in the healing waters will result in some rejuvenation or miraculous cure. No one should mock their faith, but Lourdes is not a sensitive haven where desperate people can be comforted with dignity. Rather, it is the ultimate in distasteful package tours, with religious trinkets purchased in their thousands by the pious with the same logic that went into the sale of medieval indulgences. If you can steel yourself against an over-cynical reaction, at least visit the shrine where, in 1858, Bernadette Soubirous believed she saw the Virgin Mary and had revealed to her the whereabouts of the healing spring. The pope was a notable visitor in 1983.

MARSEILLE

Gene Hackman's adventures in the sequel to *The French Connection* showed the unacceptable and dangerous face of Marseille, a city notorious for its violence, drug traffic, prostitution, and sections which are of supreme hazard to the tourist at night, such as the African quarter along the Rue Bernard du Bois. Marseille is, of course, not entirely like that: the boisterousness of its transient maritime population merely makes it vulnerable to such misconceptions. Visitors can absorb its effervescent atmosphere without going in fear of their lives and, what is more, eat some of the best food in France. Marseille is the home of bouillabaisse, a fish soup-cum-stew cooked in wine with saffron and hot peppers—never cheap, but a marvellous experience. If you need to walk it off, aim for the Parc du Pharo, which has a castle built by Napoleon III with commanding views of the city and its thriving port.

Air Marseille-Marignane Airport is 15½ miles (25km) north-west of the city.

Rail Gare St Charles.

Intricate old buildings cling to and crown Mont St Michel, a lump of rock rising sheer out of the sea off northern France

MONT ST MICHEL

If you shut your eyes as you climb the mount's steeply inclined streets, you can almost imagine you are back in the middle ages, a tired traveller running the gauntlet of pedlars and beggars before reaching the haven of the abbey. Unfortunately, you are actually being jostled by modern-day tourists in their thousands, and the clamour to buy comes from the souvenir shops. Still, the mount is so spectacular, a peninsula rising sheer out of the sea, that it is worth enduring the crowds and then taking the guided tour of the abbey with its intricate and narrow passageways, suggesting that in earlier times the abbot always had in mind resistance or flight. From the abbey gardens, on a clear day, there are superb views of Brittany to the west and Normandy to the east. Also, of the sea rushing pell-mell over the sands at the approach of high tide. Now, where did you leave your car?

NICE

None of the vulgar ostentation of Cannes here. Nice is an elegant, sophisticated resort, full of delightful architecture, meticulous parks and, around the Place Massena, a pedestrian area of open-air restaurants and late-night boutiques. But the prices are lower in the Vieille Ville, honeycombed with narrow intricate streets, full of African aromas. Sheltered by high hills behind its Bay of Angels, Nice has a gentle climate throughout the year, and a kind of relentless popularity as a tourist resort with a room occupancy rate that is every hotelier's dream. Its Promenade des Anglais, four miles (6.4km) long, is more English than the English (except, that is, when you forget where you are and buy a British newspaper at French prices), and the beach could have been acquired at Eastbourne, so familiar do its pebbles seem. But every possible effort is made to shield the tourist from the inconvenience of having to step on them: boards, rolled matting, lay-me-downs and put-you-ups, deck chairs and parasols—at a price. It is possible to spend a fortune on

The Promenade des Anglais and tree covered slopes of Nice

the beach, especially if you stay for lunch. But as seaside towns go, Nice is nice.

Air Nice-Côte d'Azur Airport is four miles (6.4km) west of the city.

Rail Avenue Thiers.

PARIS

Has a schizophrenic attitude towards motorists. A huge ring motorway, the Boulevard Périphérique, has been constructed closer to the centre than many other cities would find acceptable; a mass of underpasses maintain a speed along the boulevards more appropriate to a grand prix. But parking infringements result in cars being clamped or towed away: rescue is bureaucratic and expensive. Parking tickets pursue offenders relentlessly with escalating costs. The only sensible advice for the tourist is to find a secure park and leave the car there for the duration. This presents no hardship, as many of the real attractions of Paris are best seen on foot: the Champs Élysées, the banks of the Seine, the Latin Quarter, Montmartre. Here the view from the terrace of the Sacré-Coeur Basilica is perhaps the best in Paris. The Eiffel Tower is expensive, and has huge queues in the summer months. If you must climb, try the bell tower of Notre Dame, where

the guide delights in deafening visitors. For a real contrast, go below ground, to the catacombs or the sewers. The Paris underground, the Métro, offers easy access to every tourist sight, but the bus system is just as easy to use, with route maps posted on almost every stop and the same tickets valid for both. The Louvre Museum is of epic proportions and requires a week in itself: it is free, and saturated, on Sundays. It does, however, possess an extremely useful (and free) left luggage office, and offers cheap vintage wine—the overspill produce of great vineyards—in the cafeteria.

Air Most international flights are from Charles de Gaulle Airport, eighteen miles (29km) north; some domestic flights use Orly Sud, nine miles (14.5km) to the south.

Rail For the Channel, the Gare du Nord; for the south, the Gare de Lyon.

REIMS

He who holds Reims holds France. An exaggeration perhaps, but a coronation at Reims was always the true sign of legitimacy for the French monarchy, explaining why Joan of Arc was so determined to drag the timid Charles VII there and put a crown on his head, even if the English were but a longbow shot away. From 1173 until the Revolution almost every French king was crowned here,

following a tradition begun as early as the 5th century when Clovis, King of the Franks, was baptised on the site of the great gothic cathedral. Unlike many churches in France, the cathedral has not had a charmed life. In fact it is the third to stand in this position, and received extensive damage in two world wars. But its western façade, with a spectacular rose window of deep blue glass, is a masterpiece worth travelling many miles to see. So too, are the wine cellars of Reims, including those of Piper-Heidseck, so vast that they take you round on a tiny electric railway. The clergy of Reims were nothing if not connoisseurs of the art of storing good wine, including the local champagne, which they usually did in or beneath their own cool chapels; and the man who invented champagne was Dom Pérignon, a monk.

ST TROPEZ

Although the guide books and many visitors are coy about it, the plain truth is that every tourist hopes to see the alluring figure of Brigitte Bardot strolling about the waterfront. If the French film director Roger Vadim had not photographed the considerable charms of the young Miss Bardot lying provocatively on the beach, her place, and that of St Tropez, as a French institution might not have been secured. Even when she has disappeared into oblivion —and her durability is already the envy of many a middle-aged woman—Miss Bardot is still likely to be St Tropez's principal claim to fame. Ironically, she has always had a love-hate relationship with the place, as the walls of her villa on the secluded and exclusive nearby peninsula were never high enough to discourage peeping

Toms, Dicks and Henris. Perhaps she was closer than St Tropez's main beaches, four or five miles (some 7km) from the town, where bikinis are largely superfluous. The port itself, full of bright cafés and avaricious artists, is the one place where everyone is on public view out of choice, and it has an ostentatious charm and prices to match. But the more recent austerity of a socialist government has thinned out the number of gin palaces in the harbour, so St Tropez may need to look to its laurels as the resort of the rich.

STRASBOURG

For a city that disappeared into German hands from 1870 to 1918 and from 1940 until the final stages of the Second World War, it is a little ironic to think that the French national anthem, the *Marseillaise*, was created here by an army officer called Rouget de Lisle. The story goes that he was fired by thoughts of patriotism during a particularly drunken dinner party, and woke up in the morning oblivious of his creation of the night before to find the words written on a napkin. No matter. The *Marseillaise* was known as the *Battle Song of the Rhine Army*, until some soldiers from Marseille sung it as they stormed the Tuileries, giving the song its place in immortality. But even under German occupation Strasbourg has always been undeniably French, intensely patriotic, with unmistakably French architecture. Its most picturesque streets are bounded on all sides by a tributary of the Rhine, a waterfront panorama of timbered houses and bridges. In the cathedral, yet another Notre Dame, is a famous astronomical clock, with the twelve apostles moving across

Once an unspoilt fishing port, St Tropez has never looked back

its face. Goethe used to climb the tower, 466ft (142m) high, when he was a young student, in an attempt (fruitless, as it turned out) to cure himself of an acute fear of heights.

TOULOUSE

If you remove the students and the aerospace workers from the population, Toulouse might be half its size, so dominated is the city by its twin seats of learning. But as the political and cultural centre of the Languedoc region, Toulouse is a thriving base for tourism, and has its own fine range of historic buildings. The Basilica of St Sernin is a superb romanesque church, with sculptures well ahead of their time. St Sernin, incidentally, was actually St Saturnain, the first priest of Toulouse, who came to a particularly nasty end in 250 when he was tied to several bulls and dragged through the streets.

Air Toulouse-Blagnac Airport is four miles (6.4km) north-west of Toulouse.

TOURS

For all its pretty squares, Tours is a place from which to tour, as most of the famous châteaux of the Loire are within easy striking distance. As you will be spoilt for choice, unless you speak passable French and like plodding round on heavily organised guided walks, it may be best to concentrate on the two châteaux where you can do your own thing. Happily, they are also the two without which any visit to the Loire would be incomplete. One is Chenonceau, built in the 16th century and later given by Henry II to his famous mistress, Diane de Poitiers, who was 20 years older than her king but by all accounts ravishing and doubtless also ravished. Henry, alas, was killed in a tournament in 1559 by a lance-thrust from Montmorency (not a good way to advance one's career prospects), and his wife Catherine de Médici became Regent. She promptly removed the heartbroken Diane from her favourite château. Had she not, however, it is unlikely that its architectural masterpiece, the two-storey gallery on the bridge across the Cher, would ever have been built. The other château is Chambord, the largest on the Loire, also a favourite of Henry's with its staggering 440 rooms and a double-spiral staircase, designed so that one person could ascend and another descend simultaneously without seeing each other. Compared with such architectural feats, it was mere child's play to divert the River Cosson to improve its setting.

VERSAILLES

The most famous palace in the world, constructed thirteen miles (21km) south-west of Paris by the Sun King, Louis XIV, more as a capital than a residence. Le Vau, Mansart, Le Brun and Le Nôtre, architects, interior designer and landscape gardener respectively, created a colossus whose upkeep ruined both the exchequer and the cream of the nobility. As Louis insisted on them living at Versailles, away from their own centres of power and mischief, they were unwilling inmates of the most expensive (and probably the worst-run) hotel in history. Visiting Versailles requires real application, so consumed is it by tourists. Apart from the Galerie des Glaces, the hall of seventeen mirrors, of awe-inspiring magnificence, many visitors get more out of the gardens, which involved an earth-moving exercise more appropriate to building a dam than a palace. However, no stay in Paris would be complete without a visit to Versailles.

GERMANY

BERLIN

The Great Wall of China apart, no wall has ever been such a tourist attraction. First erected in 1961, and progressively strengthened as groups of daring, or desperate, East Germans found ways through, over or under it, the Berlin Wall meanders for almost 30 miles (50km) across the middle of the city, dividing its citizens politically and emotionally. Wooden platforms at Potsdamer Platz and opposite the Brandenburg Gate, which is cut off from the West, offer a view into the East; but there is no good reason why most tourists should not take a day trip. By rail, go through to Bahnhof Friedrichstrasse, the station for East Berlin, or enter by road at the much more famous Checkpoint Charlie. But, like Cinderella, you have to be back by midnight. Go to the East early in your visit, the more to appreciate the

contrast with the massive and exciting development in the West. The best place to see West Berlin is from the Europa Centre, arriving shortly before dusk and staying until after dark, when the lights of the Kurfürstendamm stretch almost as far as the eye can see. But the real surprise in this city under siege are its forests and rivers, which make up almost a third of the total area of West Berlin. A trip on the River Havel explains why Berliners have no real reason to feel claustrophobic, as there is countryside to spare.

Air Tegel Airport is five miles (8km) north-west.

COLOGNE

One of the great cities of the Rhine, all but flattened during the Second World War by aerial bombardment. Remarkably, its cathedral survived, a building of epic gothic proportions some 475ft (144m) long overall. The centre panel of the altar was

One of the few buildings to survive the wartime bombing of Cologne was its cathedral, seen here from the River Rhine

painted by Stefan Lochner, perhaps Cologne's most famous artist, and is a reminder of the city's reputation as a centre of medieval art. The great goldsmiths set up shop here, and produced for the cathedral the Reliquary of the Three Magi, truly a masterpiece. Climb the steps, more than 500 of them, to the top of the cathedral tower. The view is remarkable, and conveys better than any other the energy and creative wisdom that has been used to rebuild the city. But its lifeblood is still the Rhine, with its huge barges travelling almost from source to sea. Take a steamer south as far as Mainz to see the romantic Rhine of picture postcards, with the sloping vineyards and little castles, some ruined, some not, high above its banks.

Air Cologne shares an airport with Bonn, situated 11½ miles (18km) south-east of Cologne, at Wahn.

Rail Hauptbahnhof.

HEIDELBERG

A place for abandoning the car at the earliest opportunity, for only on foot can you

Both a centre of learning and home to carousing students, Heidelberg has a wonderful setting on the banks of the Neckar

appreciate its true beauty. Rising magnificently above the River Neckar are town, castle and forested hills, offering an enchanting setting. A cable railway takes you up to Königstuhl for the view in reverse of the Neckar valley, with the river flowing southwards between the Black Forest and the Swabian Mountains, two very popular tourist areas. Heidelberg Castle is a complete ruin, but it still has an undefinable charm, especially when used as a piece of free scenery for Heidelberg's many drama productions. In the town itself, walk over the old bridge, and pay a quick visit to the Kurpfälzisches Museum (if you can pronounce it, you'll find it) to look at an extraordinary wood carving, the Altar of the Twelve Apostles, dating back to the 16th century. Heidelberg University is the oldest in

Munich's main square, the Marienplatz, dominated by the town hall. Beyond is the cathedral

Germany, and still has some ancient privileges, such as separate drinking houses for the students, with specially cheap beer. They even used to have their own student jail, because being a student was a flourishing and permanent profession with the need for a source of income the only limitation on the length of your student career.

MUNICH

The capital of Bavaria, Munich has superb beer, hideous sausages, and a studied reluctance to acknowledge its contribution to the movement that brought Adolf Hitler to power. But the beer halls are now eminently respectable, though you are more or less obliged to drink a *Mass* (a litre) at a time. Be prepared for the hangover of your life if you arrive during the Oktoberfest, a kind of fortnight's drinking party from late September to early October. Otherwise you may stay sober enough to appreciate the Alte Pinakothek, with more old masters than a dozen public schools, and the Deutsches Museum, a science museum so large that you begin to suspect they are adding to the technology exhibits while you are taking in the previous room. Technology helps to keep the traffic flowing in Stachus, the main square, where the policeman on point duty sits in front of a remote television screen, pushing buttons, instead of standing on a box.

Air The airport is at Riem, six miles (9.6km) east.

Rail The main railway station is in Bahnhofplatz.

GIBRALTAR

The re-opening of the frontier with Spain is a vital ingredient in Gibraltar's future development, whatever perils it may hold in terms of political independence. Because, without direct access to Spain, Gibraltar in tourist terms has seemed rather like a stranded whale. With access to the Spanish resorts possible only by an elaborate triangular journey across to Tangier in North Africa, Gibraltar has proved a rather claustrophobic destination with pocket-handkerchief beaches and a single shopping street that saw better times during the heyday of the cruise ship. It is as though the Devon village of Clovelly had suddenly taken on the role of an outpost of the British Empire. The military base is obtrusive and the colony of barbary apes could well move on one day —but until then keep a tight hold on your handbag.

Air North Front Airport is 1½ miles (2.4km) north of the centre.

GREECE

ATHENS

Pollution and visitors are doing more to destroy the 2,400-year-old buildings on the Acropolis than ancient battles ever did. It seems only a matter of time before the monuments and the sacred

A panorama of Athens' Acropolis, crowned by the Parthenon

rock itself will succumb or finally be cordoned off from the plague of tourists that infest it from sunrise to sunset. Well, not quite. The first coachloads do not arrive until after 9am, so it is still possible for the early visitor to appreciate the true marvels on this flat-topped hill—its Parthenon, the Erechteion with its legendary Porch of Maidens or Caryatids, and the Temple of the Wingless Victory. Museums are more a matter of taste. If you have time or inclination for only one, it must be the National Archaeological Museum. However, artefacts removed from their natural habitat sometimes lack the same

appeal, and to gain a real idea of life in ancient Athens, visit the Agora, the old city market place, and find the Stoa of Attalos, reconstructed as it was 2,000 years ago. However, avoid the Plaka, a hill once tastefully adorned with true Greek restaurants, but now a hideous tourist trap. Modern Athens, sprawling below the old city, has to be seen to be believed—but only briefly. In summer it is hot, frenetic, noisy, with taxi drivers whose sense of direction mysteriously deserts them when they see a promising tourist.

Air Hellinikon Airport is six miles (9.6km) south of the city. Olympic Airways has its own terminal (West) and a coach service from its city offices. Other flights leave from East Terminal, which has connections by coach from Syntagma bus station.

Rail Larissa Station.

CORFU

Just across the straits from Albania, and perhaps offering a permanent reminder to the Albanian peasants of the true decadence of western European civilisation, Corfu is an island paradise long deserted by the angels. Tourism on a massive scale is gradually destroying most signs of typical Greek life, leaving in its place a synthetic international playground with hotels and rented villas multiplying year by year. The beaches are superb, the bathing safe, and nightlife breathless; but there is scarcely a hint of the old Graeco-Venetian culture, dating from when Corfu lay on the great trade routes to the south. Be warned, too, that hire cars, scooters and bicycles are not maintained in a manner calculated to increase their longevity. As this has implications for your state of health, it must also be said that medical services in Corfu have not increased and improved in proportion to the growth in tourism.

Air Corfu-Kerkyra Airport is two miles (3.2km) south-west of Corfu town.

CRETE

An archaeologist's dream, bristling with sites, some more than 4,000 years old and dating beyond the time of King Minos and the worship of the sacred bulls, perhaps even to the legend of Theseus and the minotaur. Somehow Greek mythology takes on a fresh hint of plausibility in this land of rugged mountains and blazing summer sunshine. Outstanding amidst all this exceptional scenery is the Gorge of Samaria, a rocky path, 12 miles (19.5km) in length, that winds its way between cliffs and waterfalls. There are two archaeological sites of epic significance, the Minoan Palace at Phaestos, and Knossos, excavated and partly reconstructed to suggest what the Minoan civilisation may have been like at its peak. It seems they had hot and cold running water and flushing toilets, which is more than can be said for every guest house on the island today. If you are

to avoid being trapped on the indifferent beaches, a car is essential and, if you hire cheaply, so is a good insurance policy. Regard inland roads marked on maps with scepticism: some of them are dodgy even for donkeys.

Air Iráklion Airport is three miles (4.8km) east of the city.

RHODES

The durability of history has a special emphasis in the medieval city of the Knights of St John, whose towering citadel still survives intact, surrounded by walls that cleverly retain heat in winter and repel it in summer. The Turks besieged Rhodes, the last Christian outpost in the eastern Mediterranean, from 1480 to 1481, but the Knights Hospitallers defended it so resolutely that the Sultan, Mehmet II, died before they could take the fortress, and the Turks sailed away. It was not until 1522 that the Turks finally took Rhodes, and then it was less to rid themselves of the Knights than of the pirates using Rhodes as a base to raid the trade troutes. But the island's recorded history stretches back to ancient times. At Lindos, along the coast, stands the ruins of a fine acropolis, with its Temple of Athena overlooking the Aegean. Alas, Lindos, once a delightful village set on the side of a beautiful bay, is typical of how the island has come close to saturation point in tourism, with its rows of cafés offering bacon and egg all day. If you are seeking solitude, go elsewhere.

Air Rhodes Airport is ten miles (16km) south-west of Rhodes town.

Rhodes has many coves as delightful as, but more secluded than, Lindos Bay, which now attracts many visitors

HUNGARY

BUDAPEST

An Englishman, Adam Clark, built the chain bridge across the Danube that linked Buda with Pest 150 years ago. The two halves of the city have a distinct style. Buda, to the west, rises above the river in sharp gradients to a series of hills; Pest, to the east, is largely flat, the commercial centre of the city. Clark's bridge, the Széchenyi Lánchid, was one of many attacked during the great siege of 1944, when the Russians and the Germans slugged it out street by street for possession of the city. Every bridge was destroyed, and 33,000 buildings were reduced to rubble. Soviet troops returned in 1956 to repeat much of the exercise. However, Budapest seems to rise above its political constraints. Margaret Island, shaped like a boat, has many outdoor activities; the zoo is outstanding; the restaurants

Dublin's River Liffey and the handsome Custom House

have a fine ambience and tasty food, providing you like goulash with goulash. On the Pest side of the Danube is the Corso, an avenue of lovely terraces and cafés with jolly waiters. For a novel experience, ride the Budapest Pioneer Railway. Don't be surprised if the driver is sixteen and the ticket collector six or seven.

Air Ferihegy Airport is ten miles (16km) south-east.

Budapest's rebuilt Buda Castle, which looks eastwards across the Danube to the half of the city known as Pest

IRISH REPUBLIC

DUBLIN

Now that the pound and the punt have gone their separate ways, the price of a pint of Guinness is enough to encourage more visitors with rather too much local knowledge to descend on the Guinness Brewery and sample the stout for free. But it is not the same as drinking it in a traditional Dublin pub, where opening and closing hours seem to have a delightful Irish flexibility, and you are just as likely to be slapped across the back or bought a drink by a woman—and one with more designs on your company than your body. A Dubliner will tell you that everything worth seeing can be visited on foot before first orders, that Dublin Castle, the old Parliament House turned into a bank on College Green, Leinster House, the Mansion House, the Customs House and the Royal Exchange, require only a brisk walk. A glance or two at the River Liffey, rolling beneath Dublin's eleven bridges, and at the Wicklow Mountains on the horizon, and you are ready to get down to some serious drinking. Be warned: tourists have been poured on to the plane at the end of a week's stay, in which their last clear recollection was pushing open the door of the public bar at O'Donoghue's or Davy Byrne's.

Air Dublin Airport is 6½ miles (10.5km) north.

ITALY

CAPRI

The island of dreams is actually closer to a nightmare at the height of the season, when tourism reaches saturation point. Avoid, at all costs, a day trip in this period, in cattle-truck conditions with just enough time to stop at the places and beaches that everyone else is visiting. When the day trippers go home, Capri takes on a different atmosphere: wonderful evening sunsets, with the sun and later the moon reflected in a blue crystal sea. The island has always been favoured by the aquatic enthusiast because of its sub-tropical underwater vegetation and its remarkable collection of almost magical

grottoes amidst rocks accessible only from the sea. To see the Blue Grotto, hire a small boat with an outboard motor, and go very early in the morning before the tourist masses arrive and when, incidentally, the light is best. Capri's roads are not for the nervous. The little buses take hairpin bends to the top of the island at alarming speeds, passing on corners with nothing to spare.

FLORENCE

Money-lending was a source of power for medieval Florence, and one of their first recorded customers was wicked King John, who needed a mercenary army to secure his return to England on the death of Richard the Lionheart in 1199. In 1262 the Florentine bankers issued the first letters of exchange, a kind of bank draft soon accepted throughout Europe, which gave an enormous stimulus to trade. Over the next four centuries, art, architecture and sculpture flourished in the city, which saw the creative genius of Leonardo da Vinci and Michelangelo. The

Dramatic coastal crags on the Isle of Capri

clothmakers' guild paid for the cathedral, completed in the 15th century; it has a prodigious dome by Brunelleschi that took fourteen years to build and is almost as high as St Paul's. The Piazza della Signoria, with the Palazzo Vecchio to its rear, is like an open-air museum of sculpture, it has so many statues. But when it comes to museums, the Uffizi is among the best in the world. It contains the Botticelli Room, with some remarkable works: the Birth of Venus, Spring and Madonnas; and the richly ornate Tribune, which displays a matchless piece of Greek sculpture, the Medici Venus. Florence is a city with a work of art on every corner; absorb its atmosphere and marvel at the creative genius collected here. Walk along the banks of the Arno—a trickle in summer but a turbulent current in winter. And cross it, as the majestic artists of history must have crossed it, by the Ponte Vecchio, where gold and jewellery have traditionally been sold since the 16th century.

Air Florence has no international airport; the nearest is Galileo, 53 miles (85.3km) away and one mile (1.6km) south-west of Pisa.

MILAN

The economic centre of Italy, Milan nevertheless offers a life of high culture and no small sophistication. The Milanese can be seen in their finery most evenings at the Galleria off the Corso Vittorio Emanuele, where the men disappear behind their copy of the *Corriere della Sera*, Milan's famous evening paper, and the women study the fashions in the nearby luxury shops. If that sounds chauvinistic, then it is: the emancipation of women has not really reached Milan, and if it comes to Italy at all, this city will set a trend. Milan's cultural centre is La Scala, home of a less male-dominated spectacle, and simply the most famous opera house in the world. Opened in 1779 on the site of the church of Santa Maria della Scala, the 2,800-seat theatre has perfect acoustics. If you cannot get in to a performance at La Scala, console yourself with a walk on the roof of the cathedral, and see its belfries, pinnacles, and, incredibly, over 4,000 white marble statues, which cast strange overlapping shadows in the setting sun.

Air Enrico Forlanini Airport, known as Linate, is 4½ miles (7.2km) east. Malpensa, used for many long-haul flights, is much further out—28 miles (45km) to the north-west.

NAPLES

At the entrance to the city is a terrifying road tunnel, down which budding grand prix drivers hurtle at unimaginable speeds, all lights and blaring klaxons. If you are not to be intimidated during your stay, this is where you must hold your own, if you come by car. It is well to remember, however, that Italian drivers become Japanese kamikaze if passed: slaloming between the lamp-posts to regain pole position is not uncommon. See Naples and die. Seriously, though, the views of the bay, with a slumbering or grumbling Vesuvius as the backcloth, are truly magnificent; and in the narrow streets, the slums, full of one-room television suppers, offer a glimpse of Neapolitan life—downtrodden, but never downhearted. The annual income of many of the inhabitants could be swallowed up in a night at the smart restaurants and hotels by the harbour, where the American Mafia families take their holidays, all with

smart-suited bodyguards by the swimming pool.

Air Capodichino Airport is four miles (6.4km) north.

PALERMO

The capital of Sicily, occasionally too hot, rarely too cold, with palaces and grand villas, surrounded by elegant gardens. The centre of the city is Quattro Canti, meaning four corners, where tradesmen and idle pedestrians crowd into picturesque alleys. Taste the true Sicilian cassata, which consists of cake, candied fruit and liqueur-flavoured icecream. But do not try too many if you intend to see the Capuchin Catacombs, in which dry air has preserved no fewer than 8,000 corpses. Stay off the subject of the Mafia if you have an aversion to being added to the list.

Air Palermo Airport is three miles (4.8km) south-west.

Rail Stazione Centrale.

An intricate mosaic at La Zisa, Palermo

PERUGIA

Protected by its ramparts, Perugia dominates the valley of the Tiber. In 1503, the townsfolk became so disenchanted by their tyrannical rulers that they helped Cesare Borgia to take over, but found him even worse. Cesare Borgia apart, Perugia's most famous son was Pietro Vannucci, called Perugino, a master painter and the teacher of Raphael. In the Collegio del Cambio are frescoes painted by the master and his even more famous pupil. They show the humanist spirit of the age, the virtues of prudence, justice, strength and temperance. What the Borgias thought of them is not recorded.

PISA

Bonnano Pisano is the man who made Pisa famous, as the architect of the Torre Pendente. Pisano put it about that he made the tower lean deliberately: more plausibly, he was as surprised as anyone when it began to lean, the

result of a defect in its foundations or settling in its subsoil. The upper part is vertical, which is just as well because, had it not been, the whole edifice would have fallen over years ago. Realising its vital part in the prosperity of the town, Pisa's authorities have tried various ways of slowing down, if not actually stopping, any further movement. The climb upwards becomes an unnerving experience around the second spiral of the staircase: you feel constantly that you are on the point of falling. The view from the top of the tower's 294 steps is attractive, but there is nothing to touch the combined sight of the baptistery, cathedral and leaning tower from the west side of the square—all marble and frescoes of alternating colours.

Air Galileo Airport is very close, only one mile (1.6km) south-west.

POMPEII

The disastrous volcanic eruption that struck Pompeii in AD79 preserved in the ashes not only buildings but a way of life: we know more about Pompeii than any other Roman city. Pompeii was an up-market resort, frequented by the emperors. It was also a place where life was lived to the full—a not altogether long life, if the surgical instruments found in the House of the Surgeon are any indication. Among the hideous collection are pliers for pulling out teeth (he was a dentist as well as a doctor), probes, catheters and gynaecological forceps that would make any modern mother-to-be faint clean away. Yet it is the graffiti discovered on the walls that underline how much the Pompeians wrote and thought about sex, with explicit illustrations that would be thought in decided

bad taste even in these enlightened times. Some are kept locked in cupboards on the site, occasionally opened for all-male tour parties by the more mischievous guides hoping for a tip.

RAVENNA

When in 402, Honorius abandoned Rome to the Barbarians and made Ravenna capital of the dwindling Roman Empire, he touched off a movement that was to leave the city with the richest evidence of early Christian art. For although the town, built on piles, was more or less secure from invasion and still had the use of Classis to the south which could harbour 250 ships, the days of the empire were numbered. The western empire collapsed, Ravenna endured the Ostrogoths and was then reconquered by the Byzantine emperors, encouraging Christianity in their wake. The new religion was dazzlingly expressed in mosaic, in particular in five surviving examples, in the baptistery of the cathedral, the Galla Placidia Mausoleum, the Baptistery of the Arians, and the churches of Saint Apollinare Nuovo and San Vitale. The mosaics are

Roman remains are found everywhere in Italy—this one is in Pozzuoli, near Naples

constructed from small cubes called tesserae, laid irregularly to catch the light. But that gives no hint of the skill employed in creating the range of colours, and of choosing precisely the right decoration for the subject: true genius.

ROME

Richer in masterpieces than any other city, Rome is infinitely capable of surprise. Turn a corner, and some unforgettable statue or building leaps out at you, as though it had been put there only yesterday. With its narrow streets, mercifully shading the summer sun, and its avenues of cypress trees, Rome has an unforgettable charm marred only by the locust-like street traders, relentlessly in pursuit of their tourist prey. The Roman Forum, the Imperial Forum and the Palatine Hill are astonishing in their grandeur, but it is the Colosseum that remains the magnet it must have been in ancient times. Once it could seat 50,000 spectators, their 50,000 thumbs held up or down to indicate life or death in the arena. Here Christians fought with gladiators, or with lions, or all with each other; here the entire arena was flooded for naval battles, bigger in some instances than the events they were supposed to recreate. In

the Colosseum, the splendour and savagery of ancient Rome came spectacularly together.

Air Leonardo da Vinci (Fiumicino) Airport is 20 miles (32km) south-west of Rome. Some charter flights use Ciampino, 7½ miles (12km) south-east of the city.

Rome's Colosseum—one of the best-known landmarks

SAN REMO

The Italian flower market is centred here, sending produce to every part of Italy and beyond. The actual flower market is a scene of demonic activity between October and June, though you have to get up very early to see it. That, in San Remo, may be difficult; its luxurious hotels and restaurants have a tradition of nightlife that goes into the small hours. Best to sleep it off under a sunshade on the beach, another one of the private retreats where your every need is catered for. With its casino, its almost guaranteed summer sunshine and its series of festivals, San Remo is the jewel of the Italian riviera; and

compared to Cannes quite cheap at the price.

SIENA

A city with two distinct advantages for the discriminating tourist. First, by geographical accident, it is just too far off the beaten track to be included in frenetic coach tours. Second, it makes few, if any, concessions to visitors—it is aware of them but certainly not obsessed with their presence. This is because in Siena a strong family tradition has survived—manifested, for example, every year in the furious, and

dangerous, horse race round the magnificent Piazza del Campo, for the *palio*, a standard inscribed with the coat of arms of the city. The costumes and the rivalry are the same as they have been for centuries, and so are the rules. That was why, in 1983, a riderless horse won the *palio* despite throwing his jockey during the last circuit. The rules that permit this go back to the era when over-zealous followers were tempted to dislodge the leading rider with a crossbow bolt if he looked certain to win.

VENICE

You can tell a Venetian because he has a pale face and lisps slightly—at least, that is what it says in the guidebook. It may well be a preposterous generalisation but one, nevertheless, impossible to expose, because there are no Venetians in Venice, only tourists. Well, not quite. However, the tourist season in Venice must be one of the longest anywhere in Europe and, in hot weather, one of the most exasperating. The key to appreciating Venice painlessly is not to stay there at all, nor, for that matter, to go on an excursion from some other resort. The only solution

Venice's Regatta is a spectacular event

is to stay on the Venice Lido, an island opposite the city, with magnificent beaches. Among the hotels is the Grand Hotel des Bains, where Dirk Bogarde played out one of his more famous roles as the ageing Englishman besotted by a young Italian boy in Visconti's *Death in Venice*. You can still stay on the Lido in style, and take a free launch, thoughtfully provided by the hotel at regular intervals, for the ten-minute ride back to Venice, ready to do battle with the corpulent pigeons in St Mark's Square and the grasping gondoliers.

Air Marco Polo (Tessèra) Airport is eight miles (12.8km) by road, less than half that by water, north-east of Venice.

Rail Stazione Santa Lucia.

Road Cars are not permitted in Venice, but you can take them by ferry to the Lido.

VERONA

The old town, with its splendid squares linked by arcaded staircases and sinister alleys, was the scene of many an affray when the young men of Verona fought for family honour or simply for fun. With pope and emperor vying for Verona's allegiance, feuds took on a more enduring and sinister connotation, including the quarrel seized upon by Shakespeare for his *Romeo and Juliet*. Romeo was a leading light of the Montecchi, or Montagues, Juliet belonged to the Capuleti, or Capulets, and their affair may well have taken place around 1302. But there is more of a mystery about the character of Mercutio, who had so threatened to steal the show that Shakespeare was obliged to write in his premature death.

LUXEMBOURG

The Grand Duchy exists only because the great powers of Europe were determined that no one among them should possess her. But there were times when the balance of power was not enough to protect her interests, which is why the city has a formidable fortress. As the risk of siege works increased, Luxembourg responded by extending her defences. Finally they consisted of 53 forts connected by sixteen miles (25.7km) of tunnels, with gun placings and man traps carved out of solid rock. Although you can walk along parts of the ramparts, and see some magnificent views across the valley, to appreciate what the citadel was like in its heyday look at the remarkable model on display in the National Museum. The fortress apart, Luxembourg still has that slightly Ruritanian air of a little world out of its time. Unfortunately the lower tariffs on many of its goods (especially petrol) have been counterbalanced by a rise in prices, due in the main to the Duchy's increasing role in the European Economic Community.

Air Findel Airport is four miles (6.4km) east of Luxembourg.

Rail The main station is in the Place de la Gare.

MALTA

If the Knights of St John who successfully defended Valetta against the Turks in the Great Siege were suddenly to be reincarnated, they would still feel at home in its narrow streets, dominated by fortifications scarcely modified since the 16th century. Malta has never been known for sudden changes: it has an impression of faded gentility that is a reminder of its colonial past. British holidaymakers find a comfortable security in its efforts to cater for visitors from the UK, down to English tinned food in the shops. However, it has few sandy beaches and its two main resorts, Sliema and St Paul's

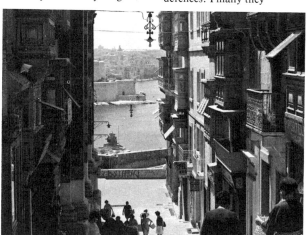

The stepped streets of Valetta, Malta, lead down to its harbour

Bay, lack any real charm. The neighbouring island of Gozo has much more appeal, but tends to be extremely crowded in the summer months. Although the authorities are making strenuous efforts to improve the position, Malta still suffers from a shortage of water, which in some parts of the island is reduced to a trickle for several hours each day.

Air Luqa Airport is five miles (8km) south-east of Valetta.

MONACO

MONTE CARLO

Principality and port, whose real independence from France is limited to an exemption from national service for the Monégasques. There are no passport checks or Customs posts at the frontier, but the French turn a not altogether altruistic blind eye to international company registrations in the principality with consequential tax advantages, provided, of course, the companies are not evading tax in France. Rents are one major source of

Risk your all in Monte Carlo's elaborate casino

revenue for Monaco; the other is the casino in Monte Carlo. Built in 1878 by Charles Garnier after the style of the Paris Opera House, its rococo art is over the top in every sense, with crystal chandeliers and gilt ceilings. But although a gesture is made at the entrance to allow entry only to people reasonably dressed, the public gaming rooms are a sad disappointment, full of scruffy slot-machine addicts losing franc pieces with monotonous regularity. For a small fee, however, you can enter the Salons Privés where the real gambling takes place after 3pm. The one other significant time on the Monte Carlo clock is 11.55am, when the changing of the guard takes place outside the palace. It is a shambles of epic proportions, not to be missed.

NETHERLANDS

AMSTERDAM

The dam of Amsterdam was created on the Amstel River back in 1275 but it was not until the 17th century that the city took on the shape that the centre has today, a semicircle threaded through with a network of canals and containing some 90 small

islands held together by hundreds of quaintly constructed bridges. The Dutch are enthusiastic cyclists, and Amsterdam has its full share. Bikes are easily hired, and provide an ideal way of absorbing the magical atmosphere of this colourful city, with its wonderful mixture of architecture old and new. The Rijksmuseum gallery has probably the world's largest collection of works by Rembrandt, including *The Night Watch*. Vincent Van Gogh has his own museum, with another remarkable collection of his paintings and letters. A reminder of more recent Dutch history is to be found in the Anne Frank House where the Frank family hid from the Nazis, and Anne Frank wrote the diary that captured the sympathy and imagination of the civilised world.

Air Schiphol Airport, famous for its low duty-free prices, nine miles (15km) south-west. The airport can be reached by rail from Amsterdam-Zuid Station in the south of the city, from where there are easy connections to the centre by tram.

Rail Central Station.

NORWAY

OSLO

There cannot be many cities that have undergone both a change of name and a change of position, but Oslo has that distinction. Founded by the Viking kings in the 11th century, it was burnt to the ground in the 17th, and recreated by King Christian IV in a less vulnerable spot under the walls and guns of the fortress of Akershus. Having gone to all this trouble, the

bridge, a veritable colossus, and a towering statue of Christ in Majesty. But west of the city, a couple of stops on the local commuters' railway, is the Belem Tower that once controlled the Tagus Narrows and, nearby, the Monument to the Discoveries, a massive tribute to Henry the Navigator, with spectacular carvings. But the real Lisbon is indoors: gloomy cafés, crowded with men doing business, or doing nothing; and, in the evening, narrow, perspiring restaurants, waiting for the singer of the *fado*, the sad song that captures the indecisive melancholy of the Portuguese mood.

Air Portela da Sacavém airport is 4½ miles (7.2km) north of the city.

Rail Santa Apolonia Station.

SPAIN

BARCELONA

The second city of Spain, but ahead of the rest in prosperity, Barcelona has a quality of individualism rare for a place of its size. Pressure groups, splinter groups and radical movements flourish here as an integral part of the city's culture. To acquire a taste of Barcelona's dynamism, meander down the Ramblas, a series of five short streets that together form a grand boulevard. Expensive shops, cheap shops, cafés, restaurants and street tradesmen offering everything from birds to flowers will slow down your progress, but the lifeblood of Catalan society will soon be flowing through your veins. Just two blocks away is a chapter of medieval Spain, the Barrio Gotico, a collection of gothic buildings with cool courtyards and outside staircases, an antidote to the

king also decided on some permanent recognition for his efforts, renaming the city Christiania, a name it kept for precisely 300 years. Renamed Oslo in 1924, the city has few traces of its past, although the Akershus fortress is still intact. A trip on the Oslo Fjord, especially in winter, offers marvellous scenery, but the real sights not to be missed are all in museums. Three of the great Viking ships, including the Oseberg, complete with its unique collection of Viking knick-knacks, stir the senses in recalling the bloodthirsty era of raids on the English coast. Then there is the more peaceful but no less famous item of transport in the Kon-Tiki Museum—the raft on which Thor Heyerdahl sailed some 5,000 miles (8000km) across the Pacific in 1947, from Peru to Polynesia, proving that balsawood is best.

The Oseberg ship, most famous of the vessels and artefacts in the museum on Oslo Fjord

PORTUGAL

LISBON

Another city dominated by its castle, in this case St George's, with an Arabic palace dating back from the days when the Moors held sway in southern Europe. They built the oldest part of the city below the castle, the Alfama, with cobbled streets, twisting alleys and steep steps. The castle, with its cool gardens, is a marvellous refuge in the heat of the day and the view from the terrace is truly magnificent. Across the wide expanse of the River Tagus is the April 25th suspension savage summer sun. The cathedral, one of the great buildings of Spain, took six centuries to complete, allowing for three centuries of total inactivity. The Picasso Museum, a reminder that the painter spent most of his formative years in the city, has the finest collection of his work anywhere in Spain. Less obvious, but delightful nonetheless, is the Museum of Federico Mares, an incredible collection of paraphernalia that defies description. Find it near the cathedral, and then look behind it for the Plaza del Rey, the courtyard of a palace belonging to the Counts of Barcelona, containing the room where the joint rulers of Spain, Ferdinand and Isabella, welcomed Christopher Columbus on his return from what he thought was the East but was, in fact, the New World.

Air Muntadas Airport, nine miles (14.5km) south-west, and linked by train to the main station.

Rail Main station is Estacion de Francia.

BENIDORM

A quiet fishing village on the Costa Blanca before the concept of the package tour in the fifties, Benidorm has become the most famous, or infamous, of the Spanish seaside resorts. Many of its hotels are concrete monstrosities, constructed in haste to meet a huge demand for accommodation that has passed the staggering total of 17,000 bedrooms. As a consequence, the downtown part of Benidorm is absurdly cosmopolitan, with fish and chip suppers and pints of English beer for the British, and similar delights from home for the Swedes and the Germans. But the nightlife is

dynamic, with some of the best discos in Europe, and the beach has soft yellow sand— imported by the ton from Morocco. Not the place for a quiet holiday, and a knowledge of Spanish is a positive disadvantage.

Air The nearest international airport is Alicante, 35 miles (56.3km) south-west.

BURGOS

In the days before skyscrapers, the grey stone colossus which is Burgos Cathedral must have been hugely intimidating to the peasants of medieval Spain, when a tall building was anything with one storey on top of another. Even today the collection of spires and pinnacles, and the huge chapels off the main cathedral nave, some of them bigger than English cathedrals in themselves, are a sombre and awe-inspiring sight. No wonder the people believed implicitly in the *Cristo de Burgos*, an image of Christ in which the face is made of stretched buffalo skin, with real human hair and nails added for horrifying realism. More cheerful is the statue of El Cid (born Rodrigo Dias in the nearby village of Vivar) on horseback. With cloak, sword and beard all flying fury, he pursues the Moors to the end of time.

CORDOBA

The commercial capital of Roman Spain, Cordoba has an old quarter of winding alleys and white houses with tiny courtyards that probably heard the tramp of Roman centurions on patrol. But the building that makes Cordoba an irresistible attraction is the Mezquita, a mosque dating back to the 8th century, which

has become a cathedral. Supported by some 850 coloured columns, the dome is the most spectacular ever constructed by the Moors, so huge that when the Christians came, they contented themselves with building a Christian sanctuary under its centre. The sense of mystical purpose is uncanny and cannot be entirely explained away by the perpetually cool interior, whose temperatures come as such a sharp contrast to the relentless sun.

EL ESCORIAL

Built by Philip II to commemorate a victory over the French, El Escorial lies 30 miles (48km) north-west of Madrid, in the forbidding range of mountains of the Sierra de Guadarrama. For a man capable of moving fleets and armies around half the known world, Philip had remarkably simple tastes. When he retired to Escorial he lived virtually the life of a monk, with a chair to support his gout-ridden leg as almost his only luxury. His deathbed was suspended at a curious angle so he could gaze down into the church where a mass was being said constantly for his soul, Philip having learned the hard way, over the Armada, that no one else was to be trusted to carry out his instructions to the full. The real challenge at El Escorial is to beat the system whereby you have to join huge parties on conducted tours. Even if you do not have to get there by bus or train, buy a train timetable, for it enables you to see when the worst of the crowds will arrive. Then leave the royal apartments, most of them far more sumptuous than Philip would have permitted himself, until last. Start with the library, a priceless collection that includes

St Teresa's personal diary. Then, alongside the sacristy, descend a staircase to the Panteon de los Reyes, tombs of black and brown marble containing most of the monarchs of Spain. For those who like the less savoury details, just above the entrance is the Pudreria, where the bodies were left to rot for ten years before their skeletons were moved to their final resting places.

Monastery of San Lorenzo de el Escorial, Madrid

marshals of Napoleon and put out the fuses already burning their way to destruction. The Alhambra's great era came to an end in 1492 when the combined forces of Aragon and Castile, brought together by Ferdinand and Isabella, took the castle after a long winter siege. The last Moorish King, Boabdil, rode away in tears until he was berated by his mother: 'Do not weep like a woman,' she said, 'for what you could not defend like a man.'

3,000 pictures are displayed, including the great works of Goya and Velasquez. But for the Madrid of the present, go on a bar crawl around the Puerta del Sol. Wine or sherry is extremely cheap, and at each bar you can sample a different *tapas*, a kind of starter without the main course, although the days when you got them without asking, and for nothing, have sadly disappeared.

Air Madrid-Barajas Airport is 7½ miles (12km) east of Madrid.

Rail Chamartin Station (near Avenida del Generalisimo) for Barcelona or Paris; Atocha Station (south of the Prado) for Lisbon or the south.

GRANADA

The Alhambra or Red Castle, on its hill, is one of the wonders of the world. The Moorish King, Ibn Ahmar, moved the River Darro several miles to give the Alhambra its beauty and serenity, safely inside the huge walls and towers. Around the Generalife, the summer palace of the Sultans, is a richly imaginative sequence of patios and walks. The Royal Palace itself, the Casa Real, is as flimsy as the Alhambra is strong, built of light wood and brick with the clear intention that each succeeding ruler would give it his own personal touch and pull down much that went before. But someone evidently appreciated the wonderful use of light and space—perhaps even the French soldier who defied the

MADRID

Devotees of high-rise concrete could have spasms of ecstasy in the suburbs of the Spanish capital, as every superfluous concrete mixer in Britain must have been sold off here. Fortunately, the centre of Madrid is quite different, especially its magnificent squares, the Puerta del Sol and the Plaza Mayor, surrounded by stylish 17th-century houses. Right in the centre is the Parque del Retiro, where formality and informality blend delightfully together. On Sunday morning it is a busker's paradise, with puppet shows for the children—though nothing as violent as Mr Punch. A couple of blocks away is the Prado Museum, one of the oldest art collections in the world, and one of the best. More than

MAJORCA

This island is one of the most popular holiday destinations for the British tourist. The price you pay for that is a surfeit of fellow Brits, a kind of middle ground in cooking that may be European but is certainly not Spanish, and packed pleasure beaches on which, on a cloudy day (and there are quite a few), if you half close your eyes, you could be back at Blackpool or Cleethorpes. The hotels are threatening to turn some parts of the coast into a kind of Costa Concrete, but out of high season—and especially if you have a car—an entirely different Majorca emerges. Find the hillside village of Deya with its delightful gardens, and visit the much smaller and more sophisticated resorts of Puerto de Pollensa and Cala de San Vicente which still have real Spanish restaurants. But the pick of the island is the Formentor Peninsula, with a string of luxury villas that leave the ugly world of the cheap package tour far behind.

Air Son San Juan Airport is 7 miles (11km) south-east of Palma.

PAMPLONA

The capital of Navarre, once an independent kingdom, and nestling in the foothills of the Pyrenees. Find the Plaza de Castillo, a magnificent tree-lined square with bustling cafés as almost everything worth seeing is but a few minutes' walk away. The massive fortress, behind the cathedral, with its original walls still intact, reflects the time when Pamplona was in the front line for attacks from the north. Pamplona is transformed from a city of passing interest into a compulsive tourist attraction during the second week in July, when the Festival of San Fermin includes the Encierro, the running of the bulls. At

Flamboyant architecture thrown into sharp relief by sunshine in Pamplona

eight each morning the bulls are released from a pen near the Plaza San Domingo to run to the bullring, escorted by the more reckless local inhabitants and a few foolhardy tourists. As the bulls are fast, heavy, and have extremely sharp horns, the wonder is that not more people are killed or severely injured. Those who survive unscathed say it is a marvellously exhilarating experience. The best, and safest, place to watch is in the Plaza San Domingo, but you would need to be in position extremely early—perhaps at 6am. Hotels are invariably booked up many months in advance and the town is packed with sightseers and pickpockets.

SALAMANCA

Whether you stop for five minutes or to while away the hours, the Plaza Mayor or Great Square of Salamanca cannot fail to please as it is the finest in all Spain. The square

is surrounded by one continuous four-storey building of mellowed sandstone, decked with black iron balconies from where the well-off survey the scene below. And what a scene it is: lively cafés under arcaded walks, where the town peacocks parade in front of eligible young men sipping cold sherry sheltered from the sun. As most of Salamanca seem to pass through the square every day of their lives, if you fail to make an appearance, it will be concluded that you are dead, or drunk . . . or have found something extremely pleasant to do.

SAN SEBASTIAN

Some of Spain's most fashionable families spend the summer here, and at weekends you are more likely to find your Consul in San Sebastian-Donastia than in Madrid—which is probably why part of the town is known colloquially as La Diplomatica. But San Sebastian is far from being totally up-market. It is a true family resort, only half an hour from France on the Atlantic coast, with chilly waters to spoil the pleasantly hot months of July and August. The waterfront restaurants are very popular, with prices to match; but in the tight little streets of the old town just behind, you can nibble away on delicious *tapas* for next to nothing and drink your fill.

Air The airport is thirteen miles (21km) east of the city.

SEVILLE

A city of marvellous contrasts, with Moorish styles adapted by Christians to create an Alcázar of unbelievable beauty. The intricate halls and courtyards of this palace lead on to gardens of breathtaking magnificence, dwarfing even those of Granada. In earlier times, however, the harmony was only on the surface. One Moorish ruler, al-Mutadid, kept a harem of 800 women in the palace, and chopped off the heads of courtiers who dared so much as to look at them, using their skulls as flower pots. After the Moors left, only the minaret of their mosque, the vast Giralda tower, was left; perhaps because even Christians could appreciate its appeal. As a compensation for such plagiarism, they constructed the largest gothic church in Christendom. Visit the town during the April fair, if you have any energy to spare after the night's revels, for Seville does really live up to Byron's assessment that it was famous for oranges and beautiful women.

Air The airport lies nine miles (14.5km) east.

TOLEDO

A city that has outgrown its natural defensive position above a gorge on the River Tagus, Toledo was capital of medieval Spain and required a cathedral to match its pre-eminence. It got one that took over 200 years to complete, with a 295ft (90m) spire and a combination of baroque and gothic architecture. The approach to the cathedral, along narrow streets in which pavements and walls alike are constructed from dazzling white stone, is a view that stays in the mind long after the visit. Two medieval synagogues also survive, recalling the time when Jews occupied positions of high power, though not without risk. One such was Samuel Levi, treasurer of Pedro the Cruel, who made the mistake of revealing the extent of his wealth to his king. Pedro murdered him and stole the

lot, and with a name like that, he surprised only poor Levi. Toledo steel, once famous for cutting throats, now goes mostly to make blunt souvenirs.

VALENCIA

The third largest city in Spain, occupied by the Moors for more than 400 years in the era before gunpowder, when the huge city walls made it almost impregnable to anything but a long siege. The only man to take it was Spain's most famous soldier, El Cid, who held the city for five years. When, after a series of fresh battles, he died within its walls, news of his death reached the Moors and their armies regathered at its gates. To their horror, however, El Cid reappeared at the head of his troops in full armour, riding his favourite charger. When the Moorish leaders told their followers it was a trick

The rooftops, towers and back gardens of Valencia

and that they were being attacked by a dead man, instead of rallying they fled in terror, giving the city two years' breathing space.

Air The airport is six miles (9.6km) north-west.

SWEDEN

STOCKHOLM

Built on fourteen islands on the edge of the Baltic Sea, Stockholm blends wide, tree-lined avenues with quaint, narrow streets from its medieval past. Gamla Stan, or the old town, has tiny courtyards and cobblestone pavements that have scarcely altered in 300 years. But even when Sweden was a great power, Stockholm was a relatively small city: it has grown tenfold in the space of a century. Examples of Sweden's warlike past can be seen in the Royal Armoury, part of the Royal Palace, with weapons, costumes, even the

Cobbled streets and dark doorways in Stockholm's Old Town

more bellicose toys of the Swedish princes. The Vasa Museum contains the warship reclaimed from the harbour where she sank in 1628. On the same island of Djurgården is the Skansen, a unique open-air museum, amusement park and zoo all rolled into one. The Stadshuset, Stockholm's town hall, shows that not all outstanding architecture belongs to the past, as it was completed only in 1923. From its tower is perhaps the best view of Stockholm, with its bridges and broad waterways, superior as a spectacle to Venice herself.

Air International flights land at Arlanda Airport, 25 miles (40.2km) to the north.

Rail Central Station.

SWITZERLAND

BASLE

Through the ages, a university town where some of the great scholars of Europe congregated, sometimes overcoming physical peril and political disapproval to live there. It you sit at one of the little cafés on the Rheinweg in the shadow of the old houses —crammed into a seemingly impossible space—you can see in the mind's eye the students of the past arguing some point of art or science over a different brew on almost the same wooden tables. From the Wettstein Bridge there is an exciting view of the entire city, spreadeagled across the Rhine and overlooked by its gothic cathedral. By climbing the medieval streets, you reach the university, attended by the famous Erasmus of Rotterdam, whose tomb lies in the north end of the cathedral. Outside is the Münsterplatz, a square that is an architect's dream, so perfect are its proportions. This northern gateway of Switzerland remains one of Europe's most important inland ports, but has lost none of its medieval sophistication and charm.

Air Basle-Mulhouse airport is situated at St Louis in France, seven miles (11.2km) northwest, but is reached by a Customs-free access road.

Rail Central Station.

BERNE

Because wars for the most part passed Switzerland by, Berne's medieval splendour survived while many other cities were less fortunate. The visitor is greeted by exceptional old buildings behind arcaded squares, an abundance of towers and, seemingly, a 16th-century fountain cascading on every corner. The city was founded by Berthold V, Duke of Zähringen, taking its name from the German for grizzly bear, killed in the nearby forests by the not-so-noble duke in 1191. Berne still has its bears, in a bear pit at the end of the Nydegg Bridge, and whatever might have happened in earlier times, they now seem to be largely vegetarian. Berne gives its name to the Bernese Oberland, one of Europe's most popular holiday areas. Jean-Jacques Rousseau enthused about its spectacular mountain scenery in the 18th century, and the Victorians, who probably had not read much Rousseau, rediscovered and developed it.

GENEVA

At the heart of French-speaking Romande, Geneva is to all intents and purposes an international city. You can use its airport in flights from Paris and Nice without leaving France, and a good many of its inhabitants actually live across the border, combining a high Swiss salary with the lower French cost of living. Indeed, about a third of the population hold foreign passports: diplomats, businessmen, tax and political exiles. Their presence is reflected in the cosmopolitan range of shops and restaurants, and sadly in the conspicuously high prices. Price does not necessarily guarantee quality, and some of Geneva's hotels have the studied indifference of establishments that are aware that their rooms will be filled in any case. Nevertheless, Geneva is a sophisticated, graceful city, with many beautiful walks—especially on the shores of Lake Léman, in the old city where buildings are immaculately preserved, and along the quayside which is dominated by a huge fountain known simply as the Jet d'Eau. The lake offers a variety of boat excursions, but Geneva, while worth a visit in itself, is too close to the frontier to be an ideal touring centre.

Air Geneva-Cointrin Airport, 2½ miles (4km) north-west of the city.

Rail Gare de Cornavin.

INTERLAKEN

Although built on a flat strip of land between the lakes of Thun and Brienz, the city has a breathtaking mountain panorama, first appreciated by the Victorians, who proceeded to ruin the place by trying to turn it into a second Bognor Regis. Interlaken has neat tree-lined boulevards, where the Victorians promenaded, and a few surviving ornate 19th-century hotels, where the British opened their windows

Interlaken under the peaks of the Eiger, Mönch and Jungfrau

every morning to breathe the crisp mountain air. You can not only see the 13,642ft (4,158km) Jungfrau mountain: you can reach it by rail—first to Lauterbrunnen, then on the cogwheel train of the Wengernalp railway to Kleine Scheidegg, which is at 6,762ft (2,061m). From there you take the Jungfrau railway to a height of 11,333ft (3,054m). This line, opened as long ago as 1912, took sixteen years to build and climbs higher than any other railway in Europe. At the top is an elevator to take you to a terrace 11,720ft (3575m) high from where, on a fine day, you can see an awe-inspiring Alpine panorama of what must be among the finest excursions in the world.

LAUSANNE

Voltaire and Gibbon (of *Decline and Fall of the Roman Empire* fame) liked Lausanne when it was a quiet, quaint little resort in the 18th century. Nowadays, it is less quiet, less quaint, but offers a relaxing atmosphere, along the lake from Geneva. Business is conducted in Lausanne with a greater sense of decorum, and even the hotels are largely pushed down the hill to Ouchy, reached by a splendid funicular. They are, however, worth seeing for their ambience of bygone days and

their mind-boggling service (with prices to match). The lake provides many languid excursions along its shores, past vineyards that stretch down almost to the water's edge. On the skyline is Lausanne's old city, clustering around the cathedral of Notre Dame; hardly Paris, but an exceptional example of an early gothic building.

LUCERNE

Both a lake and a town, and, of the two, the lake is certainly the more spectacular. It stretches for over 20 miles (32km) into an Alpine valley that leads eventually to the St Gotthard Pass, offering intensely dramatic scenery, with woods that kiss the water, and jagged, multi-coloured peaks. Steamers ply up and down the lake to a variety of stops, allowing the visitor to take in the view from every possible angle. The town of Lucerne is a step back into the past, when its prosperity virtually depended on the British holiday trade. That is no longer so—there are now more Germans and Americans than British tourists—but the Edwardian image of its hotels remains. Lucerne has spread outward from its original setting, giving the casual visitor the impression of a noisy and rather gloomy provincial town. But once you get back from the more modern streets the real charm of the place emerges. The old town is delightful, spread out on the banks of the River Reuss, connected by two covered wooden bridges—a reminder that Switzerland can indeed be wet. An abundance of cafés and restaurants distract the holidaymaker from the more serious business of museum-hunting, but even the most relentless gourmet should go to the Swiss Transport Museum, a marvel of its kind.

LUGANO

A semicircle of hotels and expensive villas marks this sophisticated resort on the shores of Lake Lugano, in a large bay between gentle hills that roll towards the Alps to the north and the Po Valley and the Apennines to the south. In the centre, the place to see and be seen is the big square with its cafés whose furniture has sprawled for so long on to the pavements that they now have squatters' rights. If you become bored with the small talk, or frightened by the prices, as well you might, there are abundant parks and gardens cared for by a whole army of gardeners. The mild climate makes this a resort for all seasons, and even the most expensive shops (definitely an arm and a leg, so be warned what it will cost you) close only briefly. Some of their profits come from lavish gifts bought by the big winners at nearby Campione, an Italian enclave entirely surrounded by Swiss territory. Campione's *raison d'être* is its casino, because in Switzerland the maximum legal stakes are too low to attract the serious gambler. In Campione, however, you can lose a fortune before your first drink has arrived and still have 20 minutes on the return boat ride to decide whether or not to throw yourself overboard.

MONTREUX

A lakeside resort, equally popular with the British and the French since Edwardian times, with a superb climate and a promenade that would not seem out of place at Eastbourne or Torquay. Although Montreux oozes respectability in the daytime, with its well-groomed gardens and over-abundant wastepaper baskets, at night it offers slightly risqué entertainment, and the perils of a casino. Just 1½ miles (2.4km) distant is the Château de Chillon, made famous by Byron. The reconstruction of the castle in the 13th century must have been remarkable—Duke Peter of Savoy had half a mountain moved into the lake to create its ramparts.

ST MORITZ

On the lake of the same name, this town was a gathering place for the rich and the famous, the so-called beautiful people, in the late sixties and early seventies. Its fashionable past is now but a comforting illusion for tourists who have paid too much for too little. St Moritz's ready access to the ski slopes from its 6,089ft (1,856m) altitude, makes it among the favoured winter resorts, though it has much to offer besides winter sport. It claims to possess waters with curative powers, and the spa facilities at St Moritz Bad are open all year, though many of

Around St Moritz, access to ski slopes is quick

the first-class hotels close for much of the summer. Half the town, including the hangers-on of the tourist trade, seem to disappear too, giving St Moritz the impression of an English provincial town on a wet Sunday. But it remains a good centre for exploring the valleys of the Grisons Canton, which until the last century was isolated not simply from the rest of Europe but from Switzerland itself. The local language is not French or German but Romansch, more familiar to the legions of Julius Caesar than it is to us.

ZERMATT

The leading winter sports centre of the Valais canton, dominated by Switzerland's most famous mountain, the Matterhorn. You can visit a museum marking the feats of early mountaineers and even climb the peak yourself if you are passably fit and have a good head for heights. This is not as preposterous as it sounds because in good weather, by the easiest route, and with a really competent guide, it is as easy as falling off a log (let alone a mountain). The Swiss have left nothing to chance, even installing, at 12,000ft (3,660m), the world's highest loos, presumably just in case you are caught short with your crampons on. Back in Zermatt, if you avoid being run over by the horse-drawn carriages, being able to say you had just climbed the Matterhorn should do wonders for your après-ski.

Rail Täsch Station, four miles (6.4km) down the valley, is the nearest to the resort of Zermatt.

ZURICH

The Reformation virtually began here when, in 1519, Ulrich Zwingli preached

Old houses along the Limmat River in Zurich

anti-papal sermons here and brought Switzerland close to civil war. Zwingli's bronze statue stands on a tall pedestal beside the Grossmünster, a church said to have been created by Charlemagne, the second great influence in this medieval city. Zurich retains its puritan streak, offering little nightlife, only a kind of staid elegance that disguises the considerable wealth of its inhabitants. It also hides away its industrial heart so successfully that many visitors would be astonished to discover that this is the hub of Swiss industry, run on hydro-electric power behind sound-proofed buildings. This allows citizen and tourist alike to enjoy the walks along the shores of Lake Zurich and the River Limmat.

Air Zurich Airport is 7½ miles (12km) north, with a direct

rail link (eleven minutes) to Zurich-Flughafen, situated under airport terminal B.

Rail Zurich Hauptbahnhof.

USSR

MOSCOW

Peter the Great is largely to blame for the distinct absence of buildings in the Soviet capital dating from earlier than 1812. If that sounds like a historical impossibility, it should be explained that Peter protected the magnificence of his own capital, St Petersburg, now Leningrad, created in 1703, by the simple expedient of refusing to allow stone buildings to be erected anywhere else. Thus, when Napoleon set Moscow on fire in his frustration at finding that anyone who was anyone had left, most of it was made of wood, and burned spectacularly. It was not until 1824 that much was rebuilt, this time in brick, in imperial style, including the Bolshoi Theatre. All that survived of note was the Kremlin, meaning fortress, in Red Square, a huge complex surrounded by red walls and towers, five of which are lit up at night with ludicrously large red stars. Heroes of the Soviet Union, who curiously included the American author, John Reed, for writing a slightly romantic account of the Russian Revolution, *Ten Days That Shook the World*, have their ashes buried in the walls; from time to time others less favoured, so the story goes, may have been interred while still breathing. Red Square stretches from the Lenin Mausoleum on the west to the large department store, GUM, in the east, where 300,000 shoppers queue for this and

queue again for that, every day except Sunday. But even though you will be looked after by Intourist as carefully as though you were a spy, resign yourself to queueing for almost everything. If you plan to make any phone calls and don't know the numbers, pack a Moscow directory in Britain. There seem to be more Soviet telephone directories in London than in Moscow.

Air Sheremetyevo Airport is eighteen miles (30km) north-west.

YUGOSLAVIA

DUBROVNIK

Walls and turrets preserved so immaculately for centuries that you can almost imagine a Venetian or a Turkish soldier on guard duty, his armour glinting in the fierce sun, as he scans the Adriatic Sea. That is Dubrovnik, a city built on a huge rocky promontory, visible for miles by land and water, for centuries a safe haven for the merchant-adventurers of Venice. Situated in the deep south of Yugoslavia, Dubrovnik can be paralysingly hot in the midday summer sun: then the circular tour of the walls, fascinating in the cool of the evening, becomes a self-imposed torture, with every retaining wall too hot to touch. Cars are not allowed inside the city walls, adding to the sense of stepping back in time. Renaissance churches and palaces are examples of serene grandeur, with few of the environmental problems of western Europe. Dubrovnik is also a harbour: from here you can hire a boat to cross the port to Lokrum, a tiny yet delightful wooded island, or sail to Venice, as the mariners did long ago.

As most hotels add a surcharge to calls made from bedrooms, using the public telephone system can save a lot of money and at the same time get rid of the coins one tends to accumulate because of unfamiliarity with the local currency. Direct dialling is now possible throughout western Europe, provided that you organise yourself properly. Make sure that you have the right coins, and enough of them (to be on the safe side, work on the basis of double the cost of a trunk call in the UK). Write down the complete number, including all the codes, omitting the first zero in the UK dialling code. Pause in the right places, but otherwise dial steadily. Expect to hear some strange dialling tones while your call is being put through, which can take one minute or more. Any persistent tone or recorded announcement will mean that it has failed to connect, so hang up, wait a moment, then try again. Usually your coins will then be refunded, except in Denmark, where you have to keep trying or lose your money. Try to avoid times of day when you will be competing with businesses for the available international lines. In some countries, for example Germany, calls at weekends and between 6pm and 8am Monday to Friday will be charged at a lower rate.

Country	Type of callbox	Which coins	What to dial
Austria	3 coin slots	1, 5, 10 sch	00 44 + UK area code (leave out 0) + no
Belgium	European flags	5, 10, 20 BF	00 (wait for 2nd tone) 44 + UK as above
Cyprus	green	25, 50, 100 mils	00 44 + UK code + no
Denmark	all	25 ö, 1 kr, 5 kr	009 44 + UK code + no
Finland	most	1, 5 mk	990 44 + UK code + no
France	metallic grey	50 c, 1 f, 5 f, 10 f	19 (wait for 2nd tone) 44 + UK code + no
Germany	'international sign'	10 pf, 50 pf, 1 DM, 5 DM	00 44 + UK code + no
Greece	orange sign on top	2, 10, 20 dr	00 44 + UK code + no
Italy	yellow sign	shop tokens	00 44 + UK code + no
Luxembourg	at roadside	1 f (Lux or Belg)	00 44 + UK code + no
Malta	main POs only	pay after call	00 44 + UK code + no
Netherlands	all	25 c, 1 g, 2.5 g	09 (wait for 2nd tone) 44 + UK code + no
Norway	most	1, 5 kr	095 44 + UK code + no
Portugal	trilingual notice	2.5, 25 esc	07 44 + UK code + no (Lisbon only)
Spain	'internacional' sign	50 ptas	07 (wait for 2nd tone) 44 + UK code + no
Sweden	1 or 3 coin slots	1, 5 kr	009 44 (wait for 2nd tone) UK code + no
Switzerland	all	10 c, 20 c, 50 c, 1 f, 5 f	00 44 + UK code + no
Yugoslavia	3 coin slots	1, 2, 5, 10 din	99 44 + UK code + no

DISTANCE MAP

LEGEND

Mileage between towns — 62

International boundary

National Boundary ————

The white lines linking towns on this map are
not roads but serve to indicate the distances
between the towns.

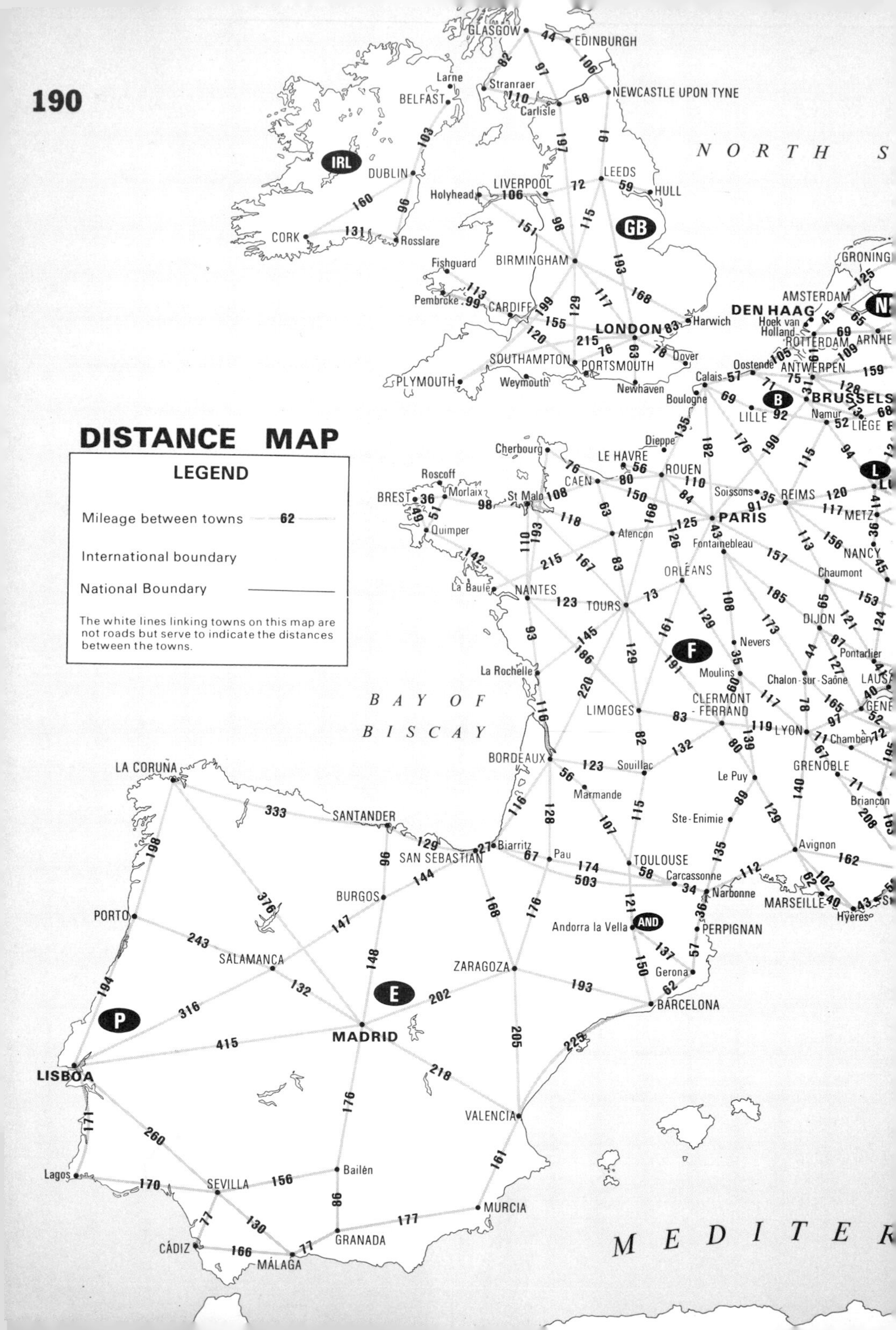

NORTH SEA

BAY OF
BISCAY

MEDITERRANEAN

IRL

GLASGOW
EDINBURGH
82
44
97
106
BELFAST
Larne
Stranraer
110
58
NEWCASTLE UPON TYNE
Carlisle
103
197
16
DUBLIN
160
96
LIVERPOOL
LEEDS
106
72
59
HULL
CORK
131
Rosslare
Holyhead
115
GB
98
151
Fishguard
BIRMINGHAM
193
168
GRONING
Pembroke
113
99
CARDIFF
99
129
117
AMSTERDAM
125
N
155
LONDON
83
Harwich
Hoek van
Holland
45
65
120
215
76
63
78
Dover
ROTTERDAM
105
69
ARNHE
SOUTHAMPTON
PORTSMOUTH
Oostende
ANTWERPEN
128
159
PLYMOUTH
Weymouth
Newhaven
Calais
57
75
Boulogne
69
B
BRUSSELS
Cherbourg
Dieppe
135
LILLE
92
Namur
52
68
LIEGE
L
LE HAVRE
56
ROUEN
182
176
190
115
94
L
Roscoff
CAEN
80
110
Soissons
35
REIMS
120
BREST
36
Morlaix
St Malo
108
150
84
117
METZ
49
51
98
118
63
168
125
PARIS
43
156
NANCY
Quimper
193
Alençon
126
Fontainebleau
113
45
142
101
215
167
83
157
Chaumont
153
La Baule
ORLEANS
DIJON
121
124
NANTES
123
TOURS
73
108
185
99
87
Pontarlier
93
161
129
173
LAUS
186
F
Nevers
91
44
127
145
191
Moulins
35
Chalon-sur-Saône
117
165
40
La Rochelle
129
Chambery
GENE
220
CLERMONT-
FERRAND
139
78
67
52
116
LIMOGES
83
119
LYON
71
195
BORDEAUX
82
80
140
GRENOBLE
123
Souillac
Le Puy
89
71
56
132
Briancon
208
163
Marmande
115
Ste-Enimie
129
Avignon
128
107
162
San Sebastián
27
Biarritz
TOULOUSE
135
LA CORUÑA
SANTANDER
129
67
Pau
174
58
Carcassonne
112
102
43
333
96
144
503
34
Narbonne
36
140
MARSEILLE
Hyeres
198
BURGOS
147
168
176
121
AND
PERPIGNAN
57
Andorra la Vella
137
PORTO
376
148
ZARAGOZA
193
150
Gerona
243
SALAMANCA
132
E
202
62
BÁRCELONA
P
316
MADRID
205
225
415
218
194
176
LISBOA
VALENCIA
171
260
161
Lagos
170
SEVILLA
156
Bailén
86
77
130
177
MURCIA
CÁDIZ
166
MÁLAGA
77
GRANADA

Distance chart 191